Masterpieces of the Musée National Picasso-Paris

art lys

PICASSO
MuséePicassoParis

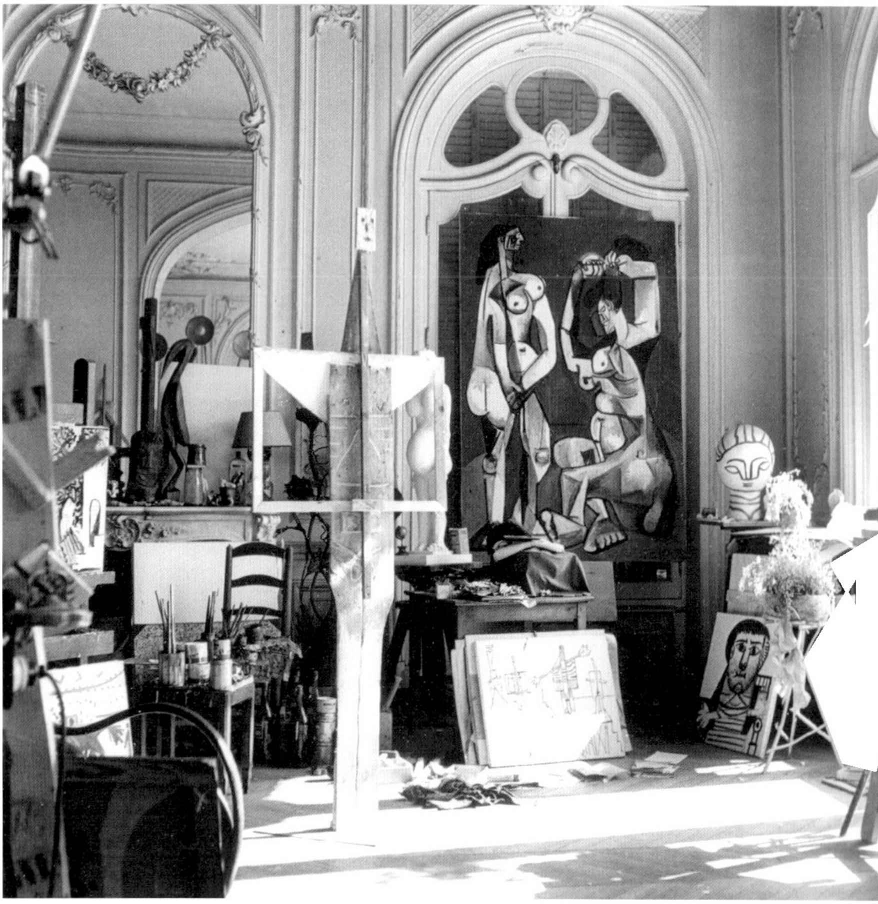

André Villers
The studio at La Californie in Cannes, with the sculpture *Man with Folded Hands* and the painting, *Women at Their Toilet*, 1958, undated print
Gift, 1987. MP1987-116

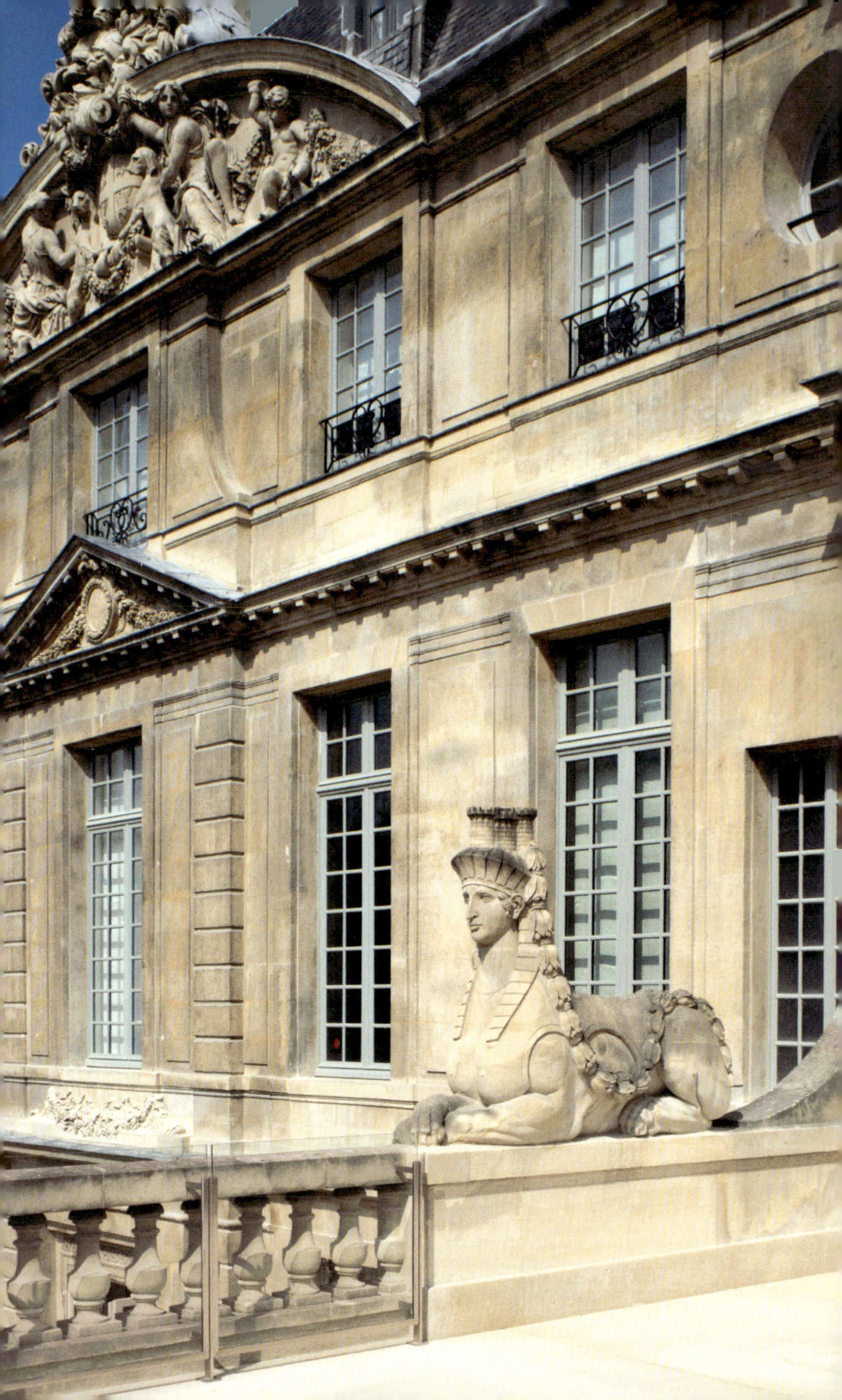

The story of the Musée National Picasso-Paris

From the La Californie villa in Cannes to the castle in Vauvenargues and the townhouse on Rue des Grands-Augustins in Paris, the story of Picasso's studios is one of mansions. Although the painter never lived in the seventeenth-century Hotel Salé, built under Louis XIV for a financier, the mansion has become part of the history of his creation, as it has hosted the collections of the musée National Picasso-Paris since 1985.

The Hotel Salé was built between 1656 and 1660, and is the only known work by the architect Jean Boullier de Bourges. The architectural and ornamental boldness he dared design is the result of two influences: on the one hand, the great architects, such as François Mansart and Louis Le Vau, and on the other hand, the growing taste in the court for the new Italian baroque. The monument comprises a main building, a right-angled wing, a courtyard and a garden. It gave the architect the opportunity to use several major innovations characteristic of the time, including its asymmetrical footprint and the angles of the semicircular courtyard.
The Hotel Salé is a lavish residence: the abundance of certain ornaments, such as the pediments, contrasts with the sobriety of the facades of homogeneous bare stone. Inside, the great staircase constitutes Jean Boullier's masterpiece and the architect gave this element a dramatic dimension, allowing for new visual games: sweeping views and perspective effects turn the flight of stairs into a true theater. The sculpted adornments add to the room's sumptuousness, with spirits, garlands, eagles and divinities.
By mid century, architectural boldness defined a class of rich men eager to show off their power and their recently acquired fortune. Pierre Aubert de Fontenay, commissioner and owner of the mansion, fits this definition. Advisor and secretary to the king, protégé of Nicolas Fouquet, he became one of the most important financiers in Paris after marrying into money and buying successive positions at court. He purchased a piece of land on Rue Thorigny and built a home to match his social ambition. Such intentions explain the edifice's monumentality—quite unusual for a private residence—and the exuberant ornamentation. As he was in charge of collecting the royal tax on salt, the house he built was thus named after his position: Hôtel Salé literally translates as Salty Hotel.
However, his wealth and power were threatened when his protector, the finance superintendent Nicolas Fouquet, went on trial. Amongst the most powerful men in the kingdom, envied by Jean-Baptiste Colbert, Fouquet was arrested in 1661 by order of Louis XIV. His downfall took with him financiers such as Aubert, who had to leave the Hotel Salé in 1663, and died five years later.

The Hôtel Salé from the courtyard

From the seventeenth to the twentieth centuries

When its first owner died, the Hotel Salé becomes a source of conflict between Pierre Aubert's family and his creditors, and it was auctioned only sixty years after his death. The succession of tenants and their various tastes and needs, changed the architecture remarkably. Several owners left their mark on the form and history of the building. From 1728 to 1749, Nicolas Le Camus, president of the Courts of Aids specializing in tax litigation, renovated the apartments, installed running water, and commissioned the ceilings and panelings. Between 1771 and 1778, the mansion bore the name of its new owner, the Marquis de Juigné, a diplomat and soldier. In 1792, the edifice served as storage for the books seized by the revolutionaries, before becoming a boarding house.
Throughout the nineteenth and twentieth centuries, several new owners radically changed the architecture of the Hotel Salé.
In 1829, the mansion hosted the brand new Central School of Arts and Manufacture, and became one of the largest teaching structures of the nineteenth century's "industrial science." New spaces were thus created: physics and mineralogy offices were set up inside the Hotel, while laboratories and lecture halls were built in the courtyard and the garden. The setting and the use of the mansion were drastically altered until the school moved out in 1884.
From 1887 to 1940, the building was rented to the bronzer Henri Vian, grandfather of the writer Boris Vian. He used some of the original decorative elements of decoration, often fancifully, to bring back several of the apartments' old rooms. There, he exhibited his own creations, aiming at well-off clients. The bronze artist also transformed the main courtyard, adding a story to the outbuildings wing. Henri Vian was well known in his time. His shop was very popular and he appeared in serial stories. He was also an art collector and he decorated the walls of the Hotel Salé with his (mainly Impressionist) purchases.
The purpose of the Hotel Salé changed once again with the arrival of a center for professional training in 1942, which soon became School of Artistic Professions. The new institution required art studios, classrooms and cafeterias. But the works caused so many modifications of the Hotel's aspect that the City of Paris expropriated the owner in 1962 for having failed to safeguard the building's heritage.
These numerous alterations also impacted the architecture. New constructions and successive reorganizations transformed the building's volumes for the long-term. The residence was finally classed as a Historic Monument in 1968.

The creation of the Musée National Picasso

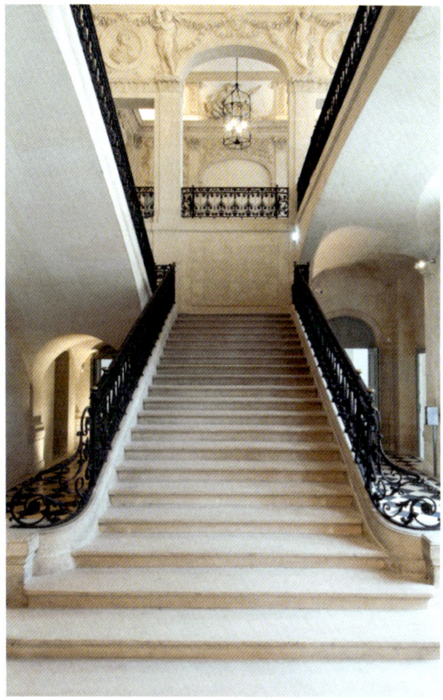

The grand staircase of the Hôtel Salé

On December 31 1968, the law on dation, payment-in-kind, is enacted. It allows such payment for inheritance taxes and intends to favor the keeping of works of art and great patrimonial collections on French territory. On April 8, Picasso dies in Mougins. His legacy is extraordinarily rich. Tens of thousands of pieces were held by the artist; works from his Spanish childhood to his latest canvases are found in his various family homes. The official auctioneer Maurice Rheims is chosen by his heirs to make an inventory, which takes him three years, for over 70,000 works of art. In order to compensate for the public collections' inadequacies and their low holdings of Picasso's paintings, the state and the master's family come to a moral agreement under which an exceptional selection is taken from Maurice Rheim's inventory, provided that it is curated in a place as grand as the artist's remarkable creativity. The Secretary of State in charge of Cultural Affairs, Michel Guy, along with Jacqueline Roque, Picasso's last wife, and Picasso's children decide together on a monographic museum, entirely dedicated to the life and achievements of Picasso. Dominique Bozo, the first director of the museum, put together the collection, by setting up a committee in charge of choosing a first set of pieces, from 1975 to 1978. 203 paintings, 158 sculptures, 29 reliefs, 88 ceramics, 16 collages, 1481 drawings, 33 sketch books, 1,618 engravings and 35 illustrated books were selected. Thus the dation gave birth to a museum.

In 1973, according to Picasso's will, his heirs donate his personal collection to the state that same year. Great masters, African and Oceanic art through to contemporary artists, this gathering illustrates quite well the atmosphere in Picasso's studios. The artist bought, received or exchanged pieces, depending on his friendships as much as on the opportunities brought by the market. Before the Musée National Picasso, his collection was exhibited for the first time at the Louvre, in 1978, including works by Le Nain, Corot, Vuillard, Cézanne, Gauguin, Matisse, Rousseau, Renoir, Braque, Modigliani, Miró, Degas, Chirico and Alberto Giacometti.

It was the Hôtel Salé that, in 1974, caught Michel Guy's attention to install, with the agreement of the artist's family, the "Musée Picasso." The City of Paris approved the decision in 1975 and the work could start, provided that they respected the architectural heritage, a task entrusted to the head architects of historic buildings, Bernard Vitry and Bernard Forquernie. They oversaw the adaptations necessary for the site's new function.

Roland Simounet won the 1976 call for projects to lead the installation of the museum in the Hotel Salé, with a bold and rigorous proposition. The great historical stairwell is the spine and central axis of the building, through which the visit starts. The walls are doubled, to hide the technical elements—"useful layering"—creating the impression of a "box" while preserving the place's coziness and pureness. The technical aspect disappears in a space discovered only through a winding path. Roland Simounet grew up in Algeria. The concept of an Arabian home with small openings is thus transposed to a seventeenth-century mansion. Simounet's architectural syntax thus resurfaces: the visit is punctuated by withdrawals and openings, allowing perspectives on to the architectural landscape. It is enlivened with the contrasting surfaces of the walls, alternately matt and glossy.
As Picasso's posthumous home, the museum must be visited like a town house. An intimate atmosphere is encouraged by indirect lighting, hidden in the dropped ceilings, or provided by Diego Giacometti's (brother of Alberto) magnificent chandeliers. The artist was commissioned to furnish the building and he made bronze and white resin chandeliers, benches and candelabra especially for the Hotel Salé. The Musée National Picasso was inaugurated in 1985.

1985–2009: the life of the collections

During its first twenty-five years of existence, gifts, donations, bequests and purchases allowed the assembly of the first exceptional groups, while exhibitions and research on the work of Picasso punctuated the life of the institution. In 1988, during the exhibition *Les Demoiselles d'Avignon*, the artist's masterpiece, today held in the Museum of Modern Art in New York, made its last appearance in France. In 1989 the museum published Picasso's *Écrits poétiques*, then correspondence between Picasso and those close to him (Guillaume Apollinaire, Gertrude Stein, Max Jacob).
In 1990, following the death of Jacqueline Roque, a second dation is given to the state. 377 new pieces extend the museum's collections and complete more specifically the group of later works.
In 1991, the state is entrusted with about two hundred thousand archival elements by Picasso's heirs. Manuscripts, letters, postcards and clippings meticulously saved by Picasso throughout his life make up most of this collection. Beyond these writings, there are also photographs by major artists such as Brassaï, Robert Capa, Henri Cartier-Bresson, Lucien Clergue, Robert Doisneau, Douglas David Duncan, Dora Maar and Man Ray. Research material and testimony to Picasso's inspirations, memories and works of art: today these archives constitute a precious library for studies on Picasso. They were assigned to the Musée National Picasso in 1992, and were shown in the exhibition *Les Archives Picasso : on est ce que l'on garde!* in 2003. The collection was enriched in 1998 by more than four hun-

dred pieces that had belonged to Dora Maar (dation and purchase) and in 2011 by around a hundred pieces that belonged to Brassaï (bequests and dation).

2010–2015: the new Musée National Picasso-Paris

In the mid 2000s, the Musée National Picasso underwent substantial renovations. From 2006, its facades, exterior ornamentation and surrounding walls were restored, thanks to a commission by the Ministry of Culture and Communication. Inside the Hotel Salé, the seventeenth-century settings as well as Roland Simounet's developments were highlighted. Three years later, an unprecedented new development program for the museum was launched: it included safety and security measures for the public and the collections, as well as a complete rethinking of the itinerary of the visit.
The interior fitting and the outside extension of the museum were designed and carried out under the supervision of architect Jean-François Bodin and his firm, Bodin & Associates. Stéphane Thouin, head architect of historic monuments, worked alongside the firm, to ensure the restoration of the classified historical parts of the Hotel Salé (in particular, its courtyard, windows, the stairwell and the outbuildings' terrace), in continuity with the work on the facades, managed by Jean-François Lagneau, also head architect of historic monuments. In 2010, it was created by decree of the Établissement Public of the Musée National Picasso-Paris.
The Musée National Picasso-Paris re-opened its doors in October 2014, with a new interior architecture. In 2015, *¡Picasso! l'exposition anniversaire* (*¡Picasso! Anniversary Exhibition*) marks thirty years of the institution's existence. It demonstrates the abundance of Picasso's experimentations, but also the richness of the collections and of their history. Site of exhibition and conservation but also of study, the Musée National Picasso-Paris is a place of memory and of a life of total creation.
In the heart of the Marais neighborhood of Paris, on Rue Thorigny, the Musée National Picasso is part of a dense grid of cultural institutions, including the Musée Carnavalet Museum, the National Archives, the historical Paris Library and the Musée National d'Art Moderne – Centre Pompidou. Situated between manifesto of mid-seventeenth century French architectural boldness and a delicate keeper of Picasso's experiments, the Hotel Salé holds two identities, now inseparable. **C.Z.**

Picasso's archives

In April 1992, after initial classification, about 200,000 of Picasso's personal papers, manuscripts, prints and photographs given to the state are assigned to the Musée National Picasso to ensure their definitive classification, their inventory, their management and their development through research. From the slightest doodle to the correspondence with Michel Leiris, as well as postcards and a collection of *L'Humanité* journals, the accumulation is miscellaneous. It is often said of Picasso that "he kept everything," but how to understand such a habit?

Picasso and hoarding

Was he one of those people who save and store so much so that they live in utter shambles? Was he incapable of throwing anything away? Hundreds of boxes of archives that arrive one morning in the offices of the soon-to-be Musée National Picasso-Paris lead one to believe so. Sabartés once asked for an explanation of this habit and Picasso answered: "Why should I throw out what graces me by coming forth?"[1]

These boxes include letters from the director of New York's Museum of Modern Art's director, and those from André Breton, as well as a myriad of incongruous objects: a mitten, a cigar box, a subway ticket, a record, a wallet, a museum subscriber pass, a dried flower ... Picasso enjoyed these everyday objects that came to him, "waste"[2] having always been a "vessel—a vehicle for [his] thinking."[3]

He made an ally out of dust, to intentionally confuse observers, while his archives, sorted in constituted categories or displayed in small bundles, held together by pegs, have their own classification. Letters are sorted chronologically, and press clippings about him and his work, as well as financial documents, are kept separately.

Picasso was one of the most prolific artists of the twentieth century. When he died, throughout his various studios and homes, about 700,000 pieces were identified, all formats and materials mixed together, from ancient Iberian art to Matisse. As the originator of Cubism and of the first collages, Picasso preached for salvaging, for his sculptures. These "archives" could have been a constant source of inspiration, infinite material on which to draw and to create.

From the man to the myth

As early as 1917, Picasso subscribed to the press service "Lit-tout" (literally, "read everything"), which sent him articles about himself throughout his entire life. When Brassaï asked, he said: "... you can't just know the works of an artist. You also need to know when he made them, why, how, and in what circumstances. There will undoubtedly be a day when science, perhaps called 'mankind science,' will look more into the man, through the creator, ... I intend to leave to posterity the most complete possible documentation."[4]
Saving his exchanges with suppliers and his correspondence thus makes sense. Saving them for posterity—why not. But then why hold on to twenty-five movie theater stubs? Was there ever a decision, a selection by a "representative panel" to allow the study of the man, but also help build a media character, a character who, over time, took on a mythical dimension, to whom people wrote by only indicating on the envelope "Picasso, painter, Vallauris France"?

Tradition and modernity

Picasso was born in 1881, under the Spanish monarchy of Alfonso XII. He died in France in 1973, under president Georges Pompidou: he went through a whole century, as proven by his archives. He also intended to keep his memories with writings and photographs in order to bear in mind people and places, to preserve a form of bond with them.
But he is also very much a man of the twentieth century, who witnessed the development of mass media. He understood very early the perks and drawbacks of a public image. He knew how to build his persona and how to control it. His archives thus prolong his observation, and they must help manage his image for posterity and unveil only what he wished to be revealed.
All of this can be found in Picasso's archives, in an apparent accumulation, in these documents more or less intentionally regrouped, for reasons more or less acknowledged. If Picasso maybe didn't keep "absolutely everything," his archives, as they are, are above anything else a work of memory. They are even, in a certain way, his unofficial memoirs, and they resemble him. **L.C.**

1. Jaime Sabartés, *Picasso portraits et souvenirs*, Paris, Louis Carré et Maximilien Vox, 1946, p. 118.
2. Claude Roy, *La Guerre et la paix*, Paris Cercle d'art, 1954, p. 27.
3. Françoise Gilot and Carlton Lake, *Vivre avec Picasso*, Paris, Calmann Levy, 1965, p. 66.
4. Brassaï, *Conversations avec Picasso*, Paris, Gallimard, 1964, p. 123.

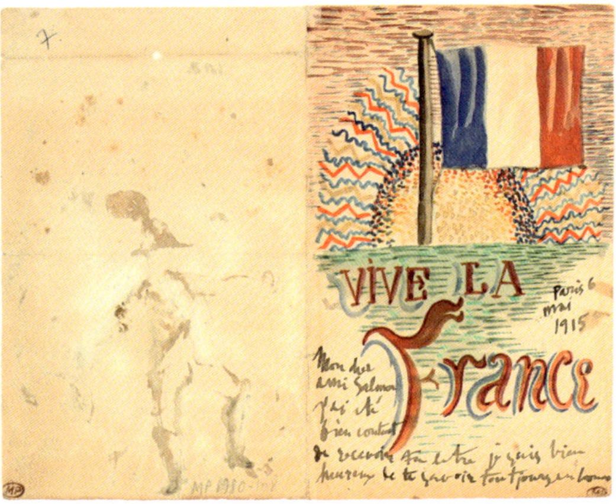

Pablo Picasso
Letter to André Salmon, May 6, 1915
Gift of Mr. and Mrs. Alain Mazo
MP1980-108

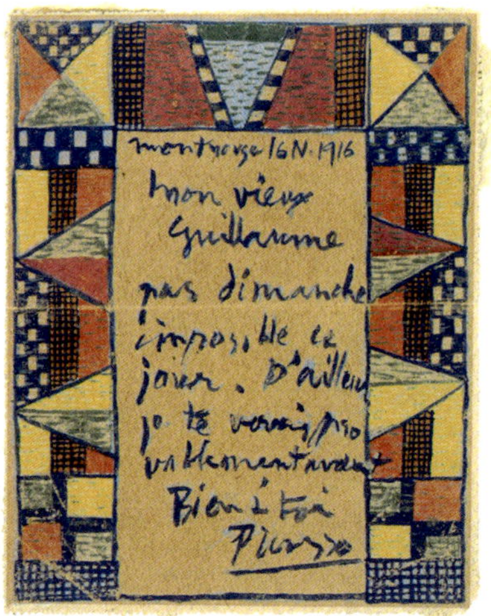

Pablo Picasso
Postcard to Guillaume Apollinaire, November 16, 1916
Purchase, 1990
MP1990-2(48)

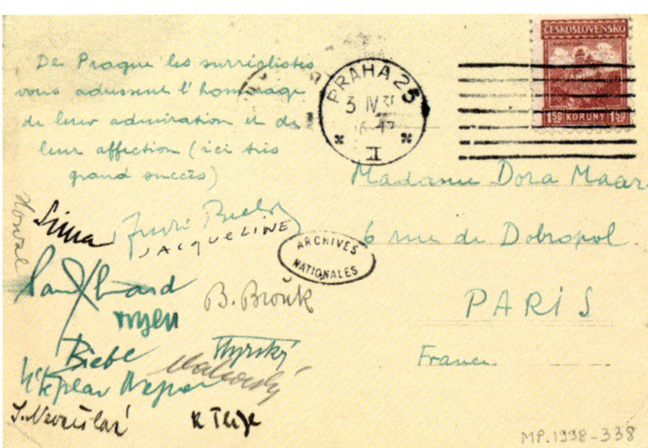

Verso of a postcard addressed to Dora Maar with multiple signatures including Jacqueline Breton, Paul Éluard and all the members of the Surrealist group in Czechoslovakia
April 3, [1934]
Purchase, 1998
MP1998-338

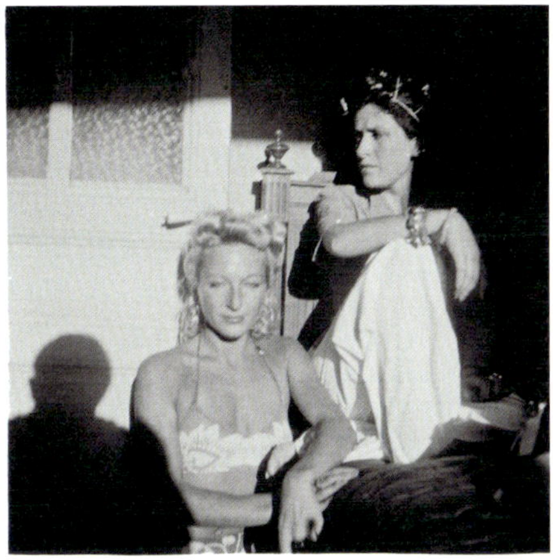

Pablo Picasso
Dora Maar with the crown of flowers and Jacqueline Lamba, [Mougins or Saint-Tropez], summer 1936
Undated print
Purchase, 1998
MP1998-153

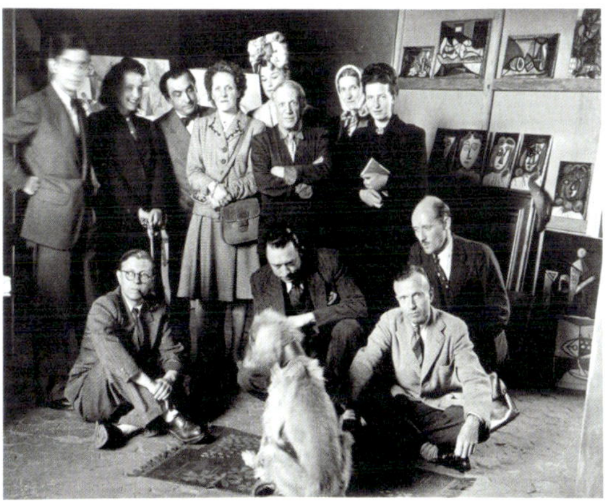

Brassaï (Gyula Halàsz, dit)
The Desire Caught by the Tail group, withJacques Lacan, Cécile Éluard, Pierre Reverdy, Louise Leiris, Zanie Campan, Pablo Picasso, Valentine Hugo, Simone de Beauvoir, Jean-Paul Sartre, Albert Camus, Jean Aubier, Michel Leiris in the Grands-Augustins studio, Paris, June 16, 1944
Print c. 1970
Purchase, 1986. MP1986-32

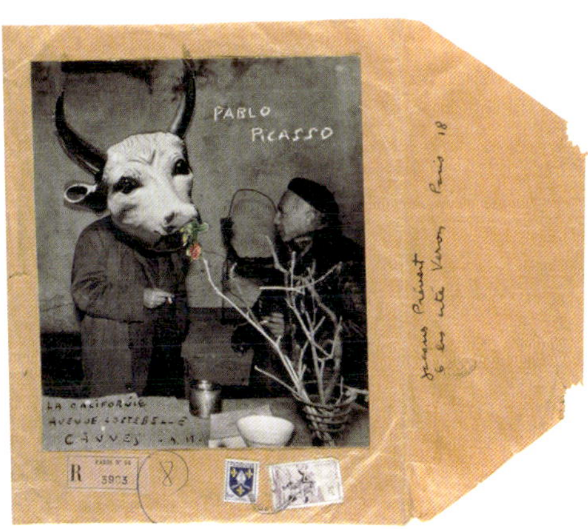

Jacques Prévert
Envelope with a drawing/collage, addressed to Picasso (La Californie, Cannes)
Gift Succession Picasso, 1992. DPCS1413

Picasso's personal collection

Picasso built a personal collection of artworks: Matisse, Braque—his partner in the Cubist endeavor—and Derain, as well as younger artists he was close to, such as Miró and Balthus, but also members of the generation before his: Cézanne, Renoir, Degas, Henri "Le Douanier" Rousseau, and even old masters and Iberian, African and Oceanian art pieces.

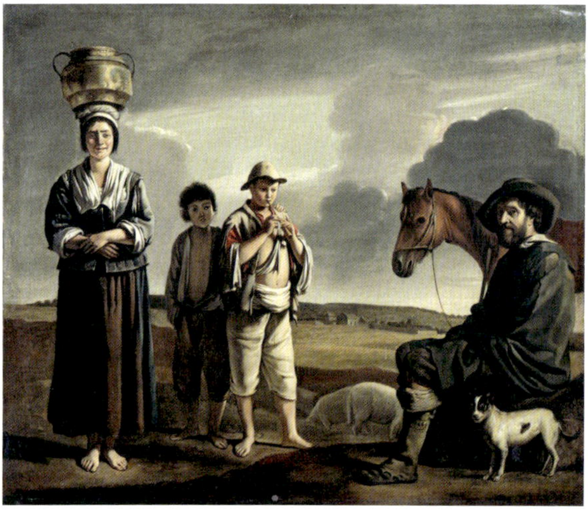

Louis Le Nain
(attributed to)
The Horse Rider's Halt,
undated
Oil on canvas
22.4 × 26.4 in. (57 × 67 cm)
Gift of the heirs of Picasso,
1973/1978. RF1973-70

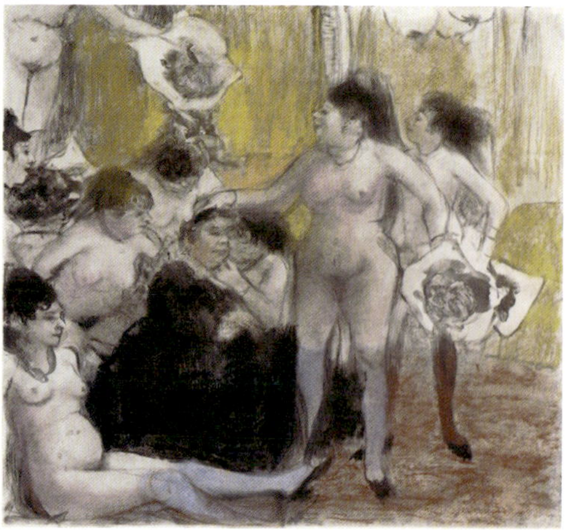

Edgar Degas
The Party, 1878–79
Monotype with black ink
and pastel, 10.5 × 11.7 in.
(26.6 × 29.6 cm)
Gift of the heirs of Picasso,
1973/1978. RF35791

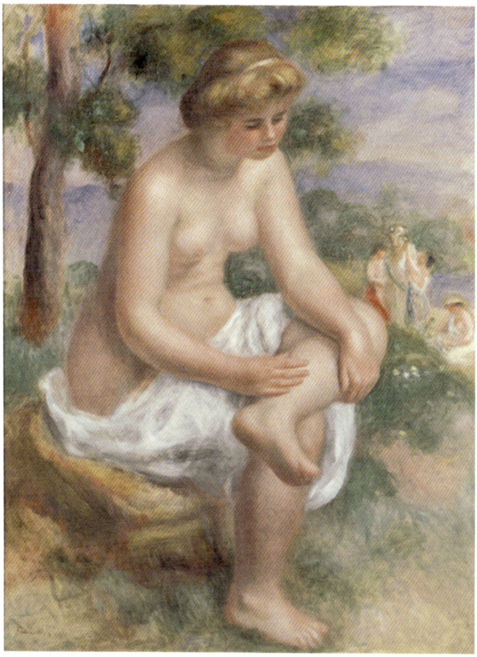

Auguste Renoir
Bather in Landscape-Eurydice, 1895–1900
Oil on canvas
45.7 × 35 in. (116 × 89 cm)
Gift of the heirs of Picasso, 1973/1978 RF1973-87

Paul Cézanne
Five Bathers, 1877–78
Oil on canvas
18 × 21.9 in. (45.8 × 55.7 cm)
Gift of the heirs of Picasso, 1973/1978. RF1973-61

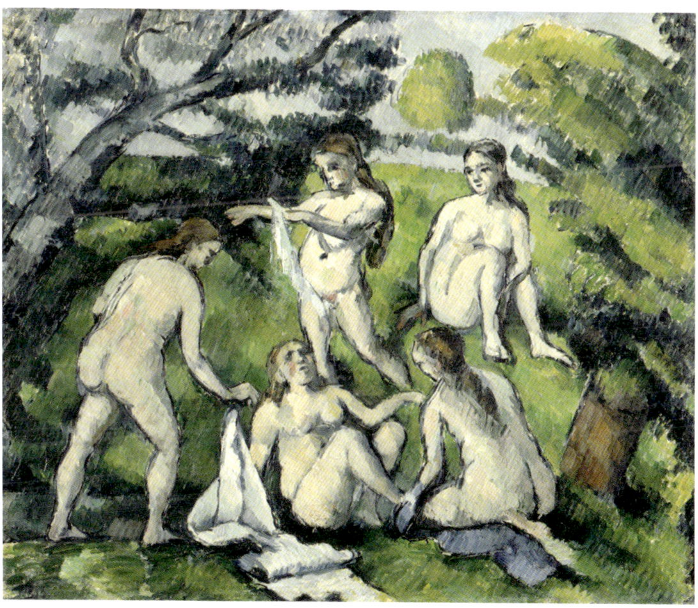

Picasso's personal collection

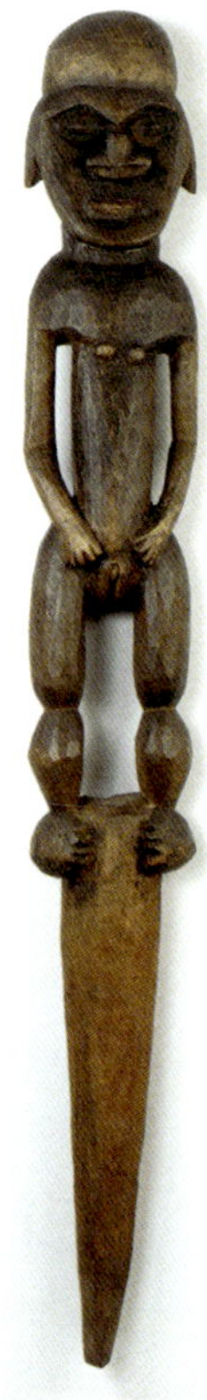

Artist Unknown (primitive arts)
Female sculpture ridge pole, undated
New Caledonia
Wood, 46.7 × 6.3 in. (118.5 × 16 cm)
Dation Pablo Picasso, 1979. MP3644

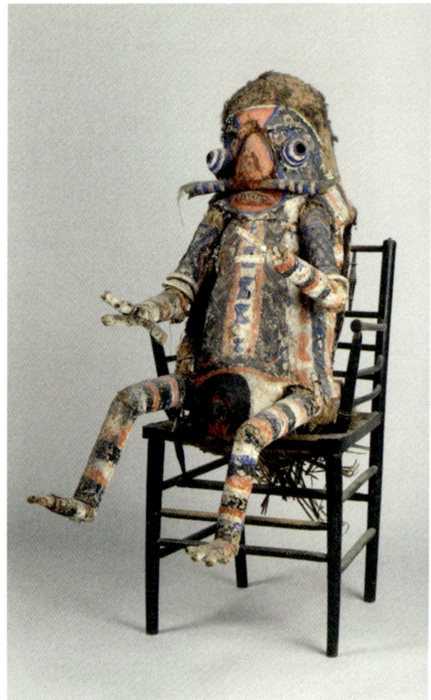

Artist Unknown
Ceremonial headdress "Nevinbumbaau," undated
Vanuatu (New Hebrides, South Malekula)
Tree fern and pandanus covered in painted glaze
44.9 × 23.6 × 36.2 in. (114 × 60 × 92 cm)
Dation Pablo Picasso, 1979. MP3624

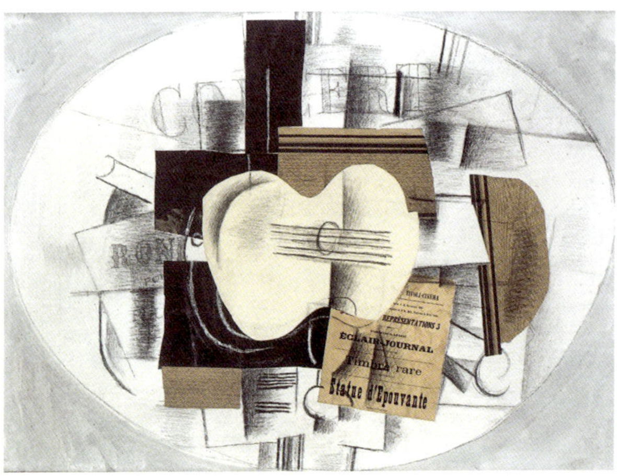

Georges Braque
The Guitar Statue of Horror
November 1913
Glued paper, charchoal and gouache on paper
28,7 × 39,3 in. (73 × 100 cm)
Dation Jacqueline Picasso, 1990
MP1990-381

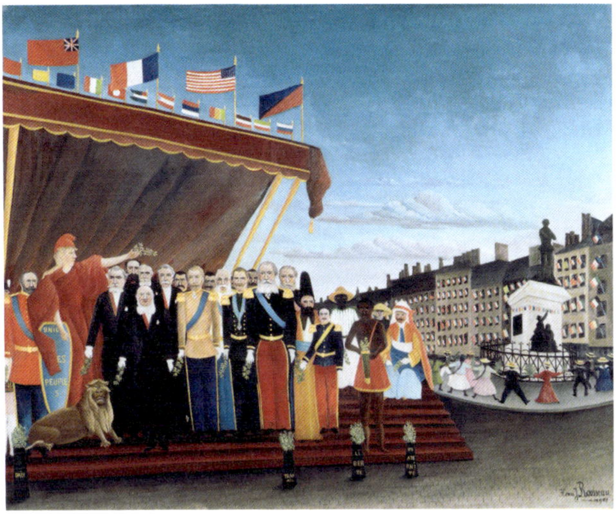

Henri "Le Douanier" Rousseau
The Representatives of Foreign Powers Coming to Greet the Republic as a Sign of Peace, 1907
Oil on canvas
51.1 × 63.4 in. (130 × 161 cm)
Gift of the heirs of Picasso, 1973/1978
RF1973-91

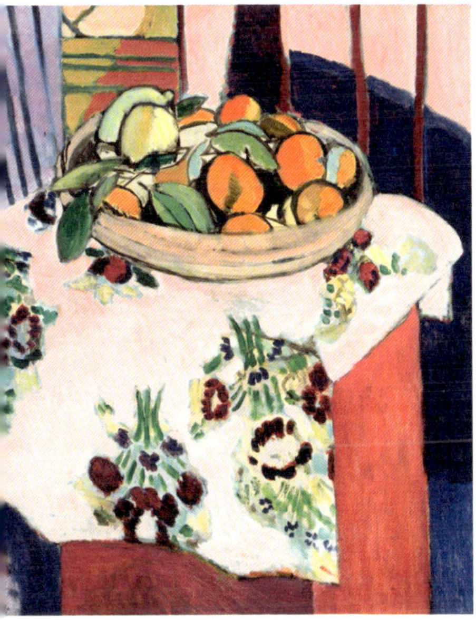

Henri Matisse
Still Life with Oranges, 1912
Oil on canvas
37 × 32.7 in. (94 × 83 cm)
Gift of the heirs of Picasso, 1973/1978. RF1973-72

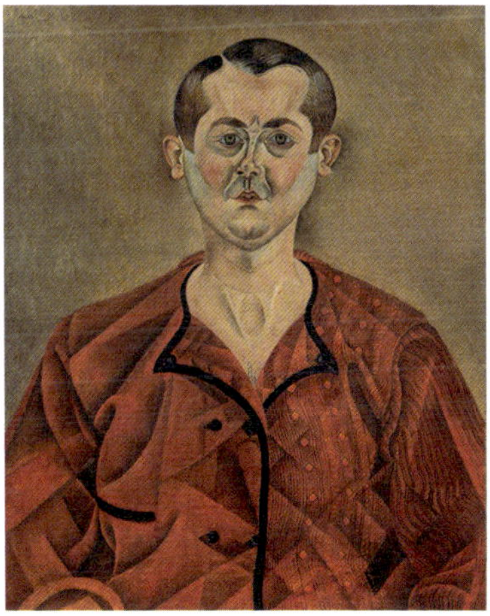

Joan Miró
Self-Portrait, 1919
Oil on canvas
28,7 × 23,6 in. (73 × 60 cm)
Gift of the heirs of Picasso, 1973/1978. RF 1973-79

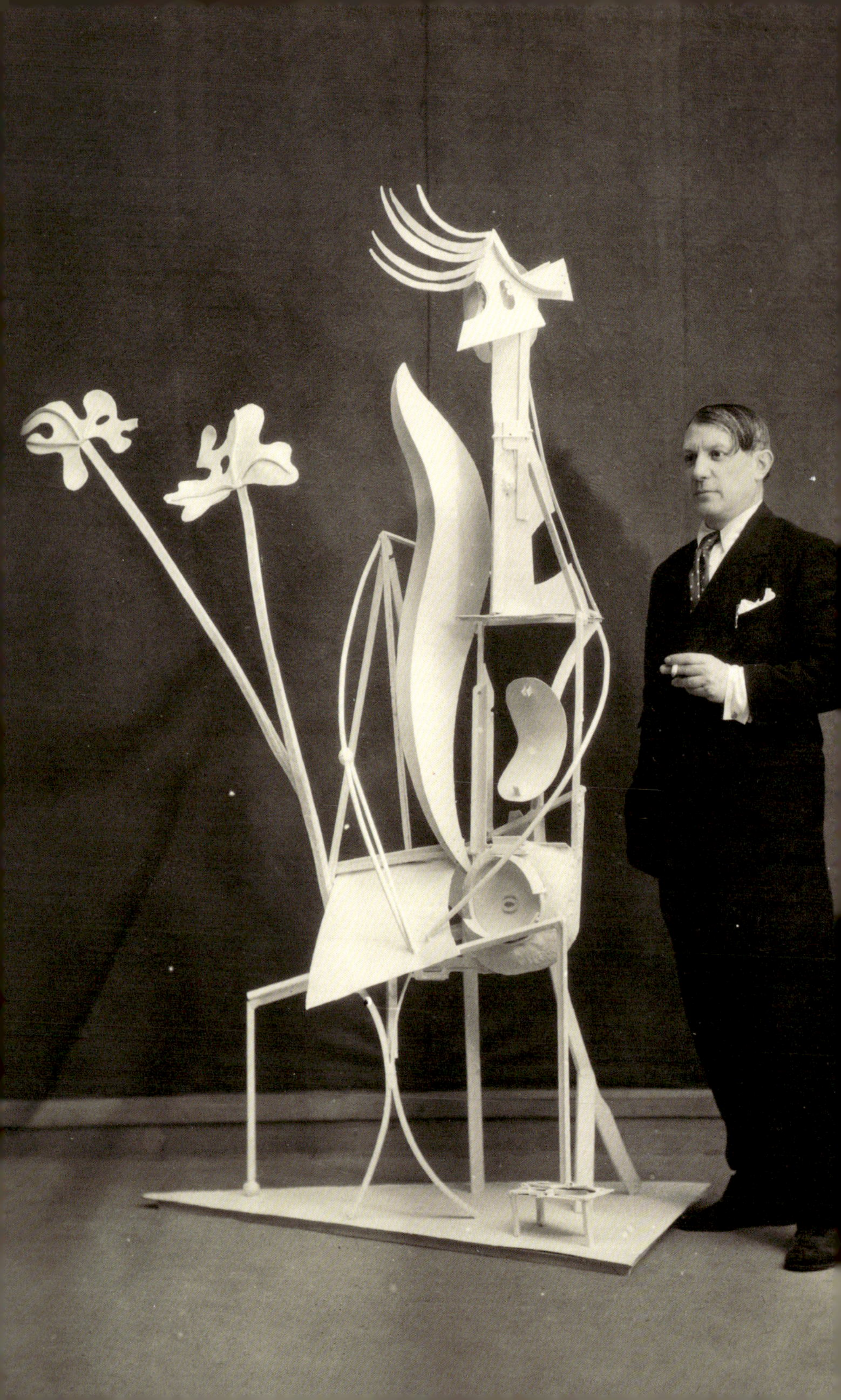

Masterpieces, 1895–1972

Unknown
Pablo Picasso beside the sculpture *Woman in the Garden*, at his first retrospective at Galerie Georges Petit, Paris, June–July 1932
Undated print
Gift Succession Picasso, 1992. APPH6652

1895

The Barefoot Girl

La Coruña, early 1895
Oil on canvas, 29.5 × 19.7 in. (75 × 50 cm)
Dation Pablo Picasso, 1979. MP2

Picasso hadn't yet turned fourteen when he painted the portrait of this young girl from Galicia, one of his very first oil paintings. Following in the footsteps of the masters of Spain's Golden Age, such as José de Ribera and Francisco de Zurbarán, Picasso portrayed popular figures and picturesque models, including this young girl with her bare feet and her sad pout. A sober pose, a neutral background, an uncluttered space, and zenithal lighting: everything adds to the naturalism. However, Picasso treats the anatomy in a mannerist style. The asymmetrical gaze as well as the oversized eyes, hands and feet convey the painter's empathy for his model, whom he observes, searches and beyond mere appearance. *The Barefoot Girl* is the first incarnation of a recurrent theme, the seated woman, observed and observant, which Picasso adapted and renewed throughout all his work. **N.L.**

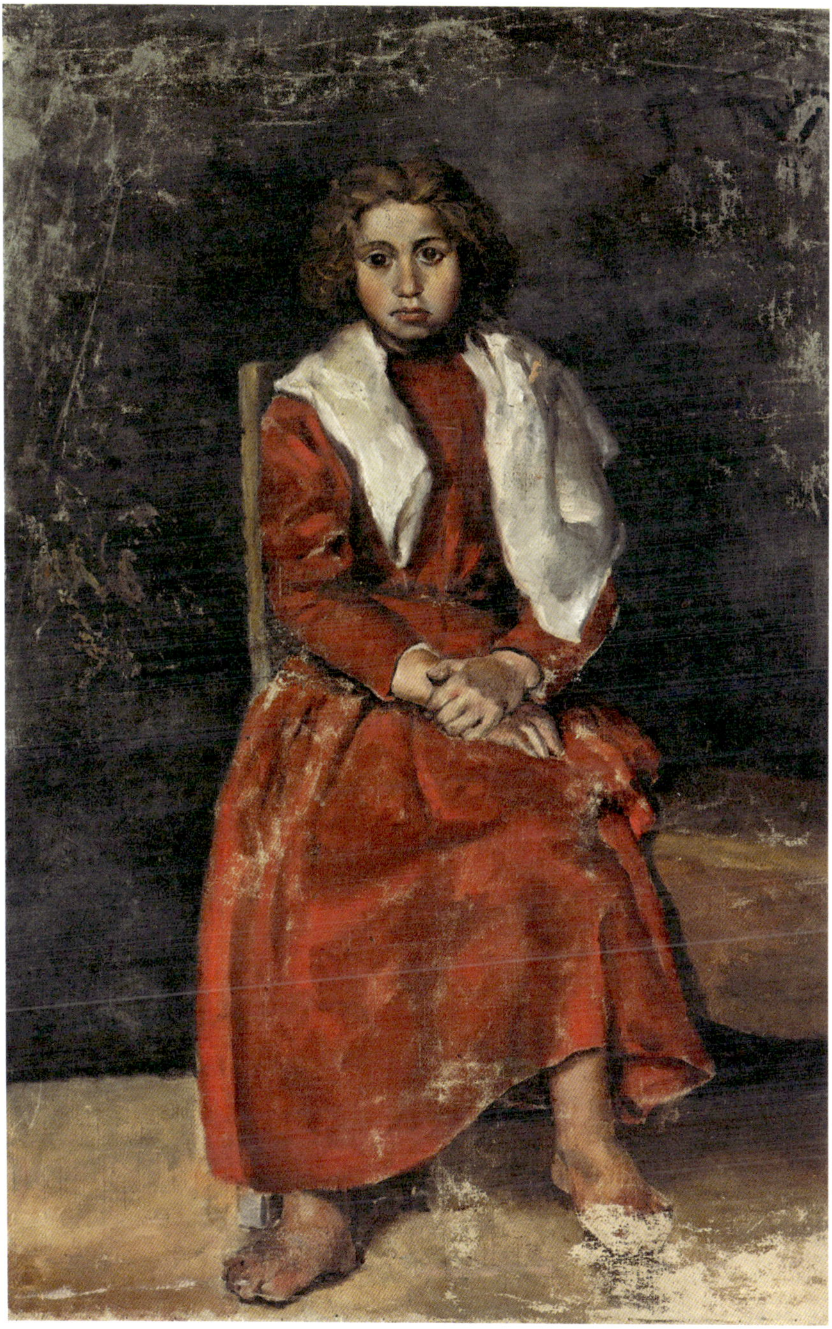

1900

El Paralelo Cafe-Concert

Barcelona, 1900–01
Oil on wood panel, 14.2 × 19 in. (36 × 48 cm)
Painting confiscated for the benefit of the state: 2008 criminal court decision in Grenoble. MP2008-2

This Spanish cabaret scene, although painted in Barcelona, gives away the Parisian avant-garde's influence on Picasso, who stayed in the French capital for the first time in 1900. Everything here is a reminder of the nightlife as depicted by painters such as Toulouse-Lautrec or Steinlen in many compositions. The scene could even seem set in Paris, if it weren't for the red flowers in the women's hair or the dresses of the flamenco dancers in the background. However, Picasso does not give in to a picturesque temptation, as he places the folk show in the back, thus focusing more on the public and placing the viewer right in the middle of the audience. His arbitrary cutting of the side characters illustrates a framing choice influenced by the new vision of pictorial space, conceived first by Degas. With its touches of paint contrasting vibrantly, the canvas is further animated by bright red and white brushstroke that recall Vincent van Gogh. *El Paralelo Cafe-Concert*, characteristic of the artist's "pre-Fauvism," wonderfully illustrates how Picasso, who was barely twenty, acts as a "painter of modern life." **E.Ph.**

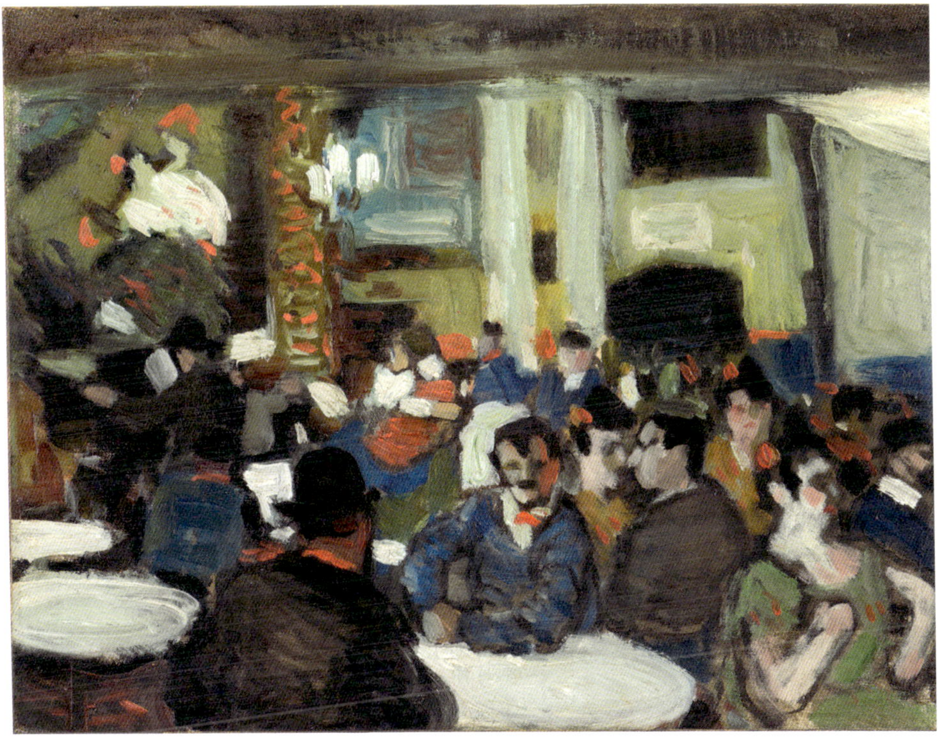

1901

Self-Portrait

Paris, late 1901
Oil on wood panel, 32 × 23.7 in. (81 × 60 cm)
Dation Pablo Picasso, 1979. MP4

This self-portrait was painted in December, 1901, right before Picasso returned to Barcelona. In June, he had shown his brightly colored works at Ambroise Vollard's gallery, in the post-Impressionist "mode," which caused a stir. Was it this success that led him to undertake a radical adventure? Over the summer, the color blue takes over the entire pictorial layer of Picasso's work, leading up to this nearly monochrome *Self-Portrait*. It may very well have been a challenge addressed to those who used blue merely for shadows, such as Toulouse-Lautrec or Steinlen. Wrapped in a typical Montmartre painter coat, the body fades into the background, made of many layers of solid colors, from which a few touches of green emerge. With its lack of structure, the body translates a world of coldness and sadness. The young man represents himself with an aged, gaunt face, underlined by an imaginary beard trimmed in the fashion of El Greco's Spanish Grandees, which Picasso had always admired. Often the melancholy emanating from this *Self-Portrait* is attributed to the death of Carlos Casagemas, a friend of the painter, who killed himself because of an unrequited love. It marks the beginning of a long, thought-filled phase for Picasso, harboring his symbolist and metaphysical "Blue period." **E.B.**

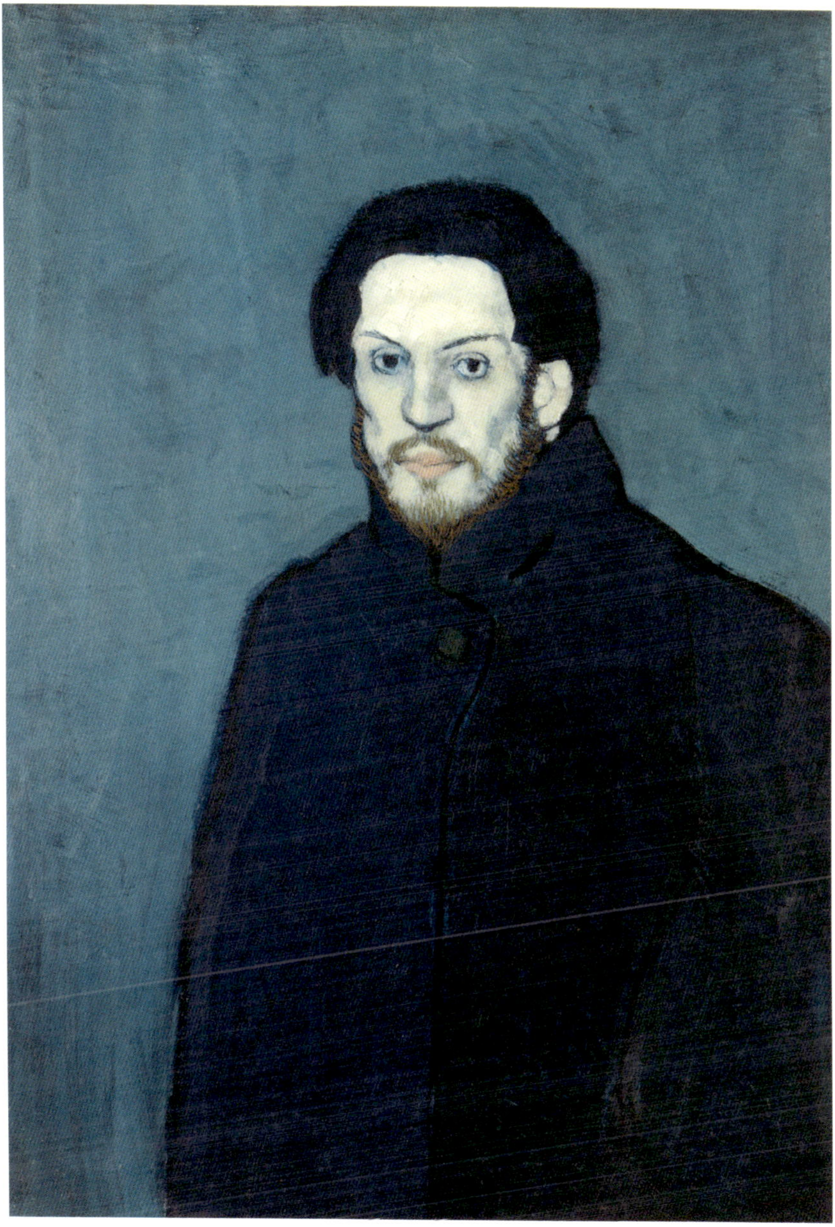

1902

Seated Woman

Barcelona, 1902
Original in Clay, 5.7 × 3.3 × 4.5 in. (14.5 × 8.5 × 11.5 cm)
Dation Pablo Picasso, 1979. MP230

Seated Woman is Picasso's first sculpture that we know of. It was most likely made from a live model. There are no other examples of it, nor any preparatory drawings, and so it conveys a unique emotion. Except for the face, with its melancholy expression that echoes the Blue period's miseries, the contours are of one compact form. This work shows astonishingly little detail: only form prevails, detached from any narrative content, stripped to its simple plastic presence. *Seated Woman*, in this way, marks the beginning of a sculptural type that Picasso would rarely deviate from: that of the individual sculpture. The image of the character set in a stone block seems tinged with religious overtones, recalling a figure from a Nativity scene, designed to evoke pathos-filled grief. The seated woman, treated here for the first time three dimensionally, inaugurating his sculptural work, shall become one of Picasso's constant themes. **V.P.**

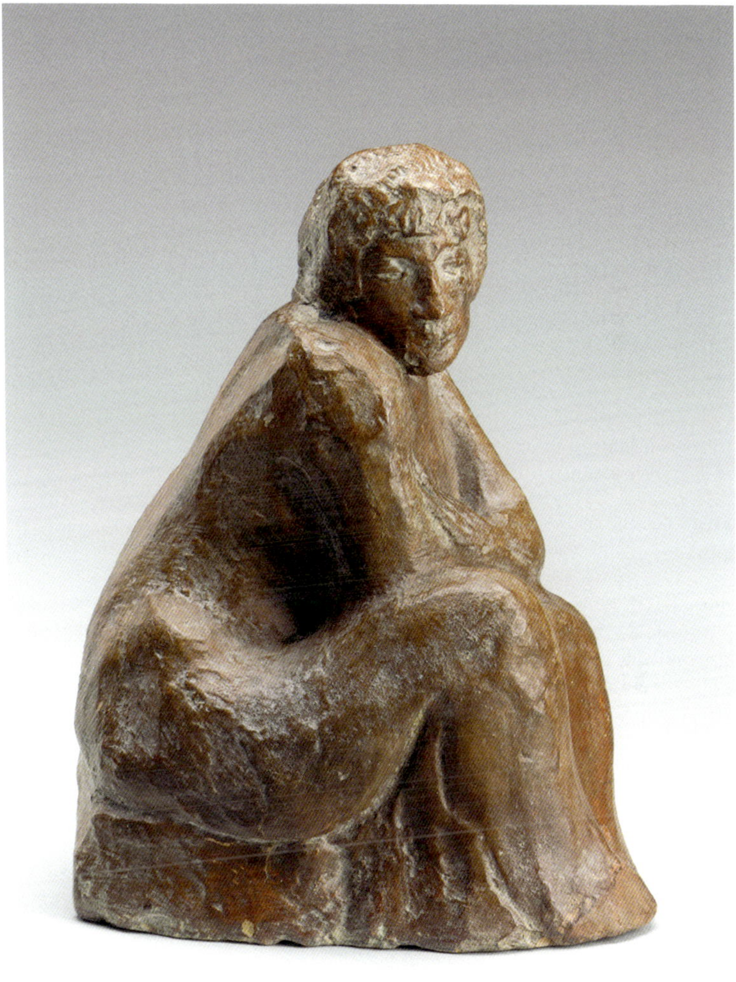

1903

Head of Crying Woman

Paris, January 1903
Pen, brown and black ink and black wash on paper, 9.09 × 7.2 in. (23.1 × 18.3 cm)
Dation Pablo Picasso. MP470

Head of Crying Woman belongs to Picasso's cycle of serious and dark drawings, begun in 1902. While in the images of groups in this series, the men and women stand closely together, heads hunched into their shoulders in profound desolation, here, the woman's face alone tells a story. Following the academic exercise of "tête d'expression" (or the mastering of facial expressiveness), Picasso uses pen and ink to exacerbate the face's misery and labor in its sunken cheeks. The delicate lines emphasize each wrinkle and echo the craggy faces of Francisco de Goya's elderly women. With this black, weeping, tense mouth, the artist explores the motif of the scream, characteristic of European symbolism, a movement he was fascinated by at the beginning of the century. **C.Z.**

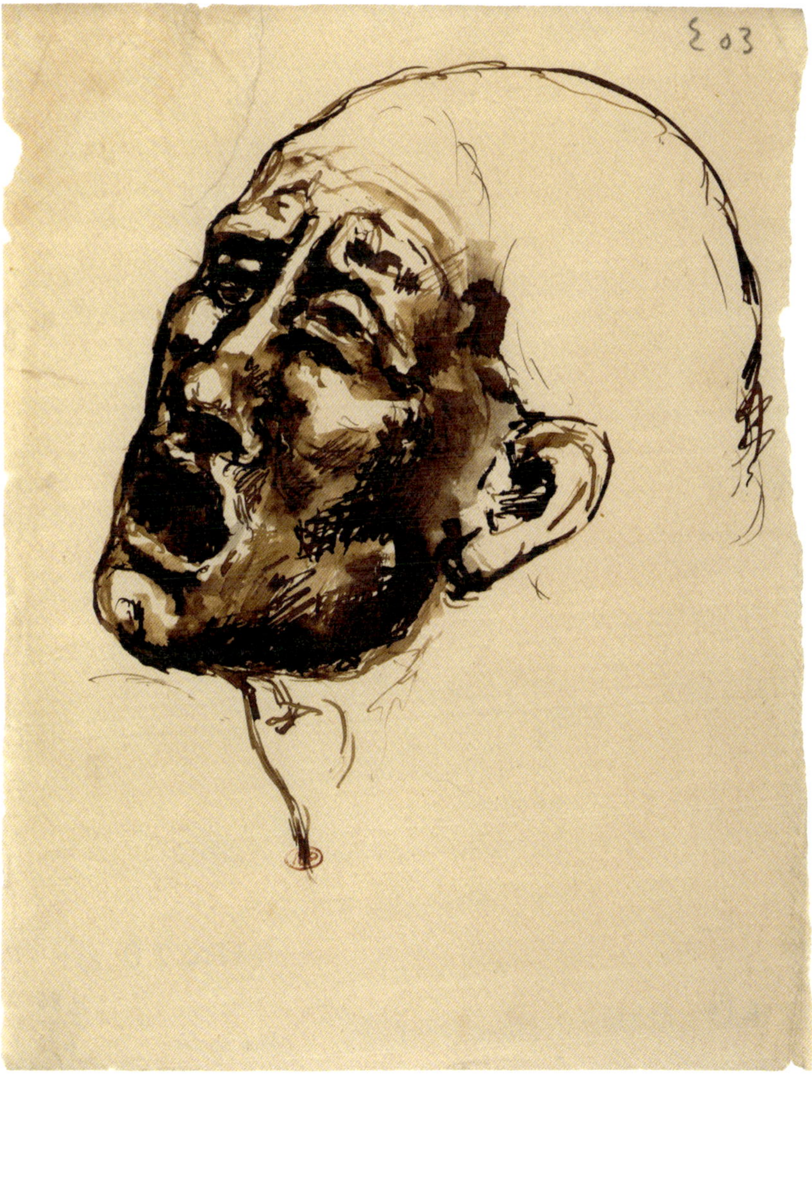

Picasso, the Spaniard

Of course ... we are led to consider Picasso as a French Cubist like any other. Wise people believe they can extricate the Spanish within him from these mechanical judgments. But they too will fall into mechanisms, those of an academic, touristic, terribly common view of the Spanish temperament and civilization. In fact, they will have discerned nothing of his profound Spanishness, nothing of the depth of the conflict under which his heritage is within and contrary to the French taste.

Jean Cassou, "Picasso and Spain," *Picasso*, exh. cat., Musée des Beaux Arts, Lyon, 1953, n.p.

Spanish roots

Picasso was born in the heart of Andalusia, in a still archaic Spain. During his youth, he experienced three very different provinces: in the south, "Arab" Andalusia, in the northwest, rural Galicia, and in the east, Barcelona and its fully European modernity. At the El Quatre Gats café, he discovered the Parisian avant-garde through art magazines and conversations with his elders who had been to Paris. These artists admired "gothic" Spain and El Greco. They collected strange objects and sculptures, including ancient ceramics. In 1906, in Gósol, Northern Catalonia, Picasso developed his first primitive pieces, after seeing Iberian statues at the Louvre. His Blue period (1901–04), his El Greco mannerism, the misery that evokes the realistic painting of Spain's Golden Age, all blossoms throughout the end of Picasso's Barcelona years. Finally, in 1909, when Cubism is invented, he retreats to Horta, the home village of his Catalan friend Manuel Pallarès.

Artistic immigration and exile

When he settled permanently in France in 1905, Picasso joined the "Spanish colony," living off of many more or less artistic jobs in Montmartre. Despite his increasing success from the early 1910s, his Spanish nationality and his status as a foreigner were never completely forgotten in a country affected by nationalism and international tensions. At the beginning of the First World War, "kubism"—as it was spelled out of mockery—was vilified in the media, and characterized as "Boche" art, or foreigner art. A judgment that included the Spanish Picasso, perhaps because his work was shown in a gallery owned by the German Daniel-Henry Kahnweiler. Between the wars, Picasso is attacked by nationalist art critics for having perverted "French art." In 1939, *Les Demoiselles d'Avignon* (1907) is bought by the Museum of Modern Art of New York, and not by the Musée d'Art Moderne in Paris. In 1940, Pablo Picasso, who had been living in France for over thirty-five years, filed for French nationality, possibly in a move to protect himself and his art. His request was denied on the grounds that he had Spanish anarchist acquaintances at the beginning of the century. The accusation that he is a corruptor of "French" tradition is then used again by Henri de Vlaminck in a collaborationist article in 1942, and Picasso makes the list of "degenerate" painters compiled by the Nazis. In 1967, he refuses the Legion of Honor medal.
Picasso was an exile, an opponent to Franco's regime as were many Spanish refugees, and he refused to return to Spain after the advent of the dictatorship. In 1967, when the regime demanded the restitution of *Guernica* (1937, Museo Nacional Centro de Arte Reina Sofía, Madrid), which had been at the Museum of Modern Art of New York since 1940, he announced that he would refuse the transfer while the dictatorship was in place. In 1963, he did not attend the inauguration of the Picasso Museum Barcelona, created with the generous donation of his friend and secretary, Jaime Sabartés. However, in 1968, to pay tribute to his friend who had passed away, he donated to the museum the "Meninas" he painted after Diego Velázquez (1957), a series of forty-seven paintings that reaffirm his place in the grand tradition of Spanish painting.

The Musée National Picasso–Paris

In 1968, André Malraux, Minister of Cultural Affairs, dation, payment-in-kind—in anticipation of the artist's death—which will help found the future Musée National Picasso. He noted that the national heritage holds only a small collection of Picasso's work, of which ten had been given by the painter himself in 1947 to the Musée d'Art Moderne, directed by the curator Jean Cassou. André Malraux thus strongly asserted that the country's heritage and culture have nothing to do with nationality. Today, the Musée National Picasso–Paris is the world's first collection of the art of Pablo Picasso, the Spaniard. **E.B.**

1904

Celestina (Woman with a Cataract)

Barcelona, March 1904
Oil on canvas, 29.3 × 23 in. (74.5 × 58.5 cm)
Fredrik Roos gift, 1989. MP 1989-5

This portrait of Barcelona madam Carlotta Valdivia became the enigmatic image of *La Celestina*, a matchmaker paid to encourage Calisto's affection for Melibea in a play by Fernando de Rojas. *La Celestina*, or *Tragicomedy of Calisto and Melibea*, is a sixteen-act dialogue that tells the misfortune of various characters, all headed towards a tragic end, as death trumps a love corrupted by money. *Celestina* was painted before Pablo Picasso left Barcelona to permanently settle in Paris, and marks the end of the Blue period, which it still belongs to. In this practically monochrome palette, the artist expresses his melancholy before the world's tragic essence. His asceticism in terms of means of expression is growing, as proven by the monochrome simplicity, the composition's austerity, the frontal face, and the absence of spatial notations or anecdotal details. A disturbing meditation on the duality of the being and the world arises from the asymmetrical gaze: one eye, wide open, signifying strength, while the left, walleyed, suggests turmoil, like an interior regard. Thus, this portrait is considered a metaphor for the creative process. **J.-Y.S.**

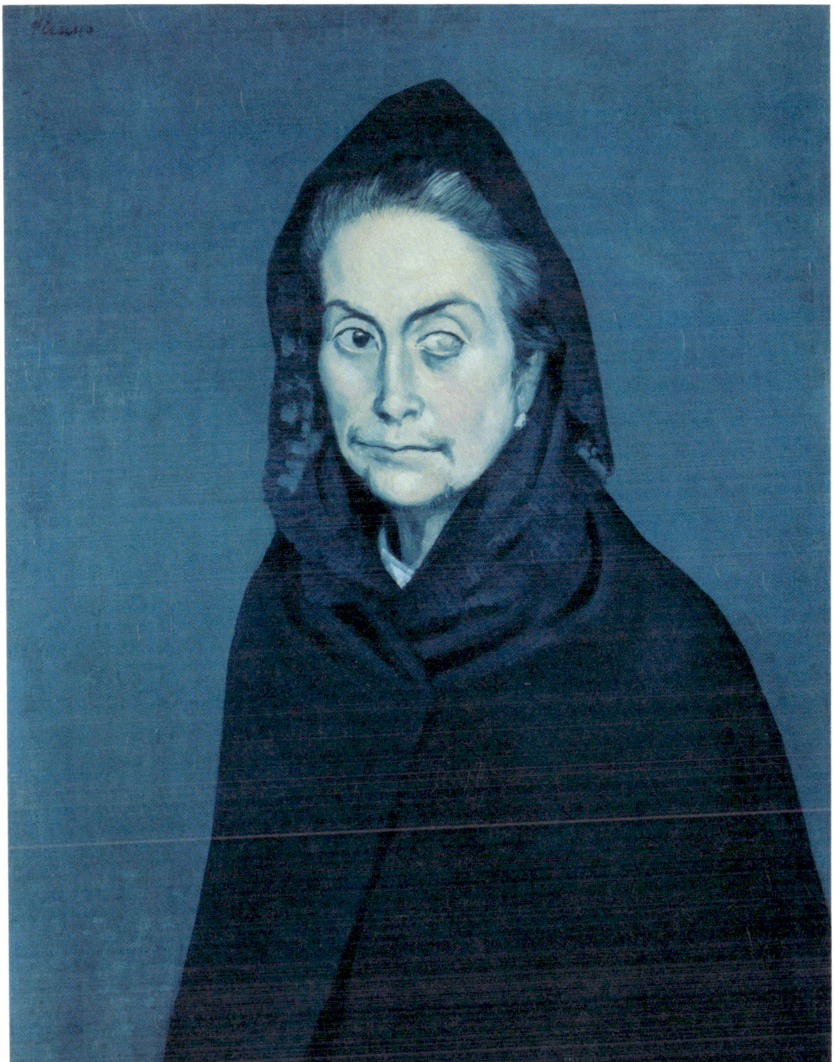

1905

The Jester

Paris, around 1905
Bronze, cast for the art dealer Ambroise Vollard
16.3 × 14.6 × 9 in. (41.5 × 37 × 22.8 cm)
Dation Pablo Picasso, 1979. MP231

In Bateau-Lavoir, Paris —his practically empty, stripped-to-the-minimum studio—Picasso explored the world of gypsies in which Harlequin, in turn fool or sad clown, mixes with a variety of eccentric characters. *The Jester* was started one evening on returning from the Medrano Circus in Paris, and is said to have originally been portrait of the poet Max Jacob, who accompanied Picasso. The modeling of *The Jester* is distinguished by its geometrical construction and its vibrant, continuously modulated surface. The strong stylistic contrast between shadow and light reveals the depth and sensibility of the introspection, while the use of clay as the original material exalts the strong expression of a character whose surface seems to bear the traces of Picasso's hands. The impression of strong plasticity comes from the structure of the hat: its triangular point, encircled with a crown, was added as in a collage. **V.P.**

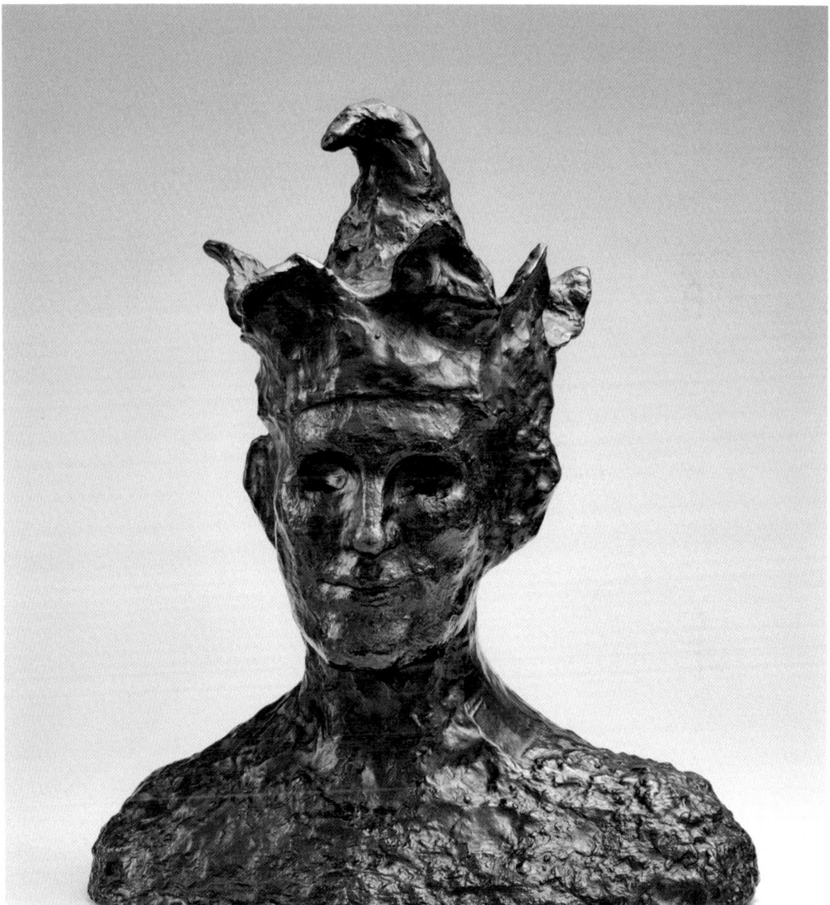

1906

The Two Brothers

Gósol, summer 1906
Gouache on cardboard, 31.5 × 23.2 in. (80 × 59 cm)
Dation Pablo Picasso, 1979. MP7

From May to August 1906, Pablo Picasso stayed in Gósol, a small village in Northern Catalonia, accessible only by mule. There, his work intertwined remarkably with the magnificent landscape of this timeless region, preserved from industrial modernity. The works achieved during this sojourn illustrate a pivotal moment, a transition from which there would be no return for Picasso. His delicate gouache is still tinged with the ochre melancholy of the grand circus wanderings, as also suggested by the not fully visible drum, a symbolic remnant of the acrobats' era. From a stylistic point of view, the painting is also representative of the new classicism arising in the painter's work. This dawning classicism is the result of multiple inspirations: first of all, that of Ingres, whose *Turkish Bath* (1862, Musée du Louvre, Paris) Picasso admired at the Salon d'Automne in 1905 and which is apparent here in the linear outline of the slender silhouettes that stand out against an almost-uniform background. The choice of subject reveals a more distant—though just as strong—influence: that of an eternal Mediterranean region, full of beautiful ephebes. Lastly, the sculptural treatment of the bodies, with stylized torsos and legs, the volumes of which are designed by a nuance of lighter shades, recalls the ancient Greek statuary tradition of the kouros. **E.Ph.**

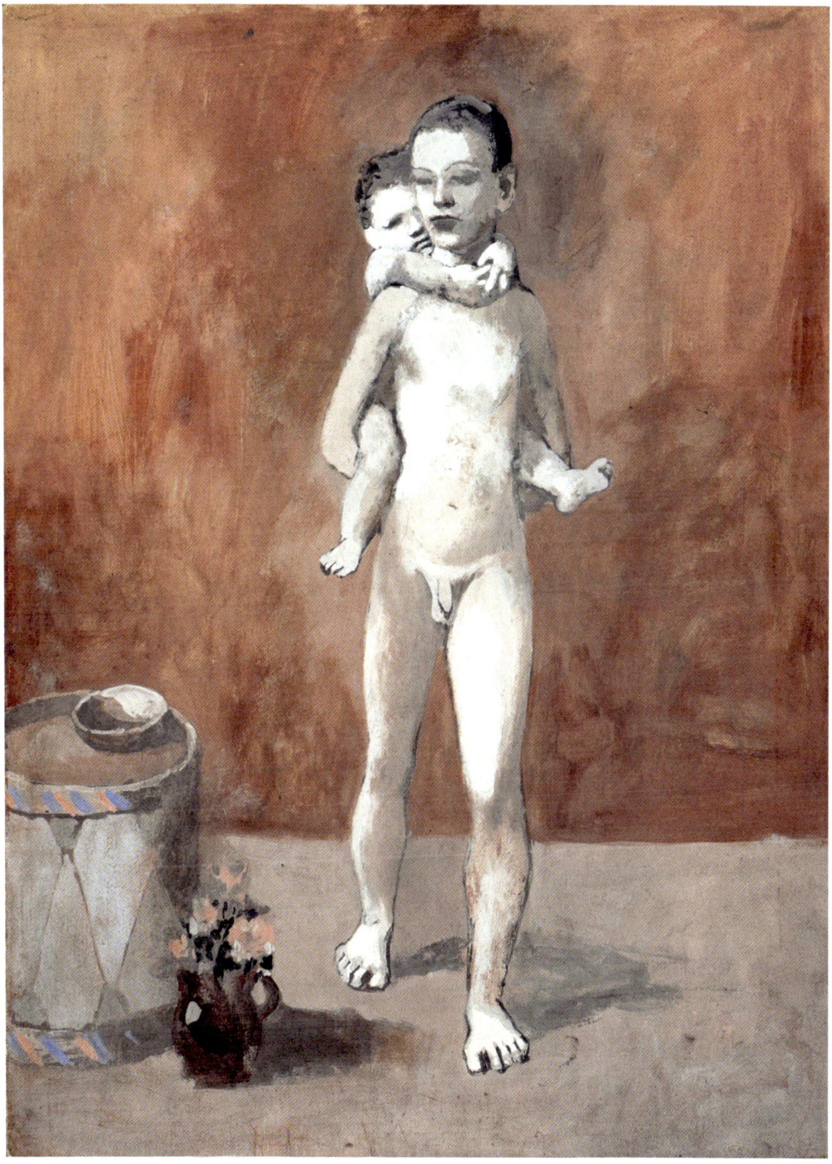

1907

Seated Nude (Study for Les Demoiselles d'Avignon)

Paris, winter 1906–07
Oil on canvas, 47.6 × 36.9 in. (121 × 93.5 cm)
Dation Pablo Picasso, 1979. MP10

This female *Seated Nude* is one of the studies for *Les Demoiselles d'Avignon* (1907, MoMA, New York) that the museum holds. In the final version of the painting, Picasso conserves this color range for the third character from the left, thus creating a contrast between ochre-pink, red and blue. He overturns, in a way, Ingres *Valpinçon Bather* (1808, Musée du Louvre, Paris), a woman bathing in the nude, with graceful curves, seated and turning her back. Picasso's nude faces the viewer, with her legs crossed in a way to offer a glance of her crotch, as would a prostitute according to photographs of the time. And yet, the eroticism is lost with the sculptural, masculine curves. While reinterpreting the geometric lessons on volume found in Cézanne's paintings, Picasso blends genders. The face becomes a triangle; the breasts become pectorals; and the round belly, abdominals. Every muscle is prominent, the hands and feet are heavy and stable. Cubism is well underway. **E.B.**

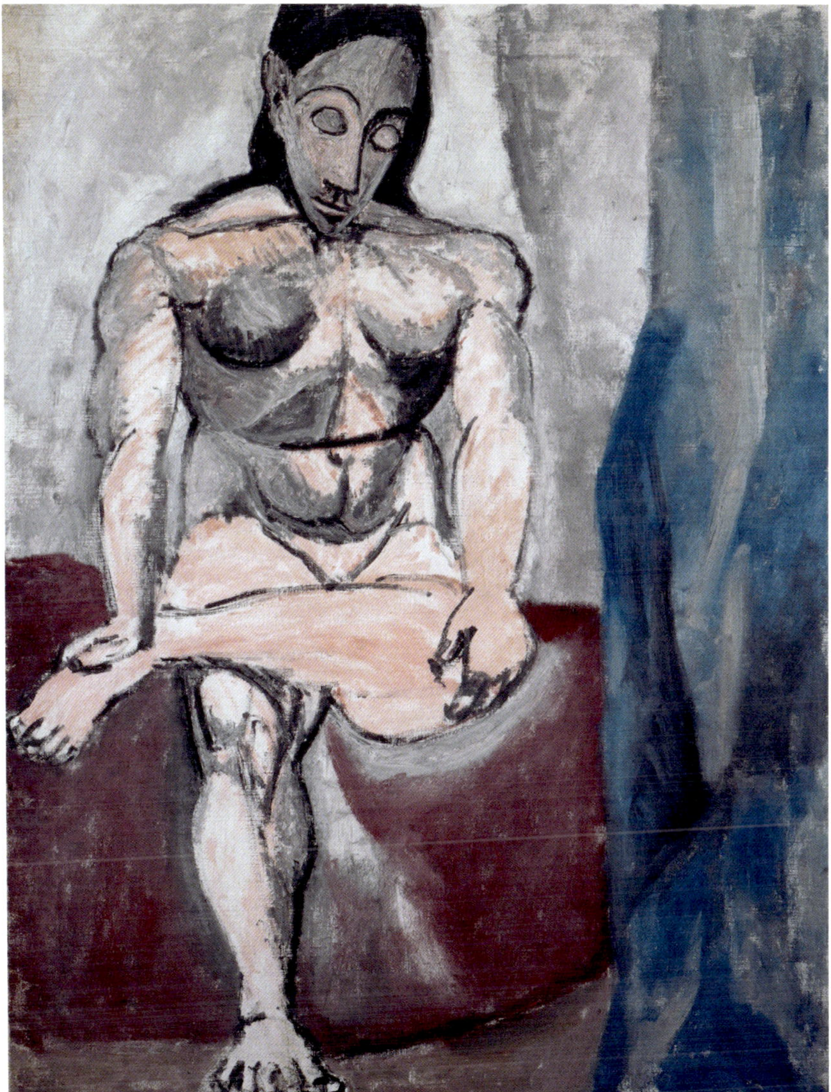

Picasso and Africa

"Negro art? Never heard of it!"

Pablo Picasso, "Opinions on Negro Art," *Action*, no. 3, April 1920, p. 25.

Discovering "African" arts

Art lovers, collectors and missionaries have long been bringing back pieces of non-Western art from their trips. France was a colonial empire that stretched into Africa, and to the Pacific Islands. Some of these objects, "fetishes," "primitive," were held at the Musée du Troacadéro, were already being studied, but were more objects of curiosity. In fact, African works were seldom distinguished from Oceanian ones, since knowledge was only in its early stages. In the early twentieth century, the gaze shifted: among the first artists to discover their artistic value and appreciate both their aesthetic and intellectual aspects were André Derain, Matisse and Vlaminck. They were in search of a new definition for art and its origins, and saw these objects as a form of novelty, following an idea formulated by several late-nineteenth century thinkers, such as Baudelaire, and later Gauguin. In a famous letter to Matisse, Derain mentions the visual, life-changing shock that was his introduction to African art, at the British Museum in 1906. Matisse was already a collector of African art, and showed Picasso a Vili statue that year. The latter saw ancient Iberian sculptures at the Louvre in early 1906—along with ancient Egyptian art—and in the summer of that same year, retreats to Gósol, in the Spanish Pyrenees. There, inspired by traditional Iberian sculpture, he begins a stylization of his drawing, which in the spring of 1907 will lead to *Les Demoiselles d'Avignon*. In the meantime, Derain took him to visit the Musée du Trocadéro, and he buys ethnographic pictures of African women (Fortier) as non-Western and non-"classical" models. All these elements come together in Picasso's art and become what is known as "primitivism." Just like his friends Michel Leiris and Tristan Tzara, he started his own a collection.

Plastic art, magic art

"African" art was a vast notion for artists at the beginning of the twentieth century, enabling a reinvention in the way bodies were represented. It marked the end of Impressionist reflections and light effects, and the end of the cerebral world of the Blue and Rose periods. The way African sculptures are structured into multiple, symbolic and geometric parts on which light shines, resonated with Cézanne's volumetric painting.
The display of volumes and the moving away from the classical, anatomical body, encouraged a sculptural aspect that helped Picasso invent new figures (see the notes for the years 1906–08, pp. 36–38). In 1912, a Grebo mask inspires a cardboard assemblage, *Guitar* (MoMA, New York). Picasso tells André Malraux,[1] that he is sensitive to the magical dimension of objects. He surrounds himself with his collections and pieces for protection, as he has a fetishistic relationship with things. He plays with them, manipulates them into various ways in his studio, and is very conscious of their power and making them a religious equivalent to art's cathartic virtues.

Arts of Africa, ethnography and decolonization

Picasso was well aware of the history between France and its colonies in the twentieth century. In the 1930s, when "negro" art became a fashion of sorts and an aesthetic in its own right, his friend Michel Leiris, who took part in the Dakar-Djibouti mission (led by Marcel Griaule) as an ethnographer, and mailed Picasso detailed descriptions of the expedition. The Surrealist magazine *Minotaure*, which often featured Picasso's artistic productions, published a special issue including the story of the expedition and its findings. Surrealist artists then tried and create a different relationship with these objects, revealing the context of their fabrication and the practices involved. In 1931, they issued a leaflet saying "Do not visit the colonial exhibition" (even though they also sell objects from their collections). In 1936, they set up the "Surrealist Exhibition of Objects," at the home of the art dealer Charles Ratton, subversively associating modern art (including some of Picasso's pieces), Surrealistic objects, and Oceanian and American art. In 1948, Picasso portrays Aime Cesaire in *African Presence*, thus showing a distant affiliation with a gradual opposition to colonialism—although it remains ambivalent in many ways. **E.B.**

1. See André Malraux, *La Tête d'Obsidienne*, Paris, Gallimard, 1974, pp. 17–18.

1908

Three Figures Under a Tree

Paris, winter 1907–08
Oil on canvas, 39 × 39 in. (99 × 99 cm)
William A. McCarty-Cooper gift, 1986. MP1986-2

In this painting, three female figures stand close together in a square—an unusual shape for Picasso. Their empty eyes and motionless faces make for an eerie lack of expression. Hinting towards the plastic forms of African masks, Picasso has moved away from the eroticism of his *Demoiselles d'Avignon* (1907, MoMA, New York), finished the previous year. He has developed a purely plastic and conceptual vocabulary, in which shadows and reliefs emerge from contrasted layers of colors, inspired by the way light underlines sculpted masses of body parts in African statuary. In the background, a forest is symbolized in a vanishing point, with the outline of a tree and branches, and dark green hatching. The colors are thus both warm and cold with ocher yellows, oranges and reds for the bark, as opposed to sea-greens and -blues. The merging of the characters and the landscape in one single pictorial space belongs to the magic of objects in African art and attempts to liberate humanity's spirituality. **E.B.**

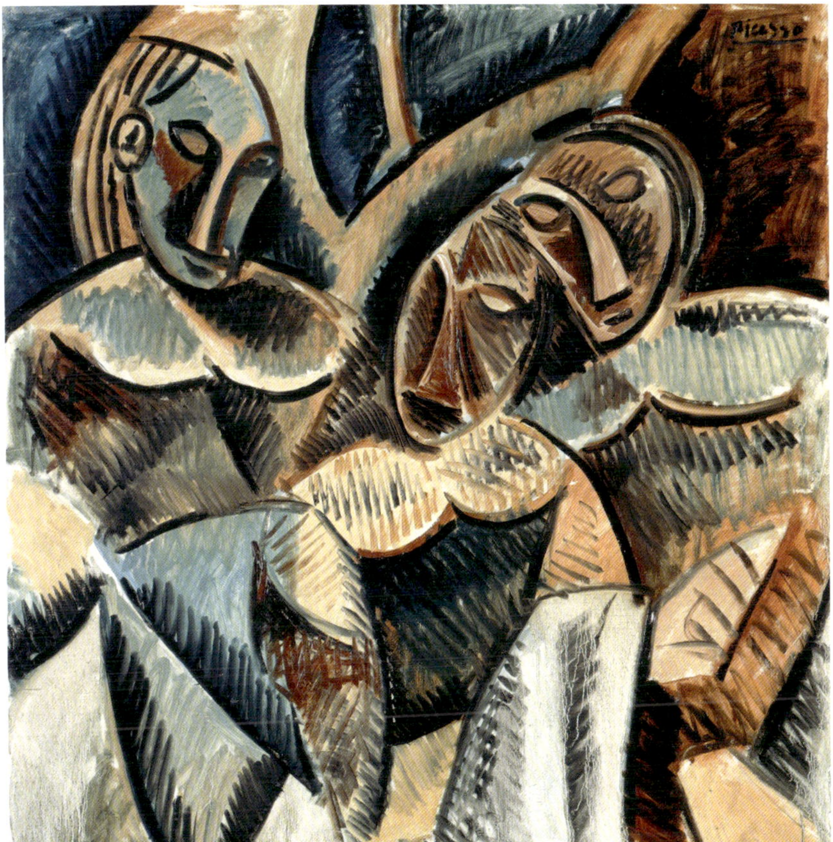
Picasso

1909

Head of a Woman (Fernande)

Paris, fall 1909
Bronze, cast for the art dealer Ambroise Vollard, 16 × 9 × 10.2 in. (40.5 × 23 × 26 cm)
Dation Pablo Picasso, 1979. MP243

In the fall of 1909, upon returning from a stay in a small village of Tarragona called Horta, Pablo Picasso sculpts a clay portrait of his partner, Fernande Olivier, in the studio of his sculptor friend Manolo (Manuel Hugué). This head brings to a three-dimensional level the graphic language he tried while in Horta, in drawn and painted portraits of Fernande Olivier. The geometrical recomposition of the human figure hereby reaches its height as it gives in to the deformation of a division into facets. The 1909 *Head of Fernande* and its treatment are a first milestone in sculptural Cubism. The volume of the round head is traversed by light, conveying a new movement to the material and paving the way for a new genre. *Head of a Woman (Fernande)* was reproduced multiple times by the art dealer Vollard and later on by Heinz Berggruen. It was immediately a huge success. This sculpture is probably one of Picasso's most famous, and proved to be a major influence on Futurist artists such as Umberto Boccioni. **V.P.**

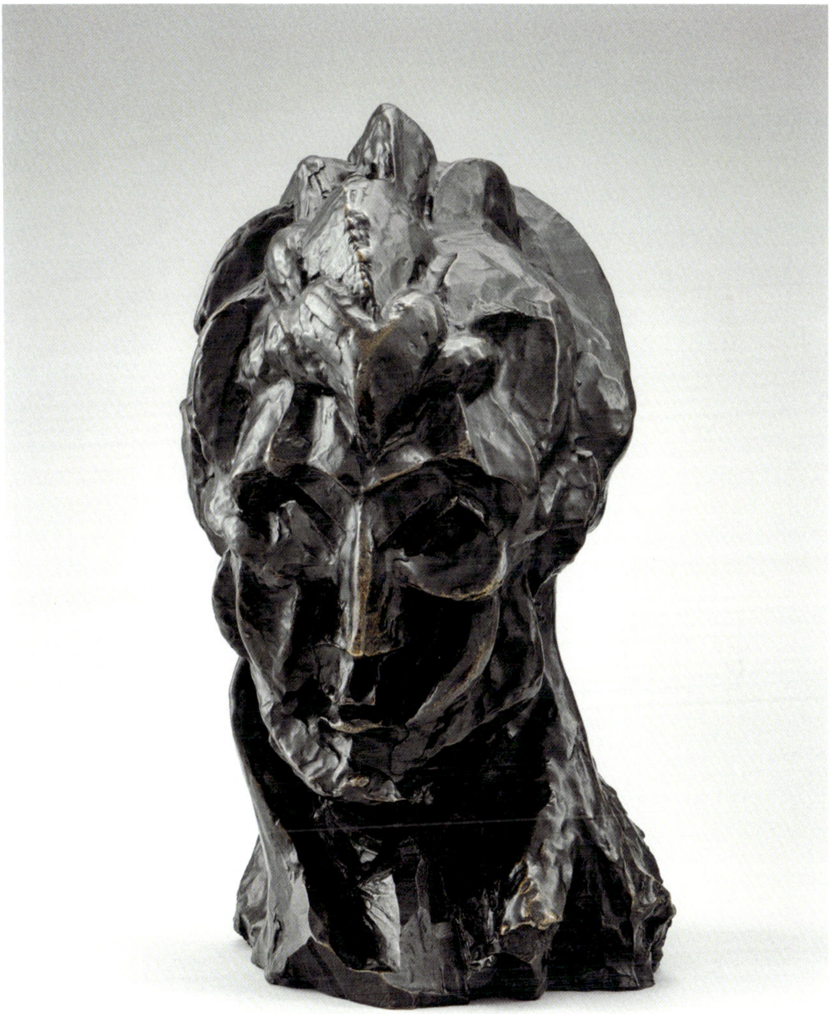

1910

The Sacré-Cœur

Paris, winter 1909–10
Oil on canvas, 36.4 × 25.6 in. (92.5 × 65 cm)
Dation Pablo Picasso, 1979. MP30

In September 1909, Picasso left the Bateau-Lavoir and moved to 11 Boulevard de Clichy. This new studio has a large window with a view of the Sacré-Cœur Church at the top of Montmartre. Here, Picasso tackles the question that has been gnawing at him ever since he found inspiration in Cézanne's paintings at the very beginnings of Cubism: how to represent a three-dimensional object on a two-dimensional surface without resorting to traditional illusionist techniques? Picasso turns to imperfect geometrical shapes, to sharp edges and to broken semicircles, thus simplifying Montmartre's mound landscape and reducing it to its mere plastic essence. The unfinished aspect of the canvas gives the Sacré-Cœur great dynamism, echoing the energy of this neighborhood where modern art is being invented. This painting thus constitutes a transition between Cubism's so-called "cézannian" phase and its "analytical" phase: the picture is still readable—the church's iconic dome emerges from the geometrical cluster—but it will become less and less decipherable until 1912, the year when Analytical Cubism peaks. The fragmentation of forms into numerous facets is underway, progressively deconstructing our habits of perception. **C.F.**

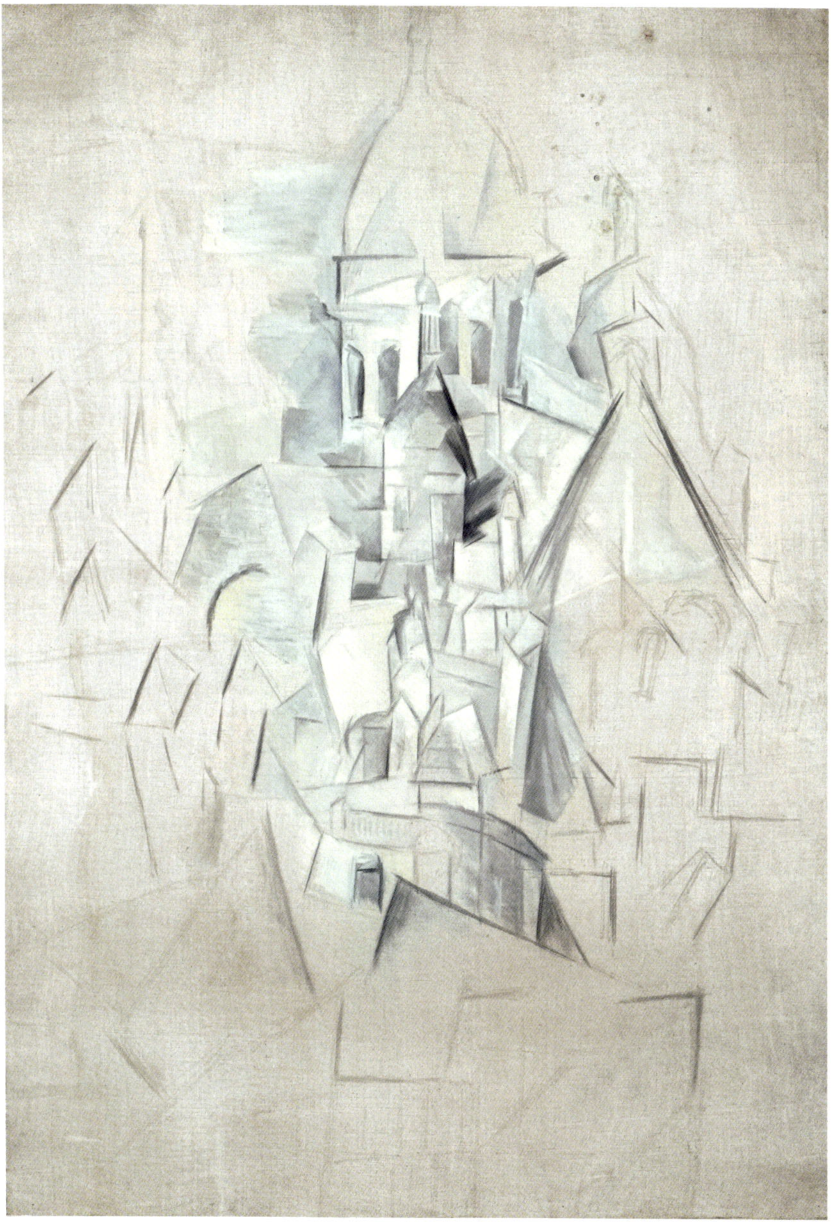

1911

Man with a Mandolin

Paris, fall 1911
Oil on canvas, 63.8 × 28 in. (162 × 71 cm)
Dation Pablo Picasso, 1979. MP35

Man with a Mandolin is a very narrow, vertical panel. Picasso recycled an existing work to which he added a canvas: the sewing is hidden under a line of small gray hatching and the lower third of the piece is indeed much lighter. It belongs to a series of famous Cubist compositions representing musicians, and shows many reliefs tangled together with lightness and transparency. The musician, who shows neither face nor personality, is disembodied. The hole in the mandolin is at the center of the frame. By painting these musicians, Picasso asserted the spiritual and inner closeness of painting and music, all the while inventing a plastic musicality: he pushes Analytical Cubism to an extreme, on the verge of hermeticism and abstraction, by painting not what we see, but what we perceive. **E.B.**

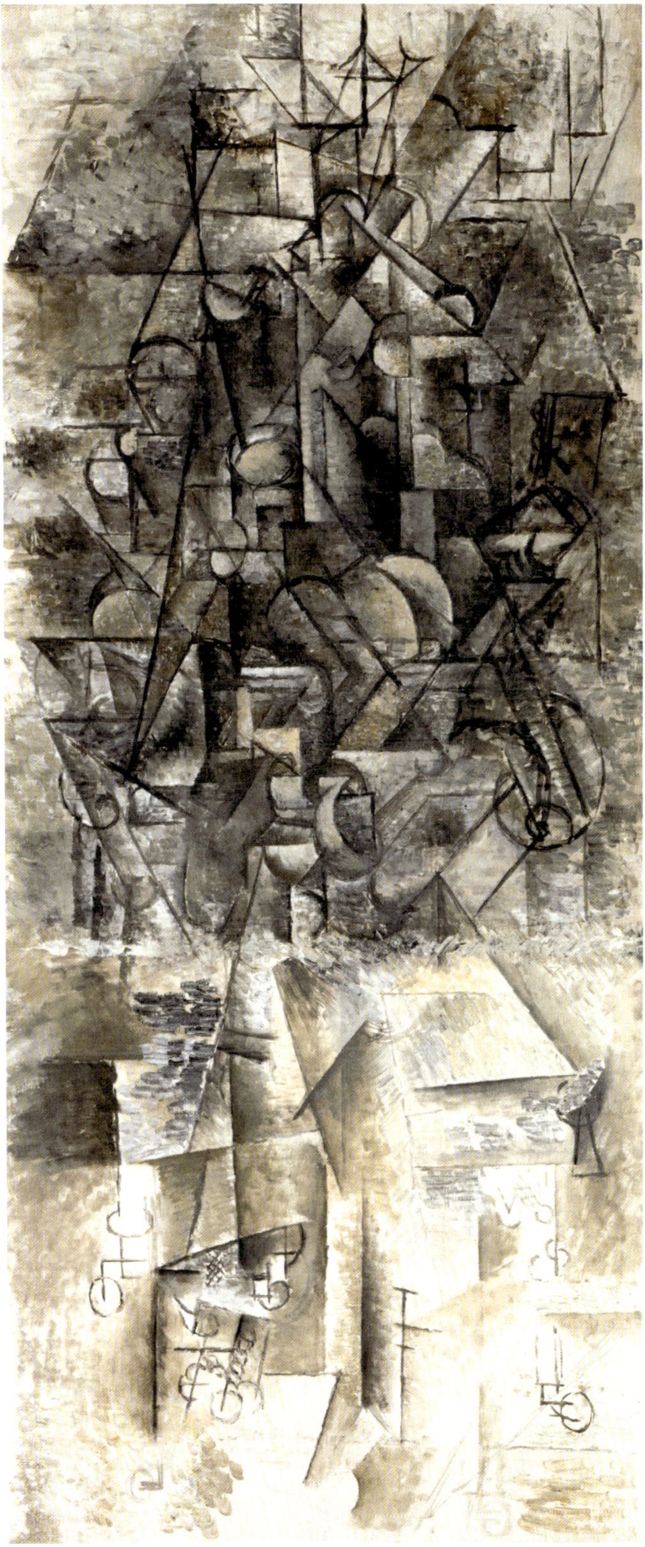

1912

Still Life with Chair-Caning

Paris, spring 1912
Oil and wax cloth on a string-framed canvas, 11.4 × 14.6 in. (29 × 37 cm)
Dation Pablo Picasso, 1979. MP36

Still Life with Chair-Caning is a mind game, a "trompe-l'esprit" (an "illusion for the mind," as opposed to a "trompe-l'œil," one for the eye) as Pablo Picasso put it. To its circular shape are joined two surprising elements: a rope and a piece of oilcloth with a pattern of chair's cane-work. Is it art or a simple object? An assemblage? A collage? *Still Life with Chair-Caning* marks a new step in Cubism, several conceptual elements of which are present: the letters JOU, as in the beginning of "journal" (newspaper) or "jouer" (to play), as well as the artistic signs for a pipe, glass, a candle, a knife, all held back by the rope in a random disorder. The rope calls to mind the ornamental string of the pedestal table with a removable top in Picasso's studio. Is the oilcloth, structured with brush strokes and a horizontal paint line, a tablecloth or the seat of a chair? How then could it be on a table? And vertically, all the more? By integrating real elements in the composition, Picasso highlights the artificial verticality of the pictorial medium, thus questioning the traditional system of representation in art. He inspired the "Tableaux-pièges" (trap-pictures) of New Realism artist Daniel Spoerri in the early sixties. **E.B.**

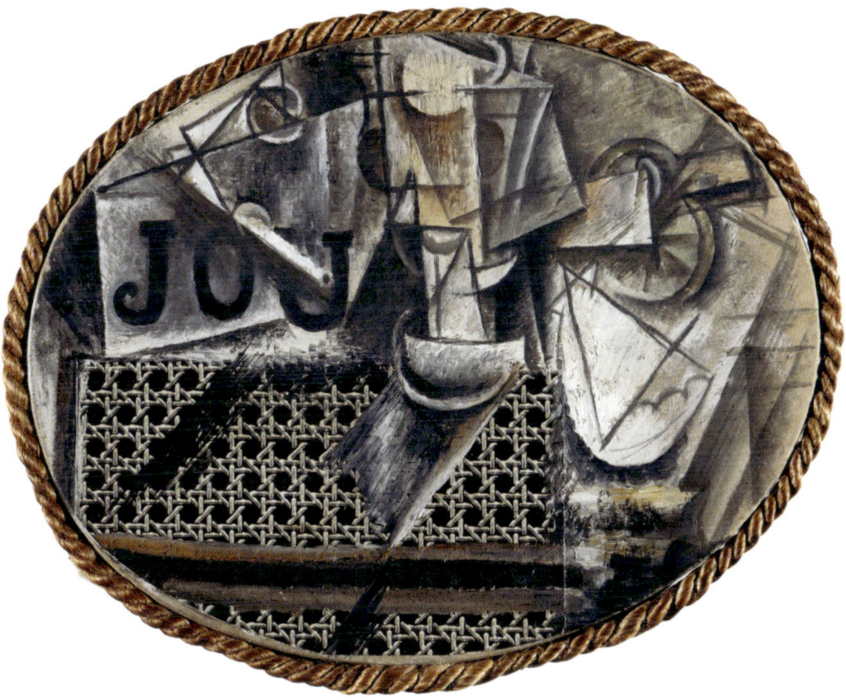

1913

Mandolin and Clarinet

Paris, fall 1913
Fir wood elements with paint and pencil
22.9 × 14.2 × 9 in. (58 × 36 × 23 cm)
Dation Pablo Picasso, 1979. MP247

The 1912–14 Cubist structures brought the earlier pictorial research into the third dimension and illustrate a shift in Picasso's work, as he turns away from the modeling technique and towards assemblage, distancing himself from classic sculptural processes and materials. In-between painting and sculpture, his relief still lives are made with poor-quality recycled materials (wood, in this case), enhanced with touches of paint. *Mandolin and Clarinet* is a perfect example of this phase: Synthetic Cubism. The musical instruments are reduced to elementary shapes and stripped of any narrative value; they simply cover all basic geometrical forms. This type of superimposition work will later be used for human figures in the 1956 group of *Bathers* (p. 149). Such straightforward and simple techniques carry a new form of expressivity and will become typical of Picasso's sculptures. **E.P.**

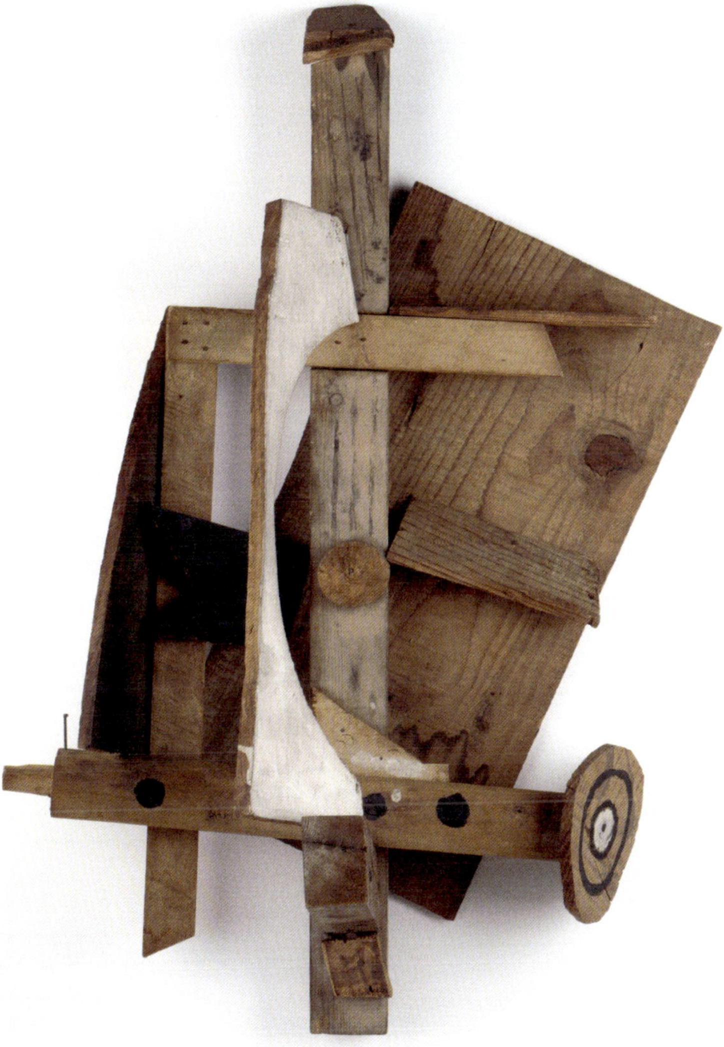

1914

The Painter and His Model

Avignon, summer 1914
Oil and pencil on canvas, 22.9 × 22 in. (58 × 55.9 cm)
Dation Pablo Picasso, 1979. MP53

Between mid-June and the end of November 1914, Picasso stayed in Avignon with Eva Gouel, painter Louis Marcoussis's former partner, with whom Picasso had been in a relationship since the end of 1911. His painting is testament to a shared happiness: the Cubist paintings celebrate the beloved woman with textual tributes—"ma jolie" (my pretty)—or with saturated colors and baroque rhythms, and rococo odes to femininity. It is then that Picasso let go of Cubism's strict structural grid, to use it as a means of expression, a style like any other. At the same time, he returned to portraits with a series of drawings of seated men: the figure of the leaning man here marks the culmination of this phase. Indeed, this small painting, long unknown, is true revelation of Pablo Picasso's legacy, illustrating the pictorial transposition of these studies. It constitutes a testimony of his return to natural shapes, initiated as early as the summer of 1914. It is also the only painting inspired by Eva's face. Unfinished, *The Painter and His Model* reveals a pure composition underneath, sketched in pencil, much like many line drawings from 1915 onward. It may have been the beginning of the war that stopped—at least until 1917—the painter's figurative momentum. **E.Ph.**

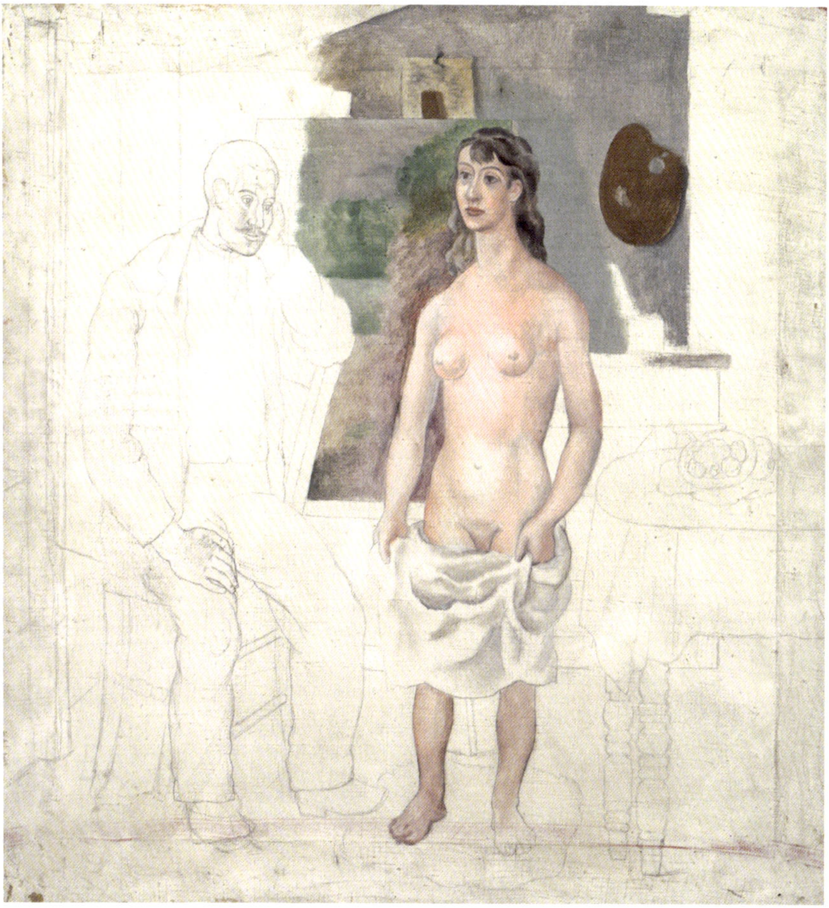

Picasso and Cubism

> *It is important to understand that he who sees triangles, cubes and cylinders in Picasso's paintings is an uneducated viewer .... [He who is able to fully grasp them] does not see geometric shapes, but things that are real in spirit, with an intensity far beyond that of illusionism.*
>
> Vincenc Kramář, *Moravskoslezká revue*, 1921, reprinted in *Kubismus*, Paris, ENSBA, 2002, pp. 12-13.

1907–1914, the Cubist Revolution

Picasso and Braque's friendship was so strong that they compared it to two mountain climbers joined by a single rope. Together they invented Cubism, a movement that opened the doors to the artistic modernity of the twentieth century. From 1907, the year of *Les Demoiselles d'Avignon* (MoMA, New York), until 1908, their painting becomes more simplified and more geometrical, drawing its inspiration from Cézanne's pictorial treatment of volume and from the plasticity of African sculpture. This would be the "proto-Cubist" phase. Analytical Cubism, between 1909 and 1911, deconstructed reality; so much so that in the summer of 1910, during a stay in Cadaquès, hermeticism comes close to abstraction. Synthetic Cubism (1912–14) brought back the entirety of the figure with incongruous materials such as pasted paper and fragments of objects. Braque and Picasso inspired followers, some of whom become the theoreticians of the movement: in 1912, Albert Gleizes and Jean Metzinger wrote *On Cubism*, but Braque and Picasso refuse to exhibit alongside them.

The two artists revolutionize painting by deciding to show the world not as it is, but as it is thought. A guitar is thus represented according to the multiple axes and points of view that the mind is capable of elaborating. Cubism is conceptual, it uses language. Stenciled words are inscribed on the painting, as a visualization of mental concepts that the two artists think of in gray ocher shades, far from reality's sensual colorfulness. But Cubism also proves to have a sense of humor and turns the world into "trompe-l'esprit" objects. Recycled materials are put together into new, incredible, and sometimes odd, configurations. A rope serves as a frame, a piece of waxed cloth becomes a chair and table (*Still Life with Chair-Caning*, 1912, MP36, see p. 50). Cubism itself dies in the trenches between 1914 and 1917 when many, like Braque, are called to the front and confronted with other explosions of shapes, very real this time.

1917–1925, Cubism and Classicism

In 1914, Picasso is still a young artist and founder of a revolutionary movement, whichis restricted to art critics and collectors. The sale of the modern art collection "La Peau de l'Ours," or "the Bear's Skin" (March 2, 1914), the *Parade* adventure (1917), selling the collection of his former art dealer Kahnweiler (May–November 1921), and working with a new dealer, Paul Rosenberg, from 1918, all gave Picasso quite a reputation as a "Cubist painter."
Just as Cubism began to be institutionalized, Picasso began to work, from 1917, on Ingres's classical lines. He painted *Studies* (1920, MP65, see p. 68), in which the classical sculptural figures of the Fontainebleau phase are juxtaposed with small still lives of the quieter Cubism he was then practicing (*Guitar and Clarinet on a Mantelpiece*, 1921, Metropolitan Museum of Art, New York). These still lives, heirs of Synthetic Cubism, seem to echo an earlier melancholy, a decade after its apogee, almost conveying an ornamental version of it. Could it be that Picasso was time traveling, as he often did, to revisit a style and add to it the mood of his new phase?

Cubo-Surrealism and Post-Cubism

The combination of Surrealist influences and of Cubist distortion begins in the late 1920s, and into the middle of the 1930s. When *Guernica* (1937, Museo Nacional Centro de Arte Reina Sofía, Madrid) is shown at the Spanish Pavilion of the Paris International Exhibition in 1937, it is characterized by some art critics as "Cubo-Surrealist." This term will remain in the history of art. Thus Picasso may well have blended the conceptual aspect of Cubism with the impulsive liberation of the subconscious in the Surrealist fantasy, between reason and emotion, a stage for haunting ghosts, constructed in the mind with the stories and photographs of the bombing. The front/profile face (see pp. 80–81), invented in between the wars, will remain until the 1970s, the trace of Cubism in Picasso's art. **E.B.**

1915

Violin

Paris, [1915]
Folded cut tinplate, paint and wire
39.4 × 25.1 × 7.1 in. (100 × 63.7 × 18 cm)
Dation Pablo Picasso, 1979. MP255

The music instrument (mainly guitars and violins) is a major motif in Cubist research, appearing in the collages by Braque and Picasso, before developing into three dimensions. From 1912, Picasso transferred to sculpture the flatness of reality that he had already initiated in painting and drawing. Assemblage—a technique derived from that of the collage—uses paper, cardboard and sheets of metal to create relief-paintings and constructions juxtaposing and superimposing planes. Objects used by Picasso lend their identity, more or less tangibly, to a recomposing autonomous in structure, material and form. The complex assemblage, *Violin* of 1915, has a powerful and paradoxical effect: its form is both homogeneous and completely fragmented. Made out of a single square sheet of metal, cut and bent, the open volume allows space into the sculpture. The paint creates hollows and reliefs in shifts of transparency and contrast. Ten years later, the first issue of André Breton's *La Révolution surréaliste* paid tribute to a white tin *Guitar* (MP260), as if to build a bridge between to avant-gardes. **N.L.**

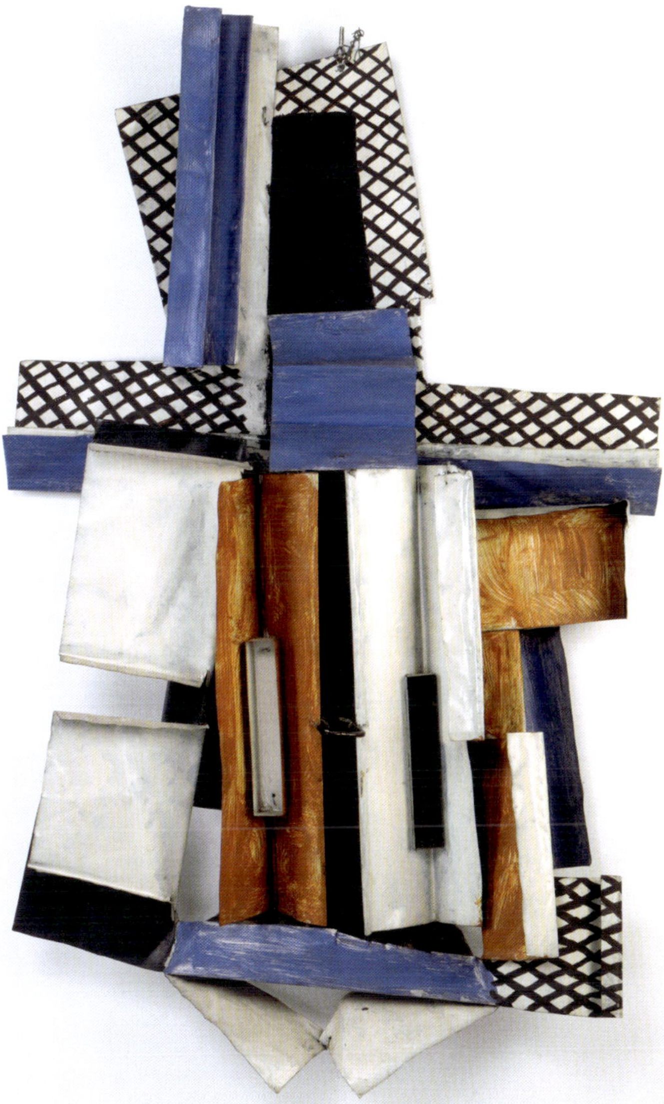

1916

Man at the Fireplace

Paris, 1916
Oil on canvas, 51.2 × 31.2 in. (130 × 81 cm)
Dation Pablo Picasso, 1979. MP54

Man at the Fireplace is a transitional work, composed by Picasso towards the end of his Cubist phase. In a pointillist and regular manner, the artist transfers to painting the glued-paper technique created with Braque a few years earlier. The illusion of a Cubist relief is created by the juxtaposition of shapes, the balance between plain and decorated layers, and the complexity of the cutting. The dismembered volumes of the full-length character bring to mind the contours of the musical instruments that inhabit Picasso's experimentations: the dark circular shape recalls a guitar's rosette, while the wavy lines at the edge of the fireplace evoke its strings. However, the large dimensions and the solid outlines of the fireplace—heavily set on the ground, yet with a distorted perspective—give the composition the impression of a new monumentality. **C.Z.**

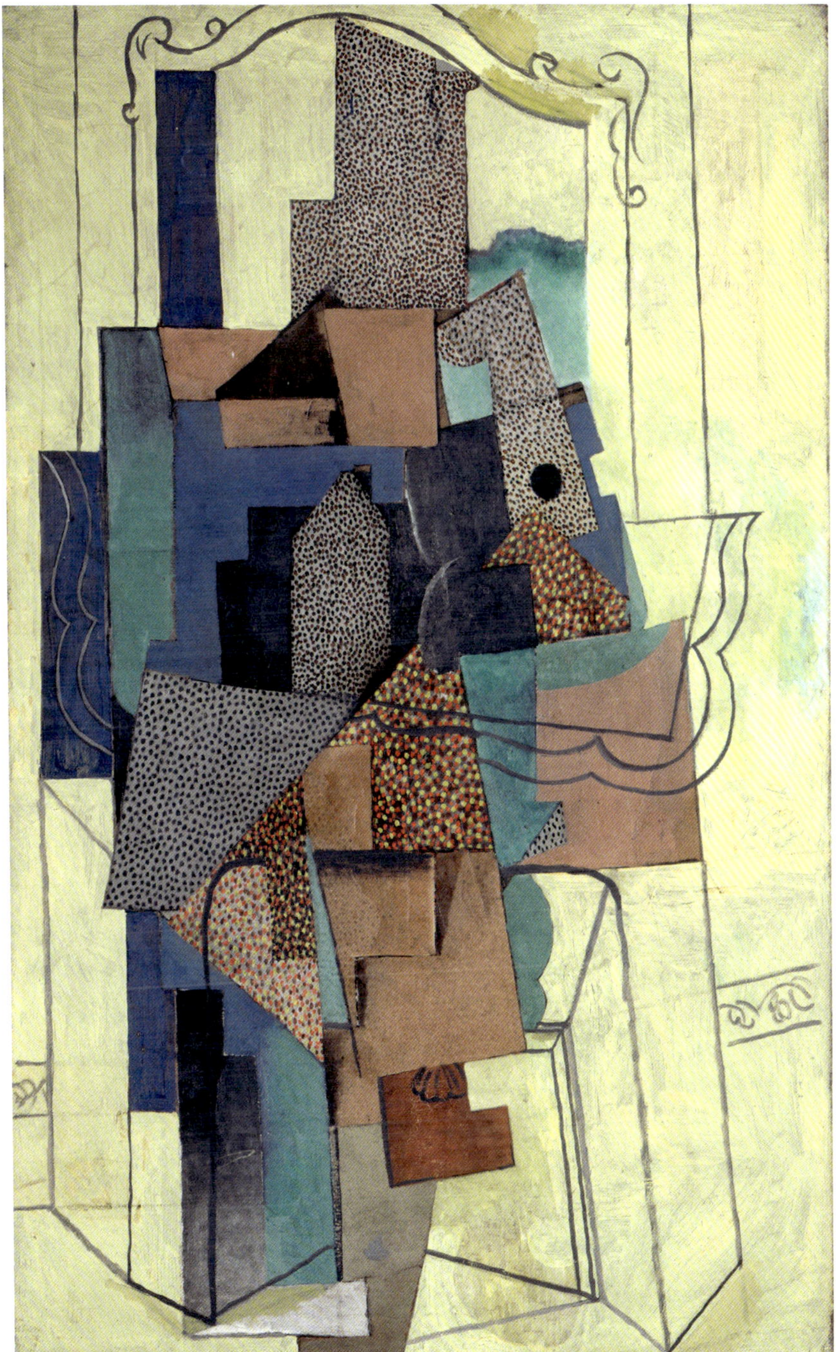

1917

The *Parade* ballet

Marked by travels and theater, 1917 also saw the beginning of Picasso's collaboration with Serge de Diaghilev and the Ballets Russes. The year began with Jean Cocteau in Rome, where the painter stayed for eight weeks, to work on the scenery and costumes for *Parade*. This ballet was choreographed by Léonide Massine, to a score by Erik Satie. It premiered on May 18, 1917, at the Théâtre du Châtelet in Paris, causing a scandal but also prompting Guillaume Apollinaire to coin the term "surrealism". While the curtain (Musée National d'Art Moderne – Centre Pompidou), with its characters from the circus and commedia dell'arte, had a classic spirit, the show is a Cubist transposition of modern life, notably illustrated by the costumes of the horse trainers. These characters were inspired by men in between sandwich boards and moved like robots, with motions deliberately held back by a very graphic costume alluding to the world of business and demands. Three trainers in the ballet—one French, one American, and one on a horse—acted as mobile advertising slogans, as they announce and punctuate each act of the parade, introducing the artists, whether Chinese conjurer, American girl or acrobats. **E.Ph.**

***Curtain design for the ballet,* Parade**

Paris-Rome, 1916–17
Graphite pencil and watercolor on paper
11 x 15.8 in. (27.7 × 40 cm)
Dation Pablo Picasso, 1979. MP1557

Design for an acrobat costume for the ballet,* Parade *ballet: acrobat costume

Paris-Rome, 1916–17
Watercolor and graphite pencil on paper
11 x 8.2 in. (28 × 20.9 cm)
Dation Pablo Picasso, 1979. MP1573

Study for the ballet,* Parade*: Pantomime horse studies

Paris-Rome, 1916-1917
Gouache on graphite pencil sketch on paper
8 x 11 in. (20.5 × 28 cm)
Dation Pablo Picasso, 1979. MP1589

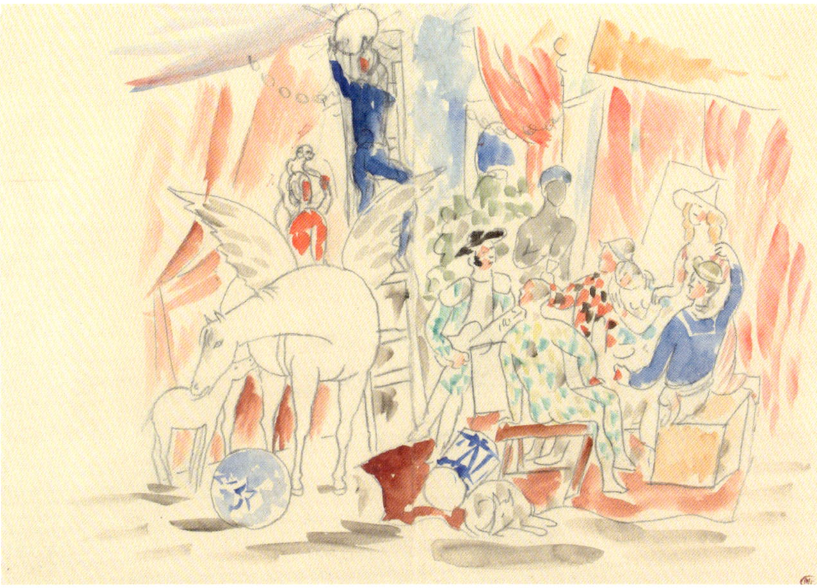

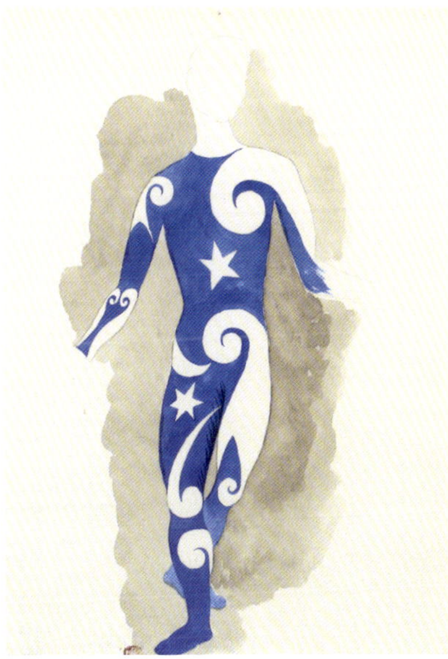

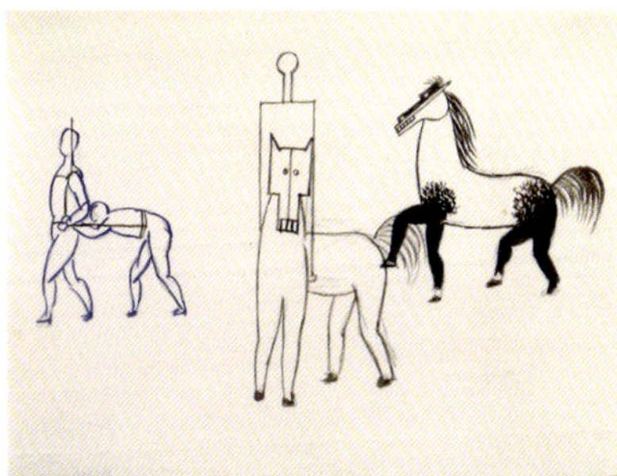

1918

Portrait of Olga in an Armchair

Montrouge, spring 1918
Oil on canvas, 35 × 11.8 in. (88.8 × 30 cm)
Dation Pablo Picasso, 1979. MP55

Picasso met Olga Khokhlova in Rom, in 1917, when he was working on the scenery for the ballet, *Parade*. She is a dancer in the Ballets Russes, managed by Diaghilev, and they married in Paris, in 1918.
During the war, Picasso has returned to the painter Ingres's classic and worldly line of work. In an elegant attire, close to the couture creations by Paul Poiret, Olga is sitting in an armchair, looking static and constrained: a pose that Picasso will use for the portraits of women his entire life. However, Olga did not sit for the painter: he painted her from a photograph. He reproduces the exact same large leaves and flowers of the chair, the pinkish petals with small green leaves, on the silky dress, the ornaments on the fan that seems dislocated and the part in the middle of Olga's hair. The background, though, has disappeared, as have the legs of the chair and the dancer's feet, making way for the raw canvas and a few coarse brush marks by way of a shadow. The woman is captured by the painting and fades into a model. In fact, an injury and her new status as a wife would prevent her from ever dancing ever again. **E.B.**

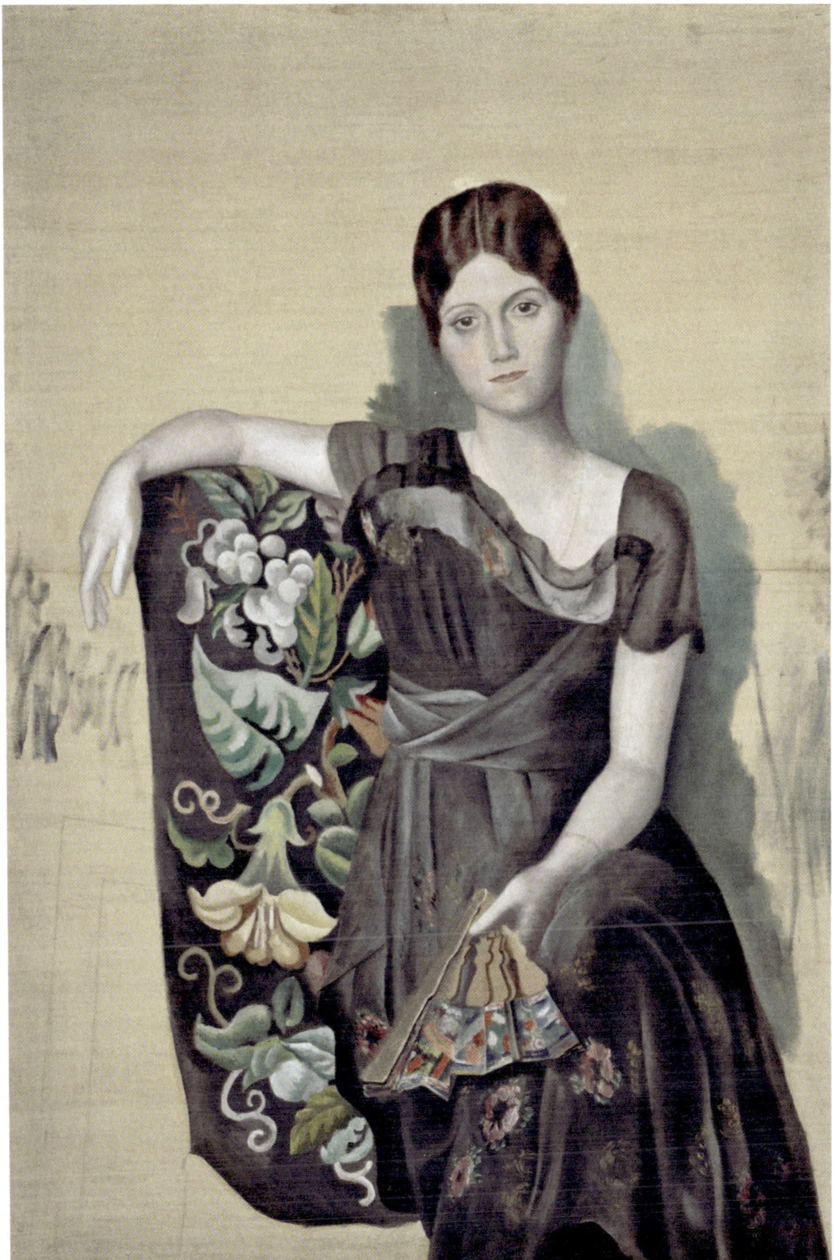

1919

Still Life with Pitcher and Apples

1919
Oil on canvas, 25.6 × 17 in. (65 × 43 cm)
Dation Pablo Picasso, 1979. MP64

Picasso painted this still life while exploring classicism. Its composition is simple, yet the piece is unsettling. On a chalky gray background, a plate with two apples sits on top of a jug, surrounded by more similar apples, randomly sitting on the table, around the pitcher. Picasso manages to increase the plumpness of the jug by slightly shifting handle and spout, and by deviating the light through the depiction of its shadows. Furthermore, the pitcher seems all the more monumental as the viewer has a double perspective, both as dominant over the table, and dominated by the plate. It brings to mind the solemn women Picasso painted at that time. For indeed this is about a woman, with ample curves, an open mouth, and a round, smooth bosom. The still-life genre has always associated symbolic, religious, philosophical and moral interpretations to compositions including objects, fruit, flowers and food. Picasso audaciously transforms the apparent simplicity of a still life close to those of Jean Siméon Chardin—one of which he will later own—into the dissimulated portrait of a sensual woman. He gives "things" a human aspect. **A.M.**

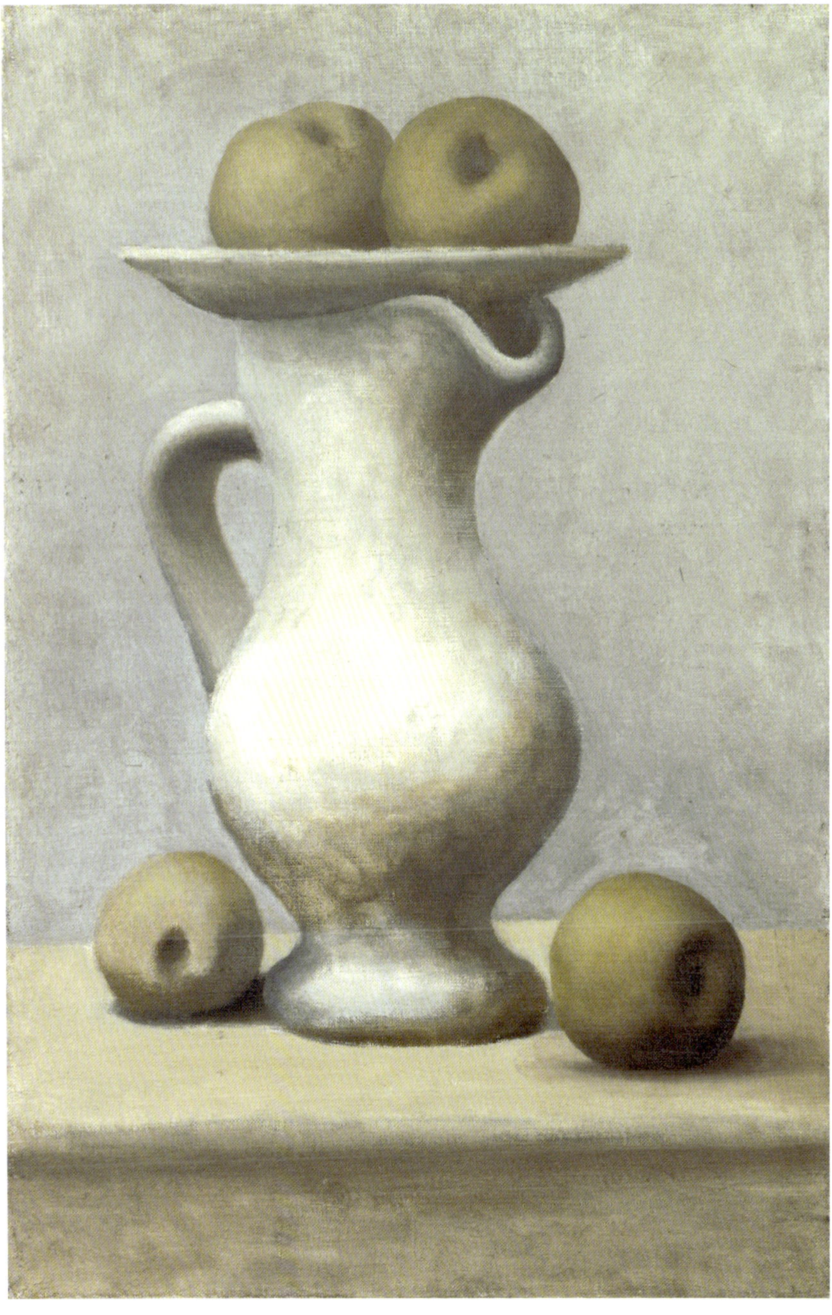

1920

Studies

Paris-Fontainebleau, 1920
Oil on canvas, 39.4 × 31.2 in. (100 × 81 cm)
Dation Pablo Picasso, 1979. MP65

Studies is an odd and emblematic piece, as it combines in one single painting all of Pablo Picasso's research at the beginning of the 1920s. It is considered a collage of all of the painter's influences, and a striking summary of his diverse yet simultaneous preoccupations, as it mixes neoclassical inspiration with the antique-like female profile, Renoir's iconography with the two dancers, and Crystal Cubism with still lives. Functioning as a manifesto, *Studies* asserts the coexistence of various approaches, and illustrates the profusion of subjects and of constituent steps in the process. Thus, the relative abstraction of the composition brings together finished and unfinished works, sketches and elaborate drawings, fragmented bodies and full-length figures, static and mobile ... much like on the wall of a studio. This *mise en abyme* does not show the act of painting itself—a topic copiously illustrated in many variations of the painter and his model—but the multiform result of the creation process. It puts forth the contemporary exploration of various paths by the artist and in doing so, challenges the strict division of Picasso's career into periods. **E.Ph.**

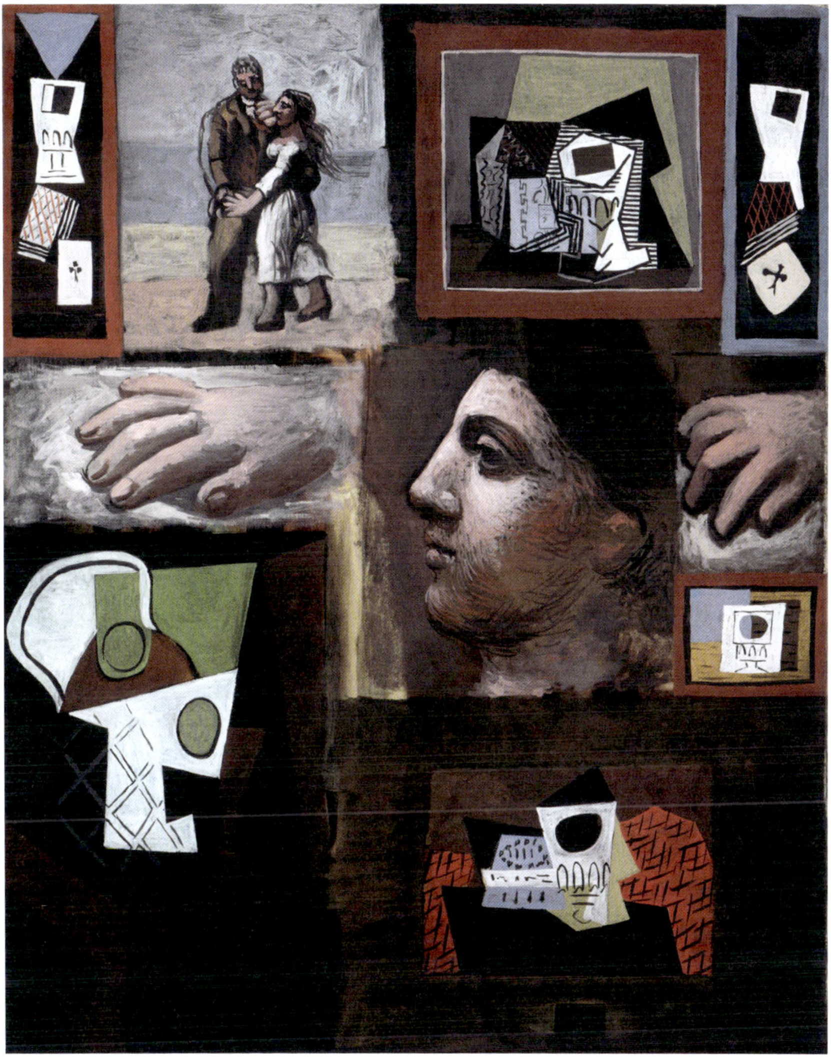

1921

Three Women at the Fountain

Fontainebleau, summer 1921
Red chalk on canvas, 78.7 × 63.4 in. (200 × 161 cm)
Dation Pablo Picasso, 1979. MP74

After multiple studies and two slightly different versions achieved with red chalk and oil, *Three Women at a Fountain* tackles the traditional imagery of the Three Graces, with three figures bearing sculptural contours, united by their movements' arabesques. This painting was inspired by several sources: antique sculpture, the classical paintings of Nicolas Poussin (*Eliezer and Rebecca*, 1648, Musée du Louvre, Paris), those of Ingres (*The Source*, 1856, Musée d'Orsay, Paris) and those—very surprising with their symbolist reinterpretation of classicism—by Puvis de Chavannes (*Young Girls by the Seaside*, 1879, Musée d'Orsay, Paris). This painting was made during the summer Picasso spent in Fontainebleau. The castle there keeps a few paintings by the mannerist Primaticcio, who inspired Picasso with his subtle deformations of the human body and his use of close framing. However, the monumentality of this composition is mainly due to the plastic treatment of the bodies in space. The canvas is practically filled with the richness of the female silhouettes, whose behavior is balanced by a meticulous disposition. The antique tunics' rigid drapery, as well as the way the bodies are depicted, seem so dense that they echo the stone on which these women are leaning. **J.-Y.S.**

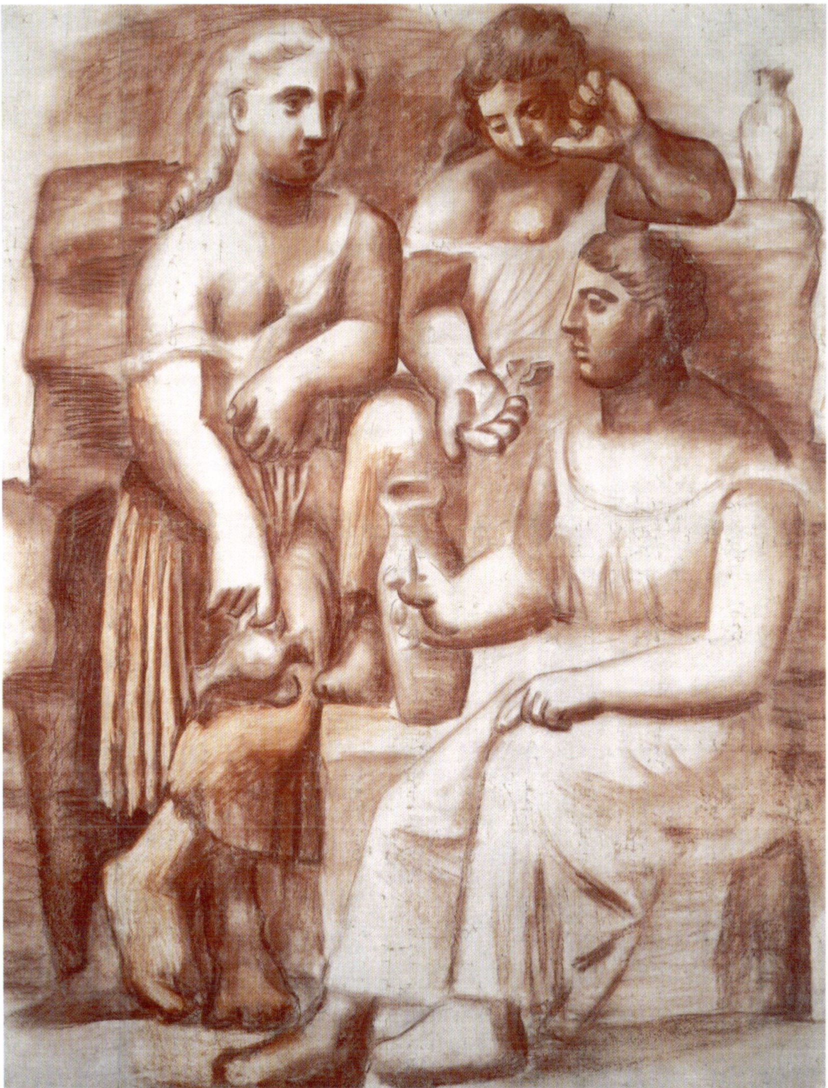

1922

Two Women Running on the Beach (The Race)

Dinard, summer 1922
Gouache on plywood, 12.8 × 16.2 in. (32.5 × 41.1 cm)
Dation Pablo Picasso, 1979. MP78

This painting is paradoxical, as Pablo Picasso uses a small size for a dynamic, powerful and unsettling scene. Two large women soar towards an azure sky, scattered with white clouds. The title mentions a race but rather, the women seem to be dancing. Neither seems bothered by her disproportionate body parts. While collaborating with the Ballets Russes, Picasso was able to observe the dancers moving. This gouache was in fact enlarged in 1924, for the stage curtain of *Le Train bleu* (choreography by Bronislava Nijinska, music by Darius Milhaud, booklet by Jean Cocteau, scenery by Henri Laurens, costumes by Coco Chanel), a ballet that evoked the Mediterranean region during the Golden Twenties, and the new trend of bathing in the sea. For these dancers are also bathers, discovered by Picasso in Dinard that summer. Lastly, their antique-like clothes and their slightly disproportionate sculptural outlines bring to mind the monumental, classic bodies that Picasso painted at Fontainebleau in the summer of 1921 (p. 71): women thus come to life as Maenads, the mythological followers of Dionysus whom Picasso first discovered on the antique bas-reliefs of the Prado Museum. In this small oil on canvas, Picasso thus combines several of his experimentations, which will eventually lead to the great "Bathers" series (p. 87), whether fun and dynamic in Dinard (1928–29), or monstrous, as at the beginning of the thirties. **E.B.**

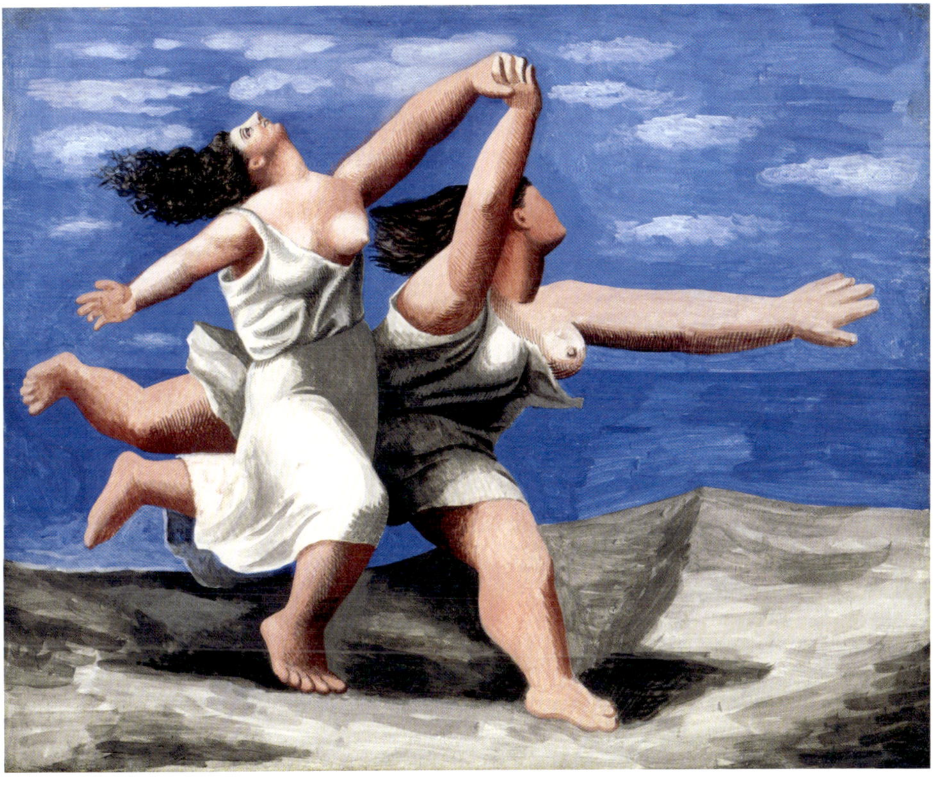

1923

Pan Pipes

Antibes, summer 1923
Oil on canvas, 80.8 × 68.5 in. (205 × 174 cm)
Dation Pablo Picasso, 1979. MP79

The Twenties were the age of a reinterpretation of the classical ideal, in art, architecture and music. The "return to order" marks the art of painting of the time, while Le Corbusier was developing a revolutionary architecture inspired by the ancient architecture's golden mean, and by a solar, Mediterranean, hygienist ideal. These men were painted during Picasso's summer in Cap d'Antibes. They represent at the same time some fishermen contemporary to Ulysses, shepherds who play pan pipes to their poems as in Virgil's *Eclogues*, and modern young men in white bathing suits. Simple and geometrical architectural elements bring to mind both the set of an antique theater and modernist architecture. The slight sway of the hips of the man on the left makes him timeless, as this contrapposto is a typical classical posture. The characters are heavy, static and concentrated—on his instrument for one, on the horizon for the other, who has an indifferent yet melancholic look. Despite the flute, the silence is deafening. The classical world is someplace else, over, forever lost, perhaps hardly even audible without melancholy by our contemporary ears. As Nicolas Poussin, most admired by Pablo Picasso, stated in his painting *The Arcadian Shepherds* or *Et in Arcadia ego* (c. 1638–40, Musée du Louvre, Paris), death prowls even in the Golden Age of Arcadia. **E.B.**

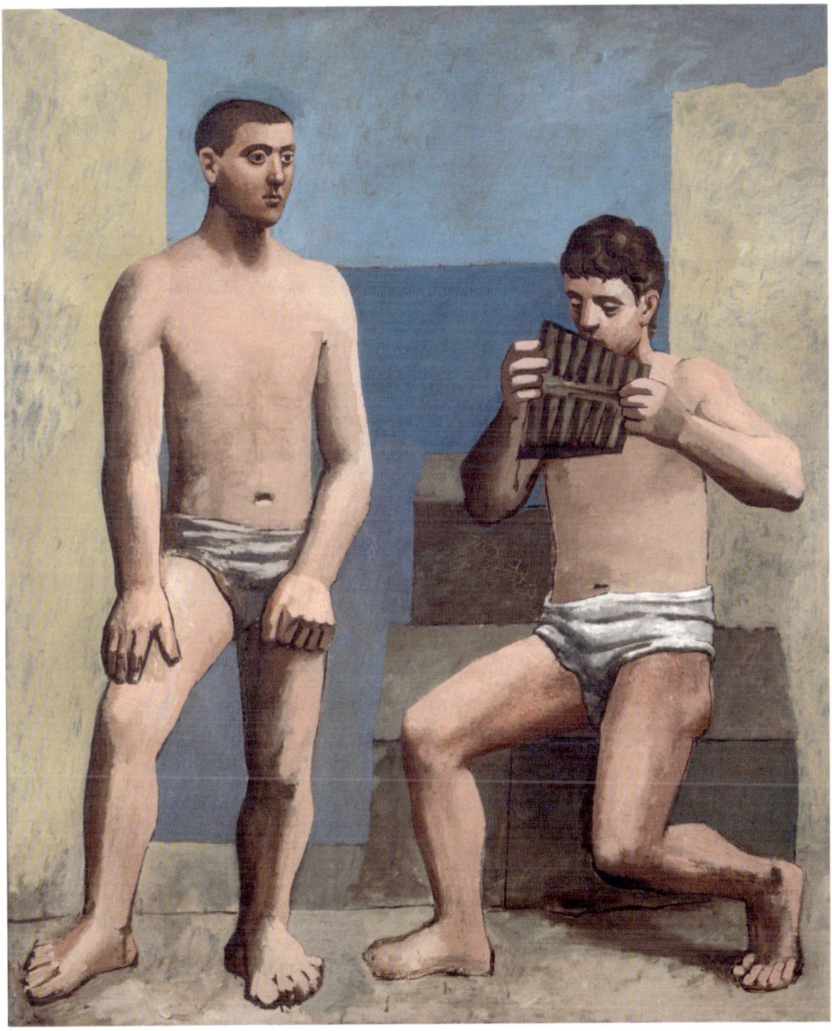

1924

Paul as Harlequin

Paris, 1924
Oil on canvas, 51.2 × 38.4 in. (130 × 97.5 cm)
Dation Pablo Picasso, 1979. MP83

The son of Pablo and Olga Picasso, Paul, was born in February 1921. At that time, the artist returned to subjects from his Blue and Rose periods: maternity, family and portraits of children. Here, the boy is elegantly dressed up, and points to the circus people the artist used to paint in 1905–06. In a simple setting, free from any ornament, the painter's son stares at the viewer. The drawing is particularly thorough and classical, but as the child is leaning on the chair, off balance, he betrays the young model's fragility. The alternation between sketch and finished painting highlights the diamond motif and the child's face. In this work, a father paints his son. And a painter hints at artistic tradition: to better frame the face, Picasso encircles it with a large ruff. While this detail makes the painting all the more realistic, it also recalls the portraits of infants by the workshop of Diego Vélazquez in the Spanish Golden Age, or Jean Antoine Watteau's *Pierrot* (formerly known as *Gilles*, c. 1718–19, Musée du Louvre, Paris). Picasso thus mixes, through this child's portrait, in a seemingly innocent disguise, centuries of Spanish and French painting. **C.F.**

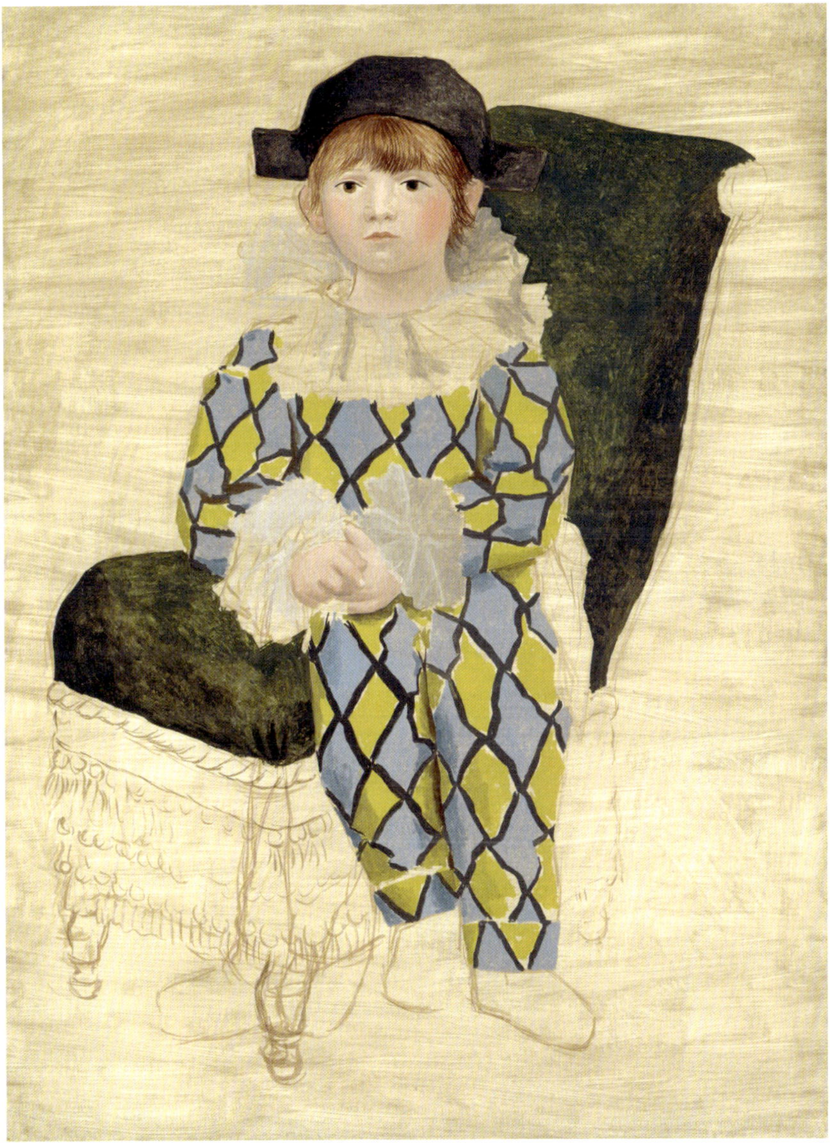

1925

The Kiss

Juan-les-Pins, summer 1925
Oil on canvas, 51.4 × 38.5 in. (130.5 × 97.7 cm)
Dation Pablo Picasso, 1979. MP85

In 1925, a year after *The Surrealist Manifesto* came out, and while the leader of the movement, André Breton, paid tribute to Picasso's precursory role in the article "Surrealism and Painting," the painter creates *The Kiss*, an exceptional yet disconcerting piece with its entangled shapes and strident colors. The young generation of revolutionary Surrealists, who soaked up psychoanalysis and non-Western arts, seems to allow a new liberation in Picasso's art. The brightly colored, wavy masks and jewelry from Oceania are met here by layers of pink, blue, green, yellow and white, with almost radiographic patterns, bound by a thick black line, revealing bodies so close that they merge. The man's two long, strong arms hold the woman. With her toes spread out, her feet no longer touch the ground. She has become captive to the embrace. One single mouth brings together the two lovers in violent eroticism: the kiss becomes sexual foreplay in which the nose/male genitals and the mouth/female genitals are uncontrollably drawn to each other, and at the same time push each other away. **M.P.**

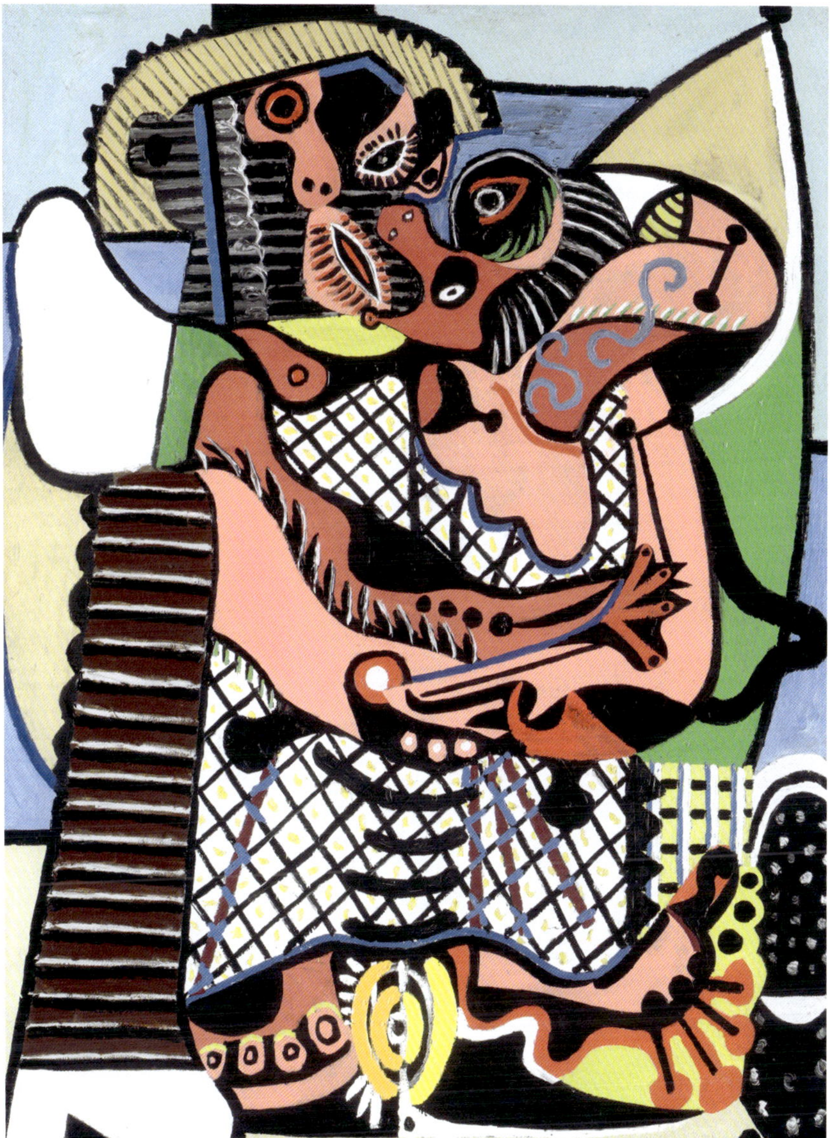

Picasso's style

In his youth, Picasso witnessed the end of academicism, or the natural death of the so-called "art pompier." But he then lived through the academic arts sparked by the Cubists, the Dadaists, the Surrealists, the Abstractionists and the Conceptualists. He knew better than anyone that art could die.

Pierre Daix, "Période finale," *Le Nouveau Dictionnaire Picasso*, Paris, Éditions Robert Laffont, coll. "Bouquins", 1995, p. 686.

Paris, 1901

When he arrived in Paris in 1900, Picasso could at last see for himself the avant-garde paintings that he had only seen in art magazines. He immersed himself in the Impressionists' bright and radiant painting, he was struck by Cézanne's reinvention of the understanding of space and volume, and by the exoticism of Gauguin's work. He most likely visited the retrospective dedicated to Rodin at the Universal Exhibition. As he settled into Montmartre, he was influenced by the paintings of Steinlen and Toulouse-Lautrec. The latter depicted the nightlife of those living on the edges, beneath the artificial blueishness of electric lights. The young Spaniard was thus confronted by varied stylistic treatments of reality, all of which questioned the possibility of truly depicting something. He first tried bright colors and strange contrasts, in his early portraits of *demi-mondaines*, the literati and overly blushed cocottes, but it does not seem to be enough for him. Picasso became Picasso with the radical choice of painting in monochrome, in blue.

His blue phase was the first of ten or so stylistic variations in Picasso's artistic production. It was followed by the Rose period, Cubism, classicism, and "Cubist-Surrealism" in the 1930s. After the war and his "Antibes phase" (1946), he underwent a graphic period, and then focused on assemblage. Navigating more and more fluidly between the old masters led him to his "Avignon period." With Picasso, the purpose of art was to show an interior world and the way in which it colors reality. Each of the artist's different stylistic phases was thus true to his vision of the world, which varied according to the period of his life. It was a process of perpetual self reassessing.

The face: front and profile

This soon to be emblematic way of depicting faces, inherited from Cubism and the juxtaposition of points of view, appears in the mid-1920s (*The Kiss*, summer 1925, M85, p. 78) and corresponds to several stylistic studies.
Picasso then returned to a multifocal representation of beings, gathering in a single portrait all the visions he had memorized. He also continued his research on the relationship between painting and sculpture, between two- and three-dimensional, between inside and outside (the "Magic Paintings" of 1926–27, studies for *Figures*, the monument to Apollinaire, 1928). His front and profile faces are one of the artistic solutions to this issue. The Surrealists were fond of non-Western art, from the Pacific Islands, Africa and Northern America, and of expressive shapes that may seem strange to the Western gaze, sometimes asymmetrical, and which inspired Picasso. With the Surrealists, he also learned how to let human urges run free and wild, shaping faces and bodies, distorting them into intentional ugliness. For Picasso, Dora Maar became "the weeping woman" because that is how she appeared to him, while Marie-Thérèse Walter was about soft curves. The "last Picasso" (1969–73) offered an ultimate, blazing occurrence of the front/profile face, as it is associated with eroticism. The body, seen from up close, is deformed by desire.

Picasso's manner

Picasso's manner varied depending on the stylistic period. However, study of his works and techniques reveals a number of characteristics. Picasso perfectly mastered classical techniques, from the choice of a very subtle touch, to the thick strokes of paint in his last phase. He painted quickly; his lines are confident, sometimes aggressive, and more and more expressive over the years; he depicts subjects mostly frontally, and rejects any perspectival effect. His mastery of stroke and line is also perceptible in his drawings—which are rarely preparatory, but instead works in themselves—and in his engravings.
Moreover, though Picasso may have modeled, he preferred assemblage and molding found objects that he unified with paint or bronze. Depending on the periods, there are also recognizable artistic signs: the nose extends into the eye from his stay in Gósol in 1906, the female genitals as "fishbone," the sun-eye and black eyes in general, the "commas" for the last musketeers' hats, and so on. Pablo Picasso's stylistic vocabulary, with all of its singularities, remains to be written. **E.B.**

1926

Guitar

Paris, spring 1926
String, newspaper, mop and nails on painted canvas, 37.8 × 51.2 in. (96 × 130 cm)
Dation Pablo Picasso, 1979. MP87

This is probably the first mop ever used in art. Usually ignored, this common object is at the center of this board and becomes, with two strings and Picasso's magic, a guitar. It is a still life made with rubbish fixed to a board. Great painting is juxtaposed with prosaic daily life, to non-noble objects, which shouldn't belong in art, according to classic, academic rules. Thus traditional values are aggressively overturned. The piece of newspaper glued to the side is an article praising the brilliance of new academic painting: can there be anything wittier than the juxtaposition of this thinking and of a regular mop used as an artwork? Nails run through the canvas and attack the viewer, reminiscent of Congolese fetish statues, which were most appreciated at the time by collectors and artists (Surrealists in particular), and which Picasso most certainly knew of. This piece, reproduced in *The Surrealist Revolution*, is dual: both executioner and martyr, violent and victim, it places the viewer in an ambivalent position, as we don't know how to look at it. The artist created this artwork vertically, but it has often been hung both ways, as if it were impossible to determine how to apprehend it. **E.B.**

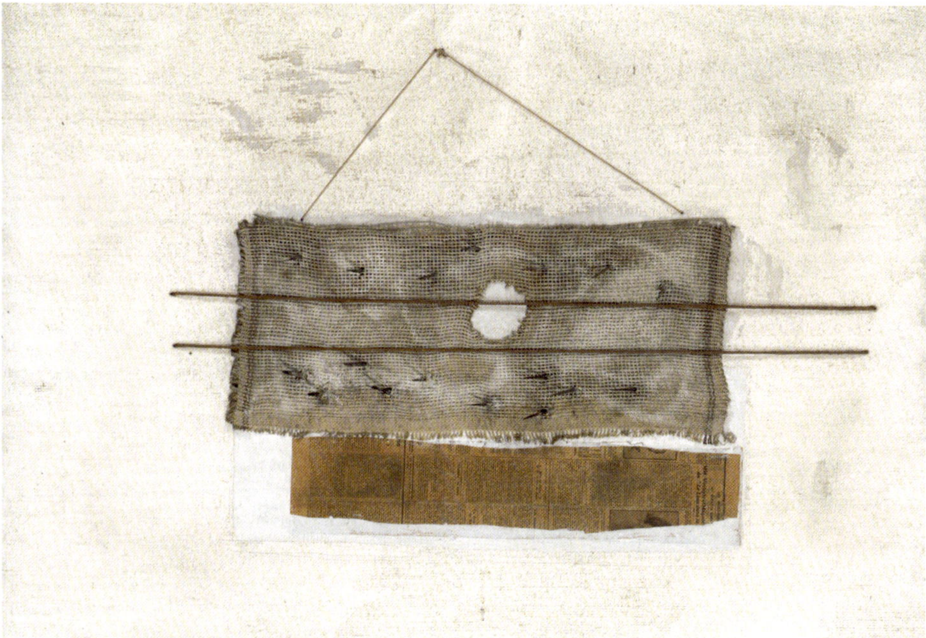

1927

Nude on White Background

Paris, 1927
Oil on canvas, 51.2 × 38 in. (130 × 97 cm)
Dation Pablo Picasso, 1979. MP102

Spending time with Surrealist artists influenced Pablo Picasso's works: shapes change and become disturbing, and the white figures he created as early as 1926 seem to float in his paintings as if ghosts. Here, the woman—recognizable by her pointy breasts—is designed with both salient angles and supple arabesques. With the same shape as *Figure* (MP101), also made that year, Picasso builds a body with a thick black outline that isolates it from the white background. The light color contrasts with the threatening black, reinforced by the deformed, almost monstrous silhouette of the nude: as Picasso is amidst sentimental confusion with Olga since he has met Marie-Thérèse Walter, the nudity he offers is aggressive, as proven by the bristly hair and the long mouth, resembling a *vagina dentata*. The influence of African masks is underlying, but mostly the piece announces a soon-to-come transition towards sculpture: these black lines will become "drawings in space" in the several studies for *Figures* and for the *Monument to Apollinaire* (MP264), as presented to the dealer Daniel-Henry Kahnweiler and the sculptor Julio González, who lent his studio to Picasso for its realization. **M.P.**

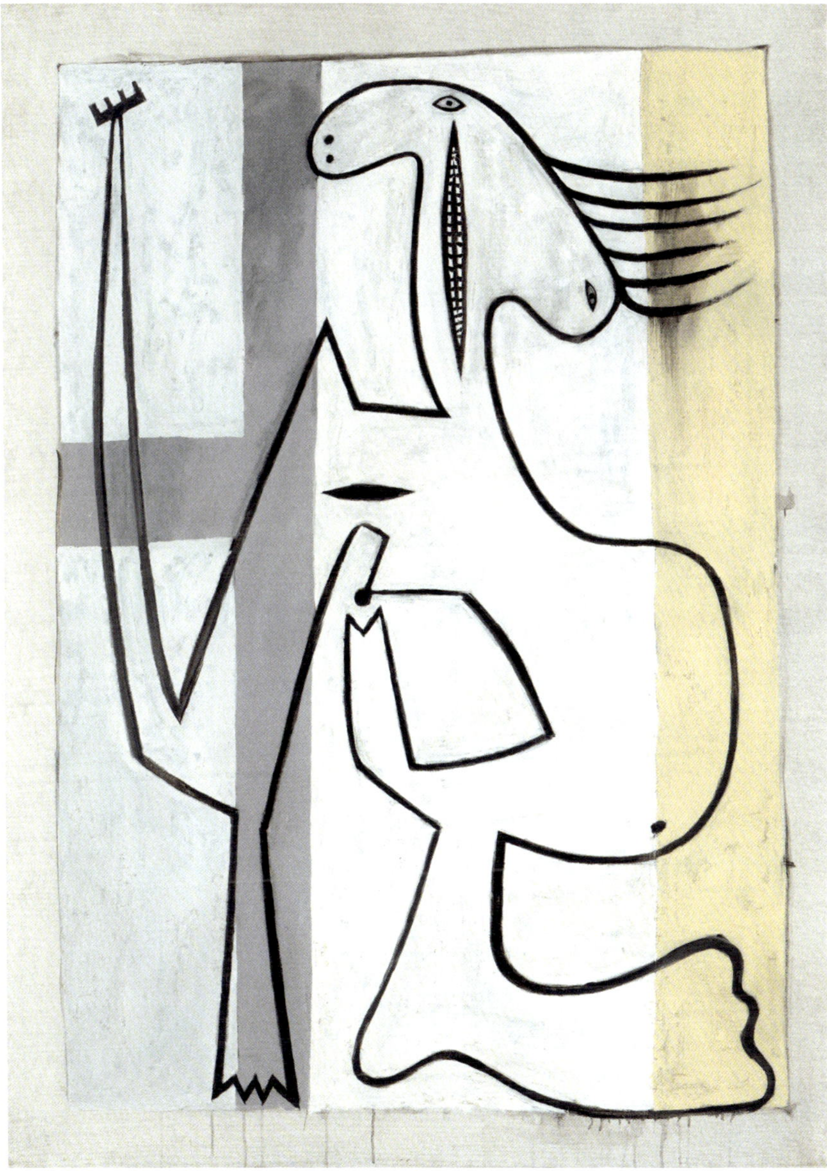

1928

The "Dinard Bathers"

While on family vacation in Dinard, with Olga and Paul, Picasso composed a series of small paintings representing bathers, a major theme in the history of art, especially in the works of Cézanne and Renoir. But Picasso's bathers are modern and belong to the everyday summer life of the time: they run on the beach, play ball, open huts. Bodies are decomposed and recomposed in a geometrical fashion. Disproportionate arms and legs contrast with tiny heads. The unstructured nudity is influenced by a surrealist, erotic violence: Picasso's mistress, Marie-Thérèse Walter, whom he had met the previous year, is secretly present in Dinard and this transpires in his contrasted bathers. They are complex and childish, erotic and monstrous, light as the wind that blows by them: they are full of contradictions, which reveal the unstable balance of this relationship. However, the transparent, vivifying light of Brittany's beaches, the bright colors with the paint still apparent and the relief left by the brushes create a poetic, light atmosphere, which announces the coming series of *Sculpted Head* with its oversimplified bodies. **M.P.**

Bather on the Beach

Dinard, August 15, 1928
Oil on canvas, 9.4 x 13.7 in.
(24 × 34.9 cm)
Dation Pablo Picasso,
1979. MP109

Bathers Playing with a Beach Ball

Dinard, August 20, 1928
Oil on canvas, 8.5 × 16.2 in.
(21.7 × 41.2 cm)
Dation Pablo Picasso,
1979. MP110

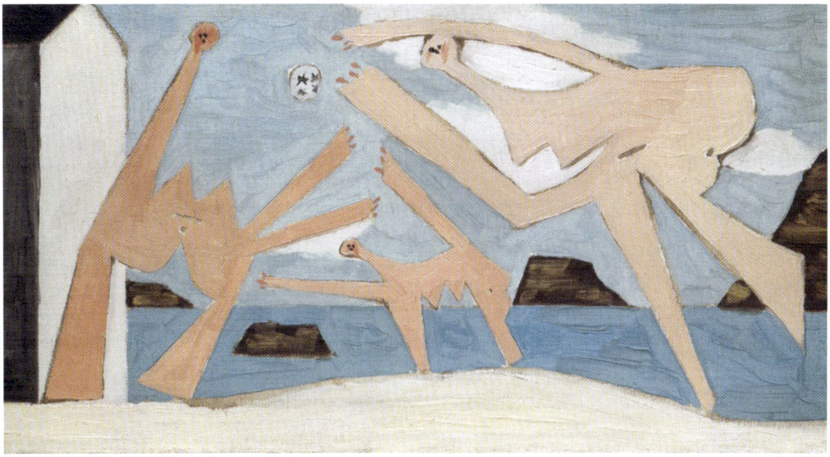

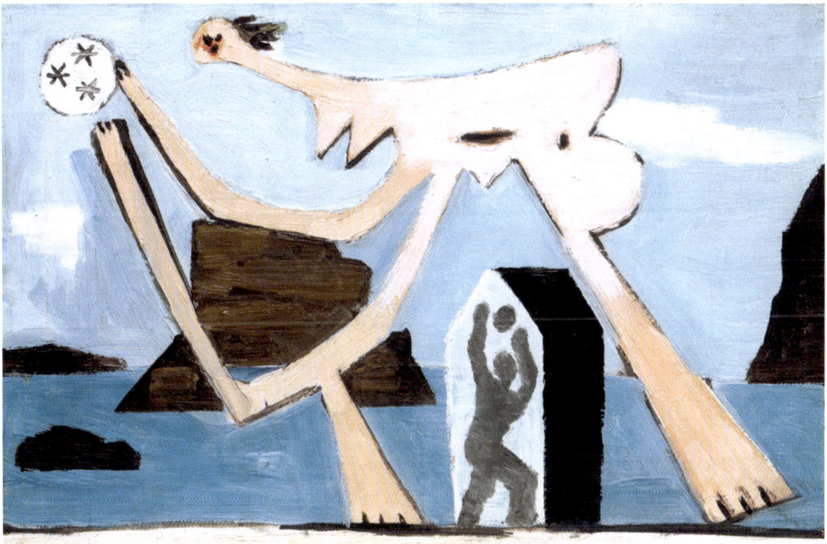

1929

Large Nude in a Red Armchair

Paris, May 5, 1929
Oil on canvas, 76.8 × 50.8 in. (195 × 129 cm)
Dation Pablo Picasso, 1979. MP113

Between August 1928 and 1929, Olga Picasso was often hospitalized for bleeding, probably genital, while Picasso is at the height of his affair with Marie-Thérèse Walter. The portrait of Olga, *Large Nude in a Red Armchair* is of incredible violence: Picasso features the theme of the seated woman, but takes the body to pieces on a red chair covered in a cloth, the folds of which recall his large 1928 black-and-white, stringy paintings. The belly is underlined with a dark ring and holds the center of the painting in an ectoplasmic manner. Behind it, the room seems "well kept." This domestic massacre brings to mind blood, flaccidity and morbidity, as opposed to the realm of stone, bone and harshness. The teeth-baring mouth, a sort of *vagina dentata*, seems to spew the red armchair, as corroborated by brownish brushstrokes: Picasso hereby suggests the disarray of a boneless, organless, without anatomy, shapeless body. And this, practically twenty years before the 1947 manifesto by Antonin Artaud: *To Have Done with the Judgment of God.* **E.B.**

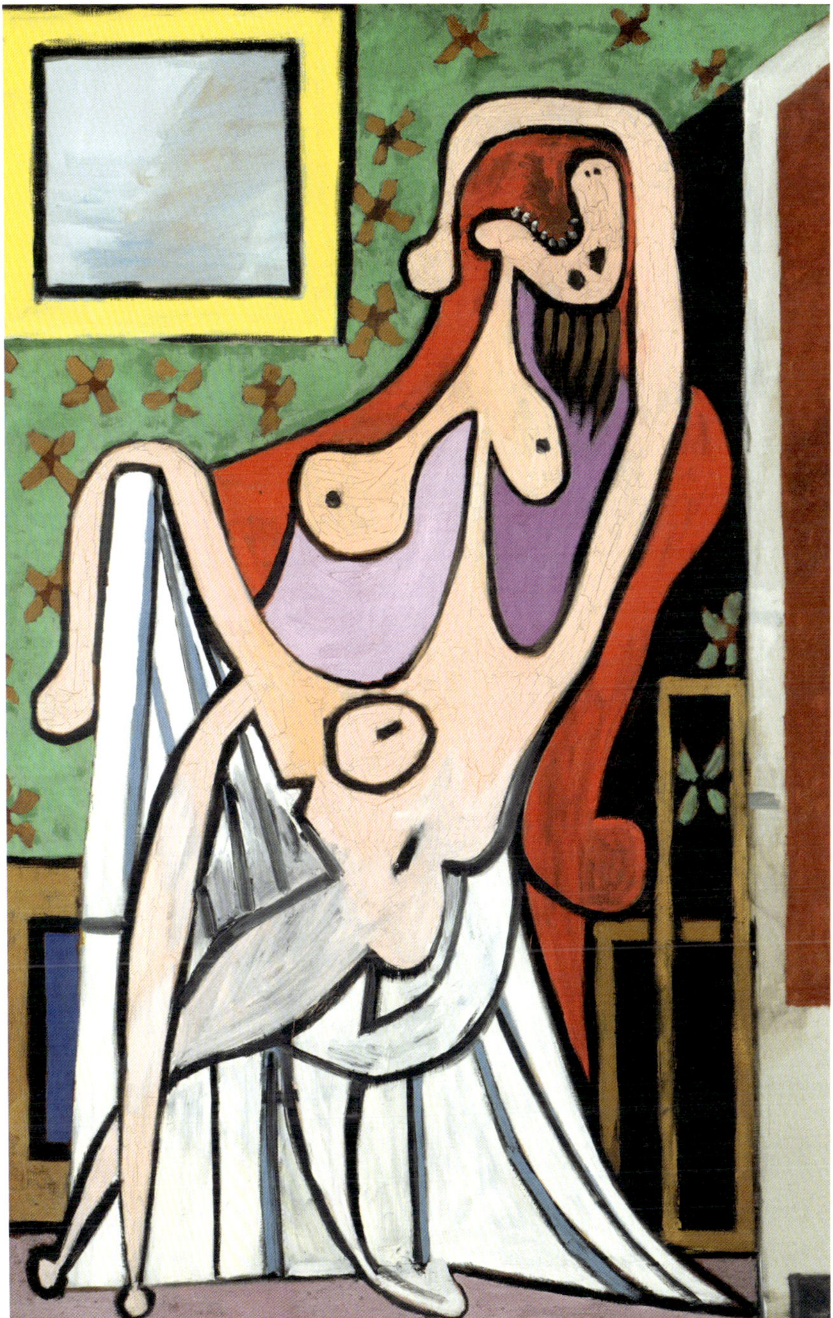

1930

The Crucifixion

Paris, February 7, 1930
Oil on plywood, 20.3 × 26.2 in. (51.5 × 66.5 cm)
Dation Pablo Picasso, 1979. MP122

While the religious is rare as such in Picasso's works, in this painting, it is linked to the expression of human suffering and to the artist's own personal obsessions. Just as in a hallucination, all the characters from the Passion are present: Christ and the Virgin, pale before the darkness, Mary Magdalene imploring, a lance holder, resembling a picador, spearing Jesus, while two centurions are betting over his tunic near two dead bodies. Other elements, straight out of Picasso's imagination, complete the Christian theme: a blue praying mantis head, a face both, frontal and in profile, a yellow triangle that recalls Mary Therese, a solar figure with a red mask and green hair, possible allusions to Mary Salome and John the apostle. A bird flies away from a green mass, whether a sponge full of vinegar, a rock, or a dark sun from the Gospel. With the brutal dislocation of the shapes and the stridency of the colors, Picasso expresses the violence of a primitive sacrifice. The painting calls to mind the pages of *The Apocalypse of Saint-Sever*, by Beatus of Liébana. This illuminated eleventh-century manuscript contains strikingly violent images with loud colors, which were published in a magazine edited by Georges Bataille (*Documents*, no. 2, May 1929). **J.-Y.S.**

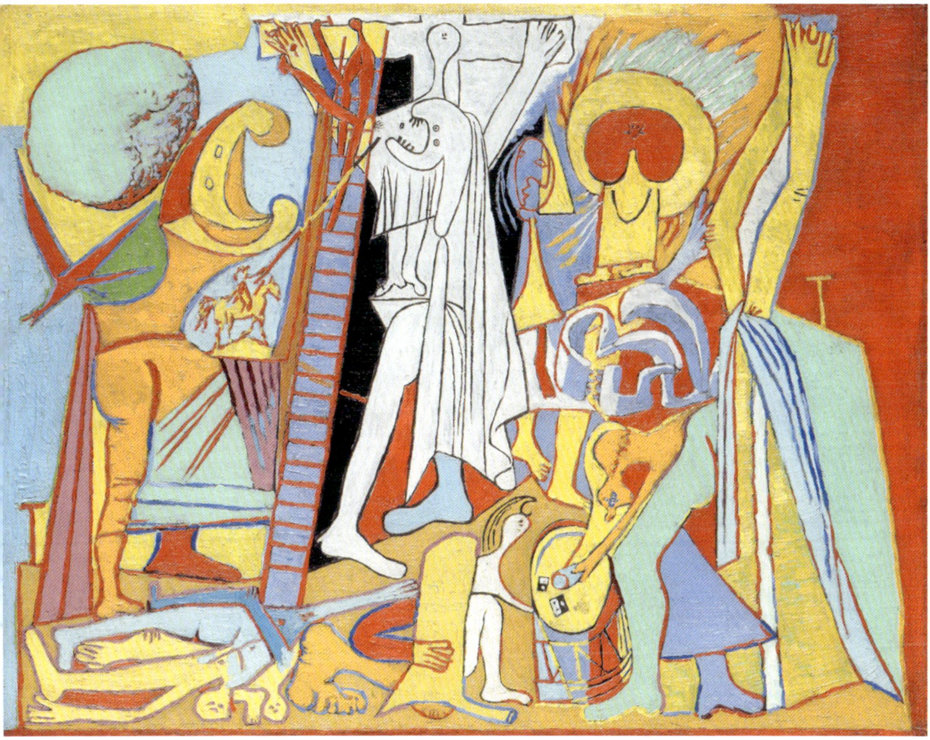

1931

Head of a Woman

Boisgeloup, 1931
Original in plaster and wood
50.6 × 21.5 × 24.6 in. (128.5 × 54.5 × 62.5 cm)
Dation Pablo Picasso, 1979. MP291

In June 1930, Picasso bought the castle of Boisgeloup, near Gisors and turned a part of it into a sculpting studio. The Boisgeloup sculptures have in common the predominance of volume, which gives the pieces much monumentality, whatever their size. The representation of the beloved Marie-Thérèse Walter, Picasso's young mistress, is shaped by a sensual, undulating language, made of sexual innuendos and the condensing of her body parts: her nose is prominent along her forehead, her eyes almond-shaped, her bosom lush. With its frontal serenity, *Head of a Woman* stands as a goddess of fertility, much like the prehistoric representation of the Venus of Lespugue, of which Picasso had two copies. Three plaster shells form the face of Marie-Thérèse evocative of the protuberances composing an African mask of a Nimba goddess, owned by Picasso. **V.P.**

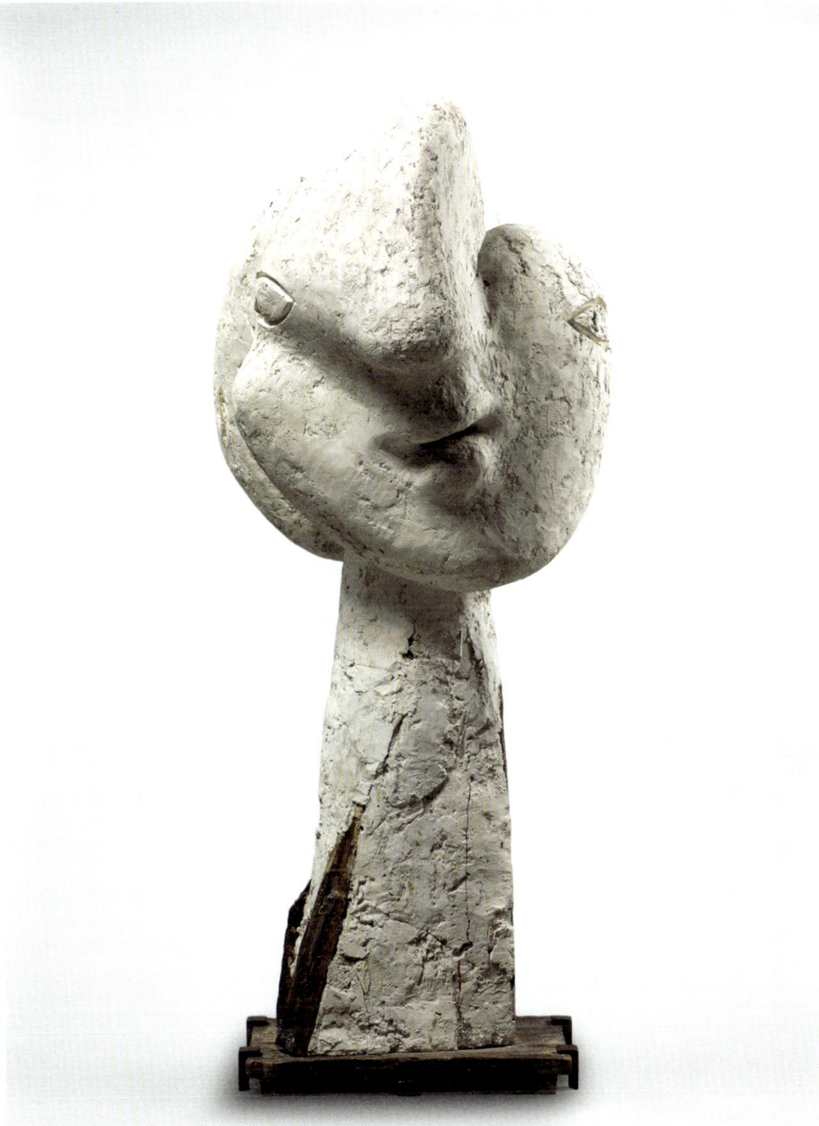

1932

Reading

Boisgeloup, January 2, 1932
Oil on canvas, 51.2 × 38.4 in. (130 × 97.5 cm)
Dation Pablo Picasso, 1979. MP137

From the moment he met Marie-Thérèse Walter, Picasso had been inserting a new pictorial language in his paintings: with simplified shapes and rounder volumes, Marie-Thérèse is recognizable thanks to her blond hair and her round breasts. Seated in a chair, as in a classical portrait, she looks straight ahead. Is she staring at the painter in the studio, even though it is known that Picasso painted from memory, rather than having his models sit for him? Or is her gaze blank as she is interrupted in her reading, in her own living room? The confusion between the body, the chair and the see-through frame causes a merging of the painting's elements: the juxtaposition of all levels creates a new perspective, typical of Picasso's reinterpretation of Cubism in the 1930s. A vertical axis splits the painting: alternating between purples, greens, reds and yellows, it forms a relief with the blurry volumes and contributes to the hazy effect of a literary musing. **M.P.**

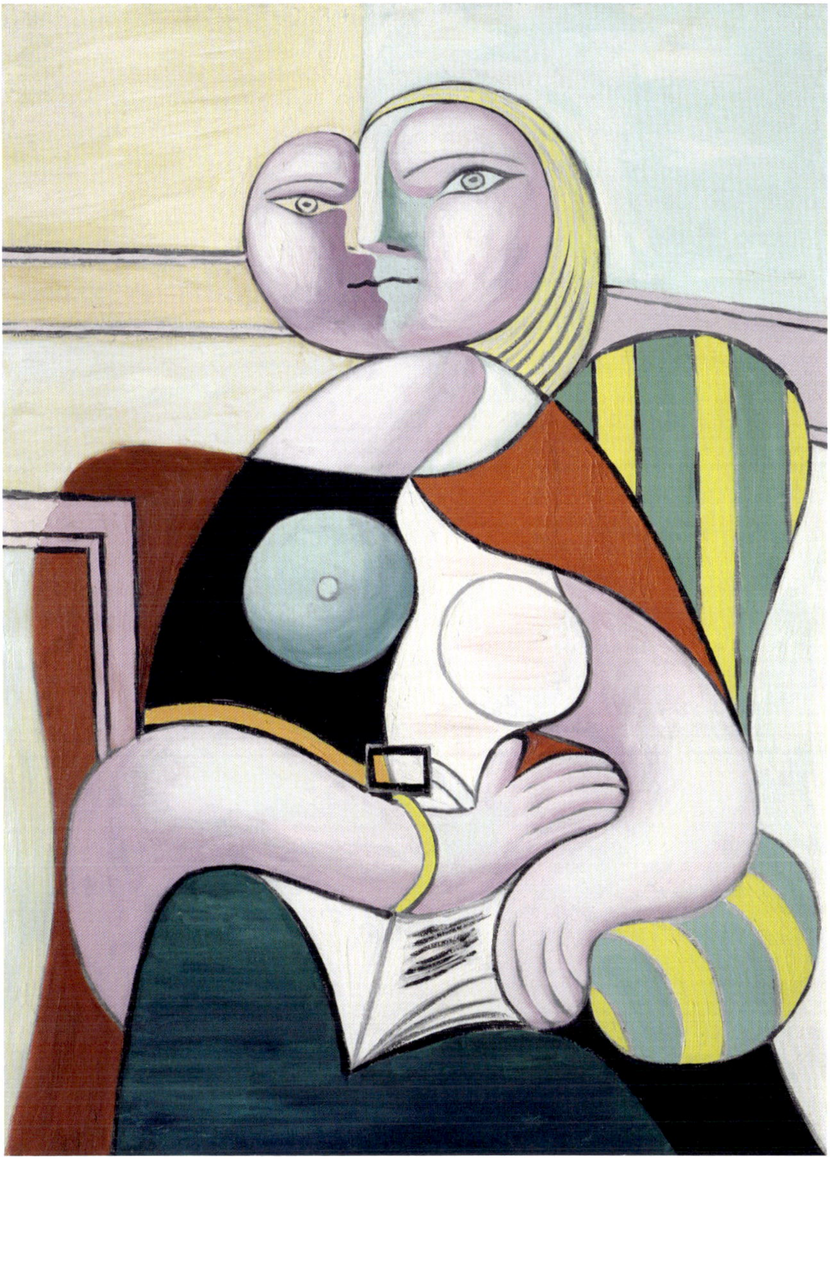

1933

Bullfight: The Death of the Woman Torero

Boisgeloup, September 6, 1933
Oil and pencil on wood panel, 8.5 × 10.6 in. (21.7 × 27 cm)
Dation Pablo Picasso, 1979. MP144

One day, Pablo Picasso told the famous *torero* Luis Miguel Dominguin that had he not become a painter, he would have wanted to be a picador. Bullfighting is a central theme in Picasso's work, and here we find all its recurring characters. Marie-Thérèse Walter is depicted as a *rejoneadora*, a horseback bullfighter with a spear. She exposes herself, naked and unconscious—or perhaps even already dead—and seems to give in to a one on one scuffle with the bull, whose horns she gently brushes against. The horse is associated with her, also a victim of the bull. The animal is so close to its rider that its pain seems to complete the woman's fragility and eroticism. A three-way dance of death is thus on display, mixing Picasso's personal life with grand mythology: the Minotaur, Europa abducted by Zeus, and the loves of Pasiphaë. Bullfighting is used beyond an anecdotal representation, to serve the expression of a complex triangle of love, lust and death. **A.M.**

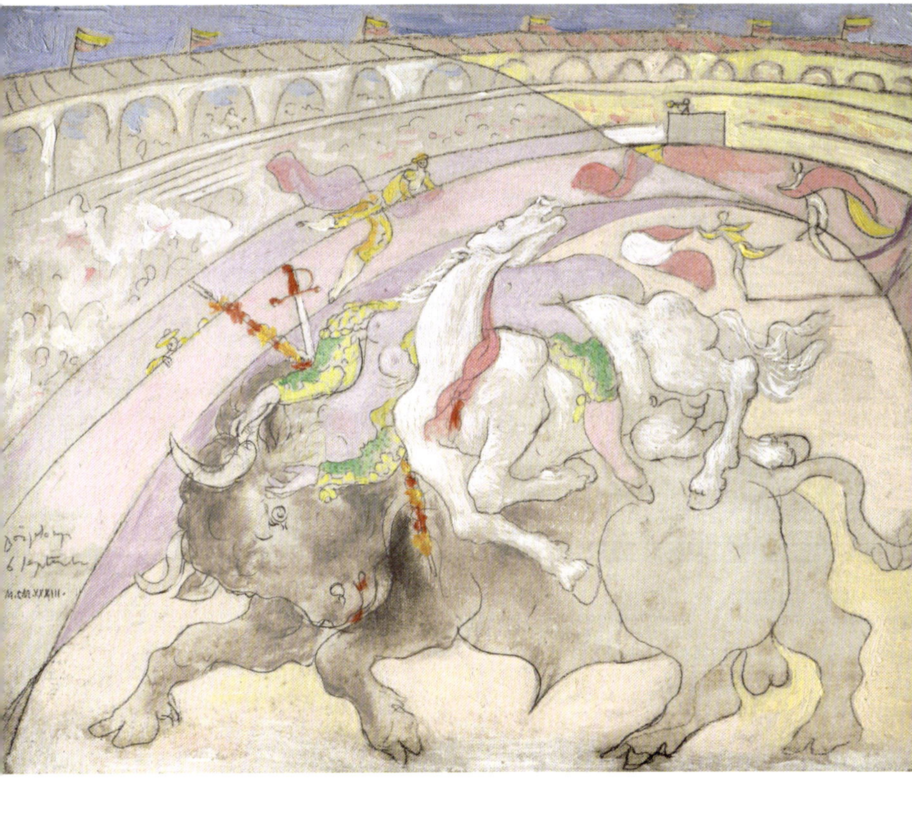

1934

Nude in a Garden

Boisgeloup, August 4, 1934
Oil on canvas, 63.8 × 51.2 (162 × 130 cm)
Dation Pablo Picasso, 1979. MP148

In this painting, Picasso expresses freely his lust for the loved one who, fast asleep, metamorphoses into floral arabesques. The woman's curves, coiled up amidst water and plants, bare the elegant suppleness of the leaves, while her soft hair becomes foliage. Within a caress, Picasso seems to reinvent the beloved's anatomy in all its aspects. The curves of the egg and moon shapes hint at fertility and tenderness. The serene harmony that Picasso has discovered with his partner Marie-Thérèse Walter illuminates his painting with fresh, bright colors, brushed in layers separated by a black line. As Picasso is fascinated by the classical profile of his model and the richness of her curves, he oversimplifies the silhouette, much like in his sculptures. The morphological elements are dissociated, while the classical profile of the model and the body's volumes are highlighted, innovatively distorted and assembled. **J.-Y.S.**

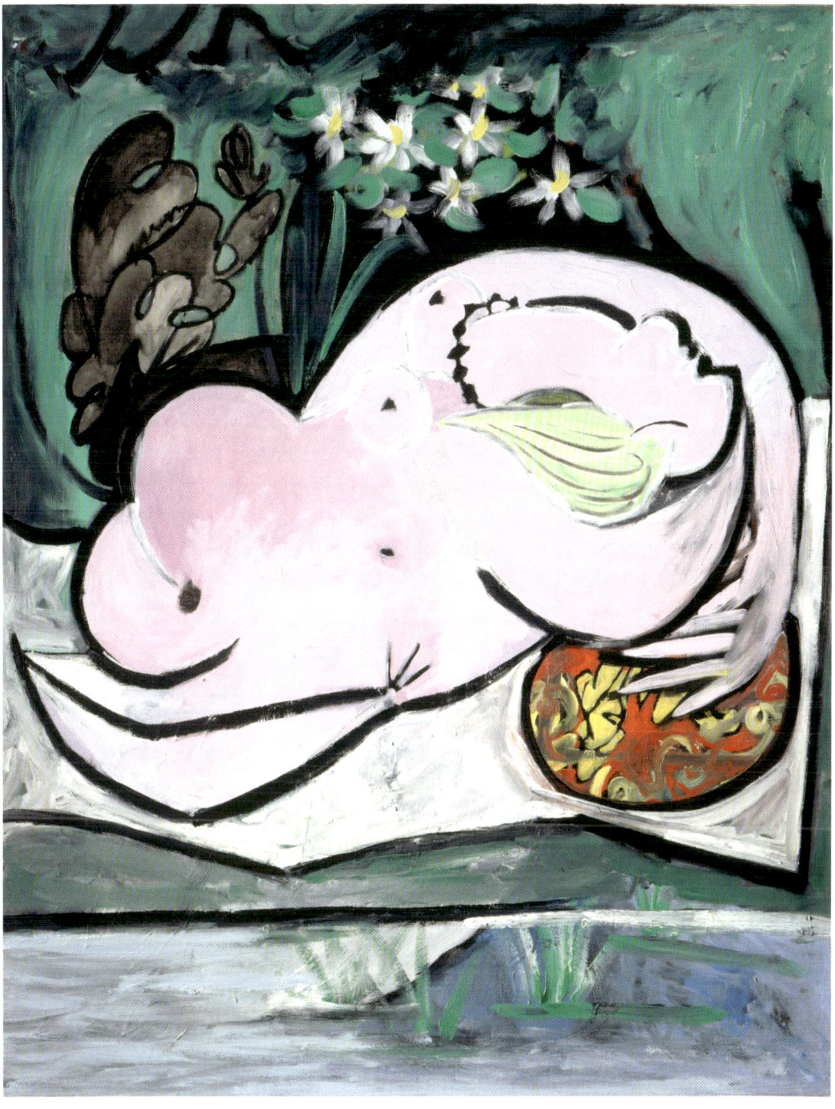

1935

Minotauromachy

Paris, March 23, 1935
Etching, scraper and burin on copper. 7th state.
Proof on Montval laid paper, after steeling, printed by Lacourière, 22.4 × 29 in. (57 × 73.7 cm)
Dation Pablo Picasso, 1979. MP2733

Several actions are on display here in a limited space, with the sea as horizon. In the foreground, a little girl with a candle and a bunch of flowers faces a suffering Minotaur. Between them, a woman toreador is thrown over her horse, fatally injured. On the left, a Christlike bearded man is leaving up a ladder, but turns around to glance at the scene. In the back, two young women with doves quietly watch from a window. The Minotaur, a monster, half-man, half-god, born from Pasiphaë's affair with a bull, appears in the "Vollard Suite" prints (a set of 100 etchings, made between 1930 and 1937 and published in 1939) as the painter's alter ego. It is also an emblem in Surrealism, especially as it gave its name, Minotaur, to a publication from 1933 to 1939 by editors Albert Skira and Teriade. This engraving masterpiece, made in the spring of 1935, is the result of vast research and dense work. It mixes Greek mythology and Spanish bullfighting tradition in a symbolic construction, and thus crystallizes Picasso's inner battles as he suffers personal turmoil. Scarred by the separation with Olga, his first wife, and troubled by the pregnancy of his young lover, Marie-Thérèse Walter, he stopped painting from May 1935 until February 1936. **E.Ph.**

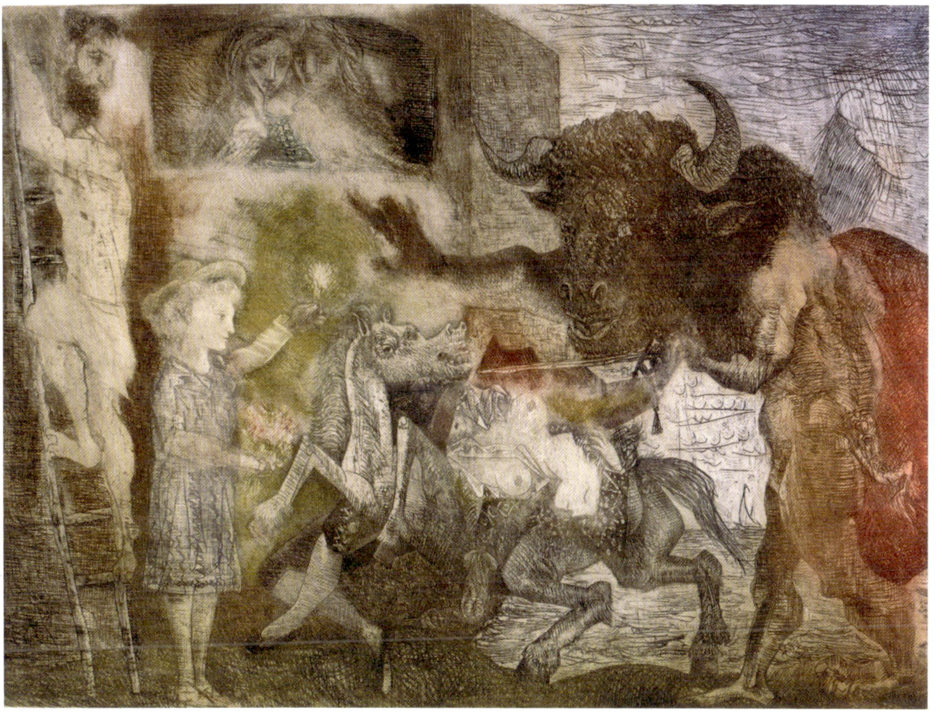

Picasso, matador or Minotaur?

If one were to mark on a map all the routes I've taken and to connect those dots, it might just design a Minotaur.

Pablo Picasso, quoted by Pierre Daix, *The New Picasso Dictionary*, Paris, coll. "Bouquins," Éditions Robert Laffont, 2012, p. 584.

Ancient rituals

The Minotaur is a mythological monster, born of the bestial love between a bull and Pasiphaë, daughter of Helios and Perse, the wife of Minos, king of Crete. According to mythology, she slipped into a wooden cow to seduce the animal. The Minotaur was locked in a labyrinth built by Daedalus. Every year, seven young men and seven young women were sacrificed to him, given by Aegeus, king of Athens. Theseus, the latter's son, ended the ritual sacrifice by entering the maze with the help of Ariadne, daughter of Minos. Thus all the elements essential to a myth are gathered: the killing of a half-human, half-bull being during a fight in which the hero risks his life, the enclosed space of the maze, the omnipresent sun that crushes people and things, and can provoke this particular melancholy in the middle of the day.

"We Spaniards go to Mass in the morning, corrida in the afternoon, and brothels in the evening. What mixes in them all? Sorrow."[1] From the Spanish *matar*, "to kill," the Matador plays the main actor in the corrida, as he is in charge of killing the bull. Bullfighting bears ritual, sacrificial, mythological and ancient dimensions. Picasso went many times to see the corrida with his father in Málaga. From the youngest age, he represented bullfighters in his art.

Surrealist ethnography

In the 1930s, the writer Michel Leiris was one of Picasso's closest friends. An ethnographer specialized in African languages and a novelist, he worked closely with Georges Bataille to create the magazine *Documents* (1929–31), which examined all forms of culture as "documents," with the eye of the philosopher, the historian and the ethnologist instead of that of the art critic. In this periodical, as in other Surrealist reviews, or in *Cahiers d'art*, art and objects from all civilizations were confronted with modern art. Picasso held a place of honor, and could see the meeting of a medieval manuscript about the Apocalypse, an ethnographic object, a photograph of Jacques-André Boiffard's toe and one of his own paintings, just as in his studio. Ancient religious rites are of particular interest to the journals' authors, who study the question of sacrificing and of solar cults.

Personal myths

This fantasized design, rich in sexual connotations, gradually takes form in Picasso's work over the first half of the 1930s. The Minotaur character then develops, before returning to simple bull in *Guernica*. He makes a dramatic entrance in the art arena when featured on the cover of *Minotaur*, another Surrealist review, in 1933. André Breton and his group pay tribute to this mythological monster, alluding here to the conflict between reason and impulse, as defined by Freudian psychoanalysis. In Picasso's works, the Minotaur carries many other connotations, linked to the painter's Franco-Spanish background, and builds a personal mythology that leads to many a great scene mixing the arena, the home, the toreador, the horse and the Minotaur, in interior nightmarish displays. This ambivalent personal mythology ranges from brute force to liberated impulse, from the apex of masculine urges to insensitivity. The Minotaur is in turn rapist and a blinded, weak creature (*Minotaur Raping a Woman*, MP115, *Blind Minotaur Guided by a Young Girl Resembling Marie-Therese with a Pigeon in a Starry Night*, MP2702), killed and killer, bull and matador, facing a horse, or rather a mare. The matador and the Minotaur make a couple, a possible role-play, which persists until the corrida works of the 1950s, and constitutes a major imaginary tension point, especially fertile for Pablo Picasso. **E.B.**

1. Quoted by André Malraux, *La Tête d'Obsidienne*, Paris, Gallimard, 1974.

1936

Handwritten Poem: "*Mathematically pure illusory image of the sickening snoring ...*"

November 4, 11 and 12, 1936
(10 × 6.8 in) 25,4 × 17.3 cm
Dation Pablo Picasso, 1979. MP3663-111

Picasso was not a regular letter writer. However, he had always written, throwing words, sentences, thoughts into journals or onto small pieces of paper. In the 1940s, he tried writing for the theater, completing two plays in a Surrealist-inspired style of his own. But for this friend of Guillaume Apollinaire, Max Jacob and Paul Éluard, fond of classical and Spanish mystical poets, writing equals poetry. Between 1935 and 1940, he wrote 280 poetic texts. Written in black ink, they include sketches, numbers and letters. Here they are crossed out; there, highlighted. Each and every note is dated. In this page from November 1936, three pieces dated November 4, 11 and 12, follow each other: the third develops in more words the thoughts of the first two and was annotated and corrected three times. This "coded" message also refers to the iconography in many of Picasso's paintings, with the woman and her tricks, the lace and the compact, the heart wounds, the bodies and their satisfactions, whether through food or sensual pleasures. On this page, his handwriting might be neat and tidy, but it also shows uncertain spelling, grammar and punctuation, whether intended or not. **L.C.**

4 novembre XXXVI.

le du morceau de dentelle detaché des regards du rot vaginal du poudrier caché
matematiquement pure image illusoire du ronflement ecoeurant petant à tire d'aile le dessin reincarné dans les plis fixé à la quille des pleurs
derriere la feuille du gateau de mensonges du pie de nez du tableau noyé dans
la raison qui grille au centre le plat d'argent de la soupe ofre son dos aux coups desesperés de l'amour detachant son bandeau

3 4 5 10 29 0 10 0 224 3 3 0

10 11 23 32 34 35 38 22 dis moi des couleurs les

preuves apportés contre

du morceau de dentelle detaché des regards du rot vaginal

matematiquement pure image illusoire du ronflement ecoeurant petant à tire d'aile le dessin reincarné dans les plis du poudrier caché derriere la feuille du gateau de mensonges fixé à la quille des pleurs la raison qui grille au centre du pie de nez du tableau noyé dans le plat d'argent de la soupe ofre son dos aux coups desesperés de l'amour detachant son bandeau 3 4 5 10 29 0 10 0 224 3 3 0 10 11 23 32 34 35 38 22 dis moi des couleurs les preuves apportés contre

matematiquement pure image illusoire du ronflement ecoeurant du morceau de dentelle detaché des regards du rot vaginal petant à tire d'aile le dessin reincarné dans les plis du poudrier caché derriere la feuille du gateau de mensonges fixé à la quille des pleurs la raison qui grille au centre du pie de nez du tableau noyé dans le plat d'argent de la soupe ofre son dos aux coups desesperés de l'amour detachant son bandeau 3 4 5 10 29 0 10 224 3 3 0 10 11 23 32 34 35 38 22 dis moi des couleurs les preuves apportés contre

11 novembre XXXVI.

splin du quart de brie dans son skin-car

12 novembre XXXVI.

l'une anonime à l'autre bat son plein la fête à plat de côte

1937

The Weeping Woman

Paris, October 18, 1937
Oil on canvas, 21.8 × 18.2 in. (55.3 × 46.3 cm)
Dation Pablo Picasso, 1979. MP165

The Spanish Civil War had been raging since July 1936: Picasso had just finished *Guernica* (1937, Museo Nacional Centro de Arte Reina Sofía, Madrid), which refers to the bombing of the town of the same name, while the country is burning. He got his hands on the pictures taken by photographer Agusti Centelles of the bombing of Lérida, which inspired this painting. The black dress, the swollen cheek and the gaping mouth suggest grief in this new form of Pietà, following the Spanish traditional representation of suffering. This woman, with her tear-shaped eyes, illustrates the pain of the Iberian people, alluding also to the tradition of Spanish baroque statues in which tears are represented with ostentatious sparkling glass beads. Pain has etched her face as suggested by the incisions of the brush into the thick paint. The character holds her hands together as if to pray, and seems to be bringing a white tissue to her nose, signified by a simple sharp triangle. Or is it a blank left in the canvas, to stress the idea of despair? Long free black hair, going white with tragedy, tell the viewer that this *Weeping Woman* is also a Dora Maar, characterized by her tears in Picasso's representations. **M.P.**

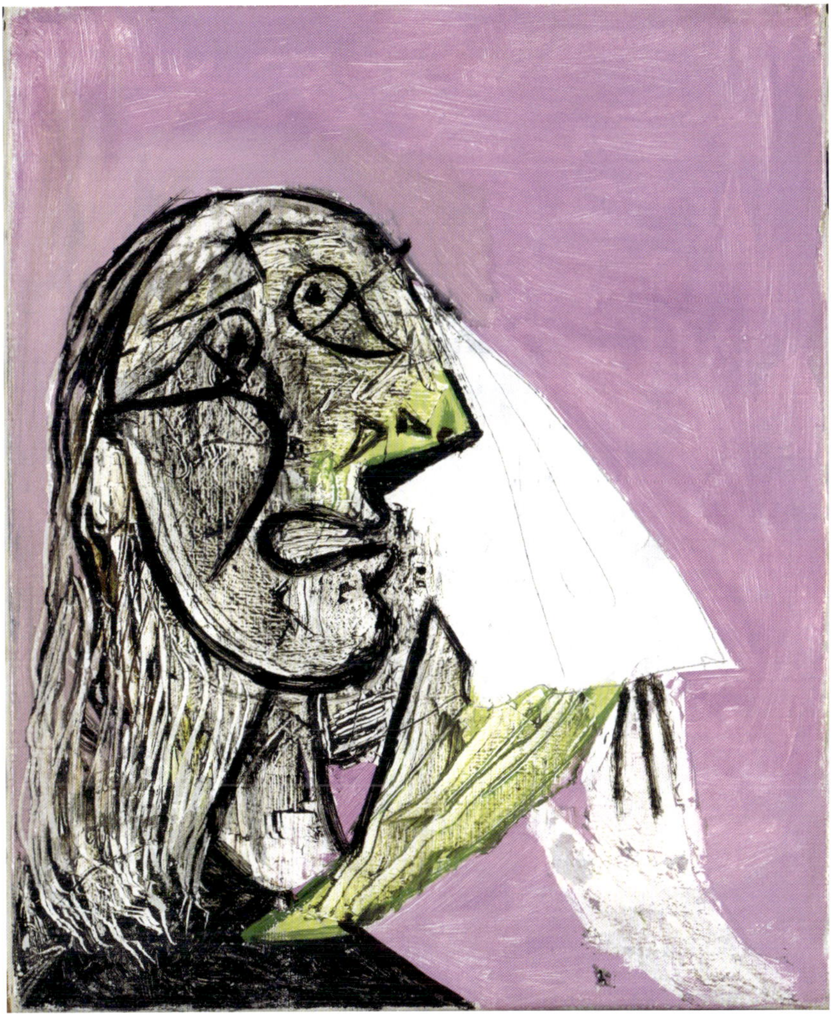

1938

Women at Their Toilette

Paris, 1938
Collage of pieces of wallpaper
and gouache on paper pasted to the canvas
117.7 × 176.4 in. (299 × 448 cm)
Dation Pablo Picasso, 1979. MP176

Painted in the Grands-Augustins studio over the winter of 1937–38, this monumental work directly descends from *Guernica* (1937, Museo Nacional Centro de Arte Reina Sofía, Madrid), in which Pablo Picasso had considered integrating wallpaper.
The artist drew the various motifs he had selected for their signifying role, with his scissors. The brick-patterned paper is thus used to represent a wall in the background, and the fake-wood motif imitates the floor and the frame for the mirror.
Picasso organizes his composition of women combing their hair with three characters that echo his personal life of the moment: on the right, Olga has already almost disappeared and turns away from the others; in the middle, Dora is ill and tightens her hands like bird claws; and on the left, Marie-Thérèse holds a mirror. An enigmatic flower head appears in its reflection: is it an image of the model transformed in the painter's eyes? Is it a fantasized reflection of the beloved woman? Or the representation of the viewer in a tribute to Velázquez and his famous *Meninas* (1656, Prado Museum, Madrid)?
Women at Their Toilette is the only tapestry cartoon Picasso conceived as such. However, it took over thirty years before it was woven at the Gobelins, at the initiative of André Malraux, then Minister of Cultural Affairs. Four copies of the tapestry were made (two in color, two in black and white), between 1968 and 1976. Each took between 12,000 and 16,000 hours to complete. **E.Ph.**

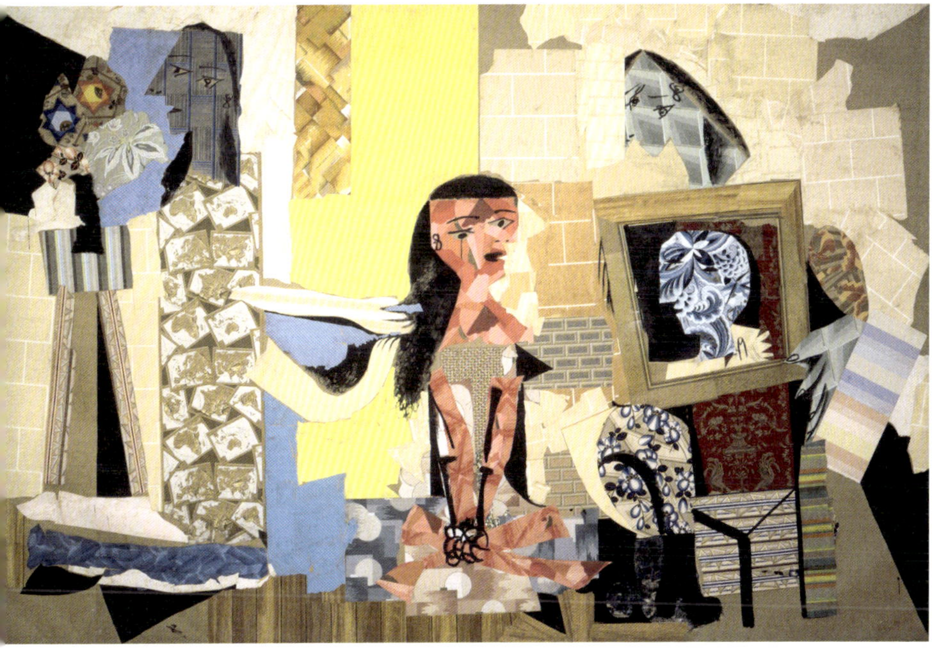

1939

Cat Catching a Bird

Paris, April 22, 1939
Oil on canvas, 31.9 × 39.4 in. (81 × 100 cm)
Dation Pablo Picasso, 1979. MP178

Political news and current events appear in Picasso's works through metaphors or allegories that support a reflection on the human condition. Conflict and violence are often symbolized by animals, as here with the cat as attacker and the bird as martyr. Picasso told Brassaï during the Occupation: "I love bristling cats become wild ... They hunt birds, walk around, run on the streets like demons ... They throw fierce looks, ready to jump at you ... And have you noticed how stray female cats are always pregnant ?" This description of a feline is faithful to the representation Picasso had made a little earlier, right up to apparent pregnancy. The making of the painting, in layers and contours, is radical, with its basis and background designed to highlight the confrontation. A cruel contrast of black and red for the injured bird resonates with the hypnotic contrast of the black cat with white eyes, borne on his face like the ambivalent mask of a voodoo sorcerer, in harmony with its irradiating claws. In the spring of 1939, while Spain has become Francoist on April 1, and Nazi Germany was dangerously getting ready for the fray, executioners and victims had found their place in all of Europe. **N.L.**

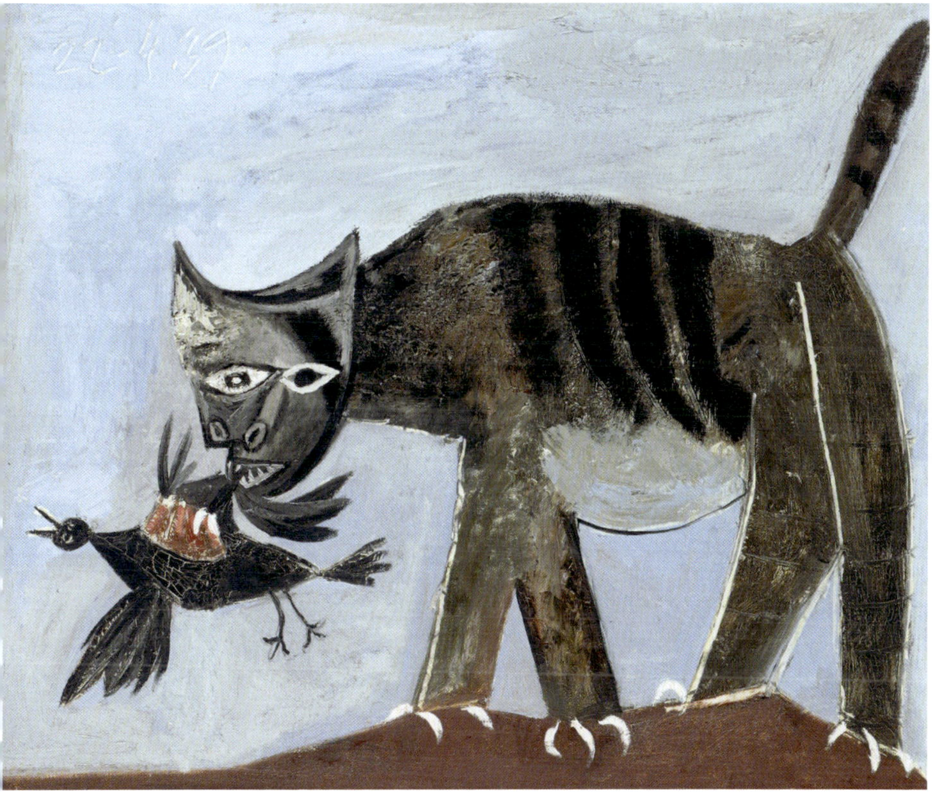

1940

Head of a Woman

Oh how Dora Maar has changed! The woman we have seen adorned with bright colors and nail polish (*Portrait of Dora Maar*, 1937, MP158) has become a skull. So much so that the issue of the model is in fact incidental for these two oil paintings on drawing paper. They were made in Royan, on June 10 and 11, 1940, where Picasso had set up his studio: he had settled in the Les Voiliers villa in January, where he returned periodically, during the Phoney War. In March, he was denied French citizenship because he was found to have been described as an "anarchist" in an old 1900s file. The German offensive started on May 10. On June 10, the French government fled Paris to Bordeaux, while the capital is declared open on the 11th. Charles de Gaulle gave his Appeal speech on the 18th and Capitulation was signed on the 22nd. These *Heads* are thus painted during one of French history's most troubled times. Picasso, hiding out in Royan since May 16, following the exodus like many others, did not yet know if he would ever be able to go back home to Paris, to his studio and his paintings. The German invasion grew along with the casualties. These *Heads*, with their washed out colors, echo the contemporary tragedy. **E.B.**

Head of a Woman
Royan, June 10, 1940
Oil on laid drawing paper
25 x 17.7 in. (63.5 × 45 cm)
Dation Pablo Picasso, 1979. MP1228

Head of a Woman
Royan, June 11, 1940
Oil on laid drawing paper
25.5 x 17.7 in. (64.8 × 45 cm)
Dation Pablo Picasso, 1979. MP1229

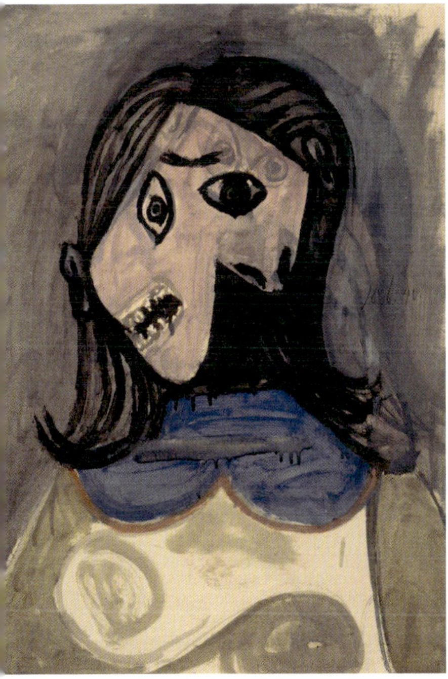

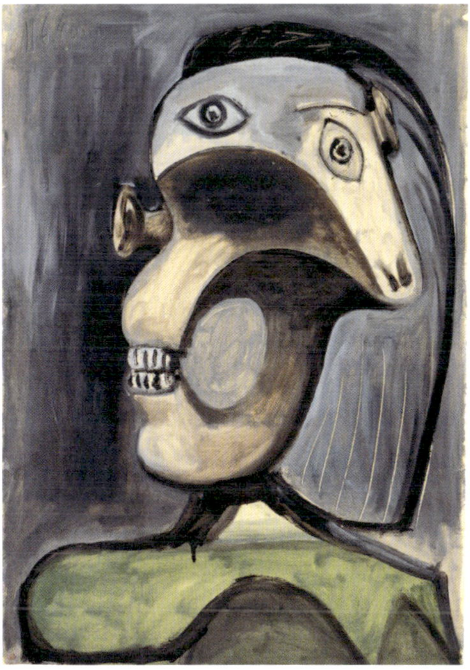

1941

Study for *The Serenade*: Reclining Nude with Her Arms Behind Her Head

Paris, December 12, 1941
Oil pastel on paper, 10.7 × 13.9 in. (27.3 × 35.4 cm)
Dation Pablo Picasso, 1979. MP1278 recto

This drawing is a preparatory sketch for *The Serenade*, a major painting made in 1942 in the Grands-Augustins studio and part of the collection of the Musée National d'Art Moderne – Centre Pompidou. It is one of fifty-five studies belonging to the museum, a series that shows the slow maturing of the subject, over almost an entire year. From May 19, 1941, to January 6, 1942, Picasso engaged in a major study, which included graphite pencil, ink, gouache, watercolor and oil pastels. He progressively determined the general composition (a naked woman reclining and a woman with a mandolin), and kept refining certain details (the meridians, the decor) and the postures of the figures. The sprawling woman is by far what interests him the most: with her twisted body, headless or sometimes two-headed, she illustrates the suffering during the war. The body's angles and the bright color contrasts spell the violence imposed upon the model, which immediately resonates with the historical context. This funereal serenade constitutes a radical transformation of the classical theme it represents, inspired by Titian. It incarnates and denounces the tragedy of the Occupation in France. **E.Ph.**

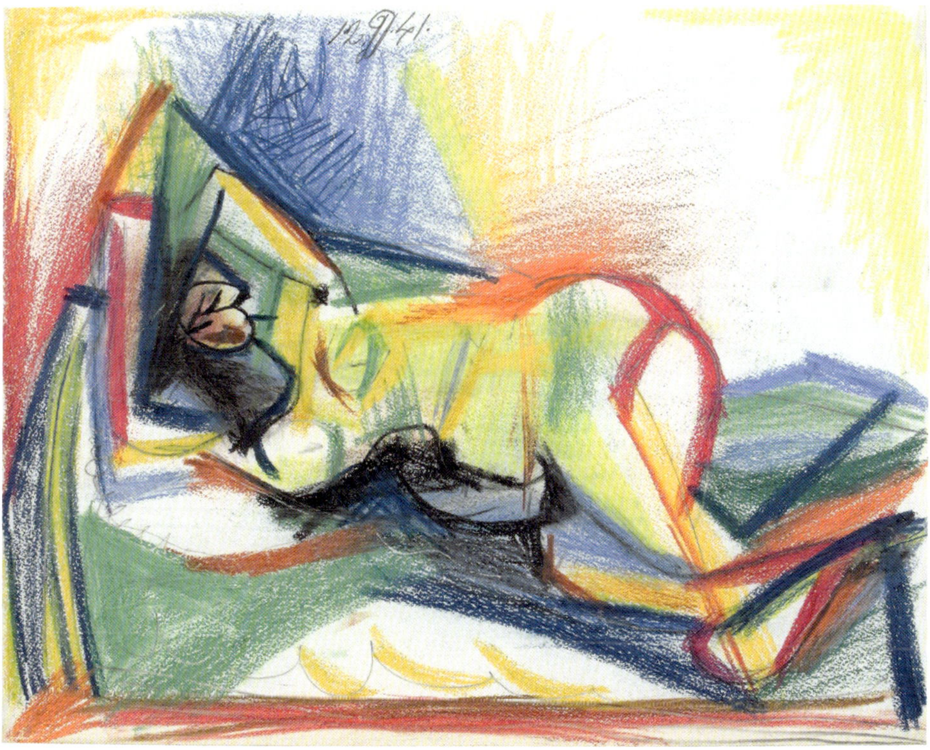
12.9.41.

1942

Bull's Head

Paris, spring 1942
Saddle and handlebars, leather and metal
13.2 × 17.1 × 7.5 in. (33.5 × 43.5 × 19 cm)
Dation Pablo Picasso, 1979. MP330

Bull's Head is probably the most famous reinterpretation of a found object in Picasso's work. It is said he found the bicycle saddle and handlebars in a dump, in the spring of 1942, as he was on his way to the funeral of his friend, the sculptor Julio Gonzalez. Thus the sculpture is considered an artistic tribute to the man who taught him soldering. The basic association of two objects without any intervention from the artist brings to mind Marcel Duchamp's ready-mades, and especially his 1913 *Bicycle Wheel* (Musée National d'Art Moderne – Centre Pompidou, Paris). However, the intention is different. Through the recycling of things that lose their primary meaning, Picasso aimed at creating a new reality. The sculpture becomes a sign, and the trivial object metamorphoses into an archetype, reduced to the very simplicity of plastic expression. Two bronze copies of *Bull's Head* were made (private collections). **V.P.**

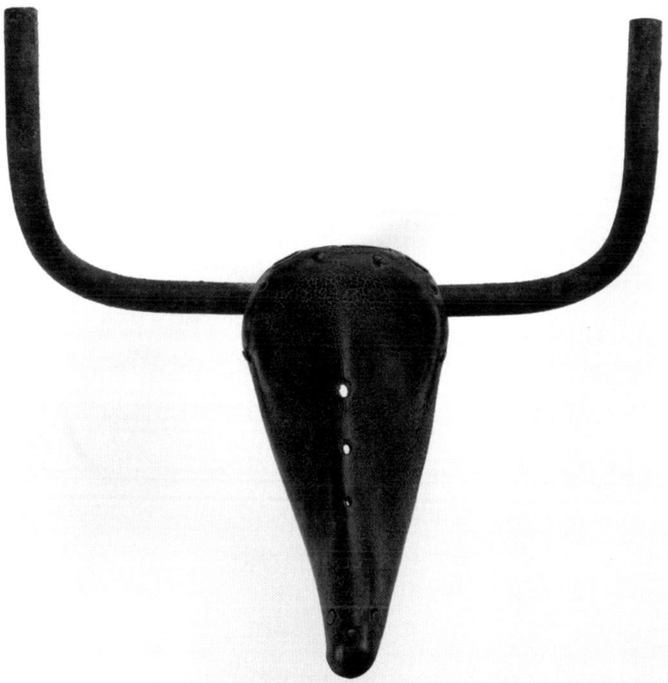

1943

Man with Sheep

Paris, 1943
Bronze, C. Valsuani foundry between 1948 and 1950
87.6 × 30.7 × 30.7 in. (222.5 × 78 × 78 cm)
Dation Pablo Picasso, 1979. MP331

Man with Sheep is one of Picasso's rare full-length statues. It comes from a long series of drawings and studies. In February 1943, in the Grands-Augustins studio, it was rapidly, yet hazardously, modeled out of plaster, with the help of Paul Éluard. As it was made during war time, it was interpreted as a representation of the Good Shepherd, symbol of peace and generosity. After the war, Picasso gave a copy of the statue to the town of Vallauris. It was then that Tristan Tzara compares it to the ancient Greek cow-bearer Moschophoros. However, Picasso denied any symbolism in the piece. The details of the face bring to mind a classic masculine portrait, perhaps a self-portrait. But classicism is set aside by the disproportionate body parts, the roughly sketched legs, the unbalanced volumes of the animal and the surprising distribution of the piece. The unfinished aspect is due to the quick execution of the sculpture, according to Picasso. **V.P.**

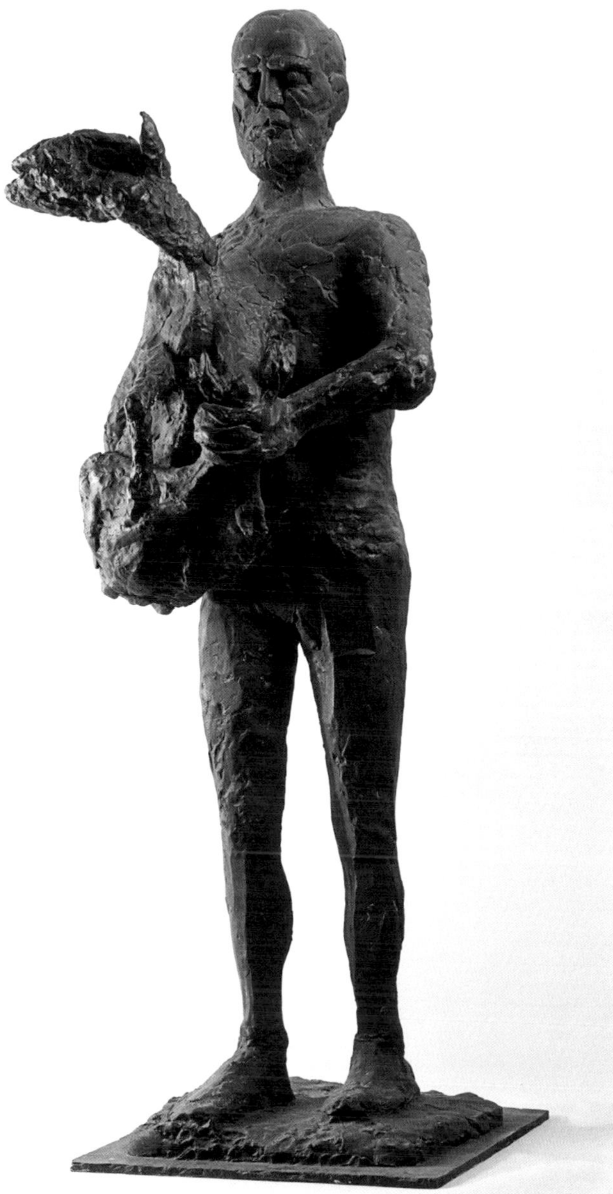

1944

Bust of Woman With a Blue Hat

Paris, March 7, 1944
Oil on canvas, 36.2 × 23.7 in. (92 × 60.2 cm)
Dation Pablo Picasso, 1979. MP193

Since the mid-1930s, Picasso had been obsessively painting a series of women sitting in armchairs, seemingly cramped in a closed room with neither door nor window. Such portraits are linked to the representation of Surrealist photographer Dora Maar, with whom he was involved with from that time, and who also sought, in her photographic work, strange, oppressing points of view. A famous picture by the young woman shows an installation by Picasso during the Occupation: up against a wall at his Grands-Augustins studio, about twenty such portraits of her are displayed on top of each other, all the way to the ceiling. An artistic game that proves her dual role as an active, creative subject, and in turn an object, when modeling for the painter. This dangerous, surrealistic game mixes life and art. Dora Maar would lose in the end, sinking into depression following her break up with Picasso. This portrait is almost the last of the series. It comes right after the arrest, on February 22 and 24, of Picasso's poet friends, Robert Desnos and Max Jacob, who died both died after their deportation. And it comes right before the reading of Picasso's play *Desire Caught by the Tail*, which took place on March 19, in the home of Louise and Michel Leiris. This event displays a form of intellectual resistance against dark times. **E.B.**

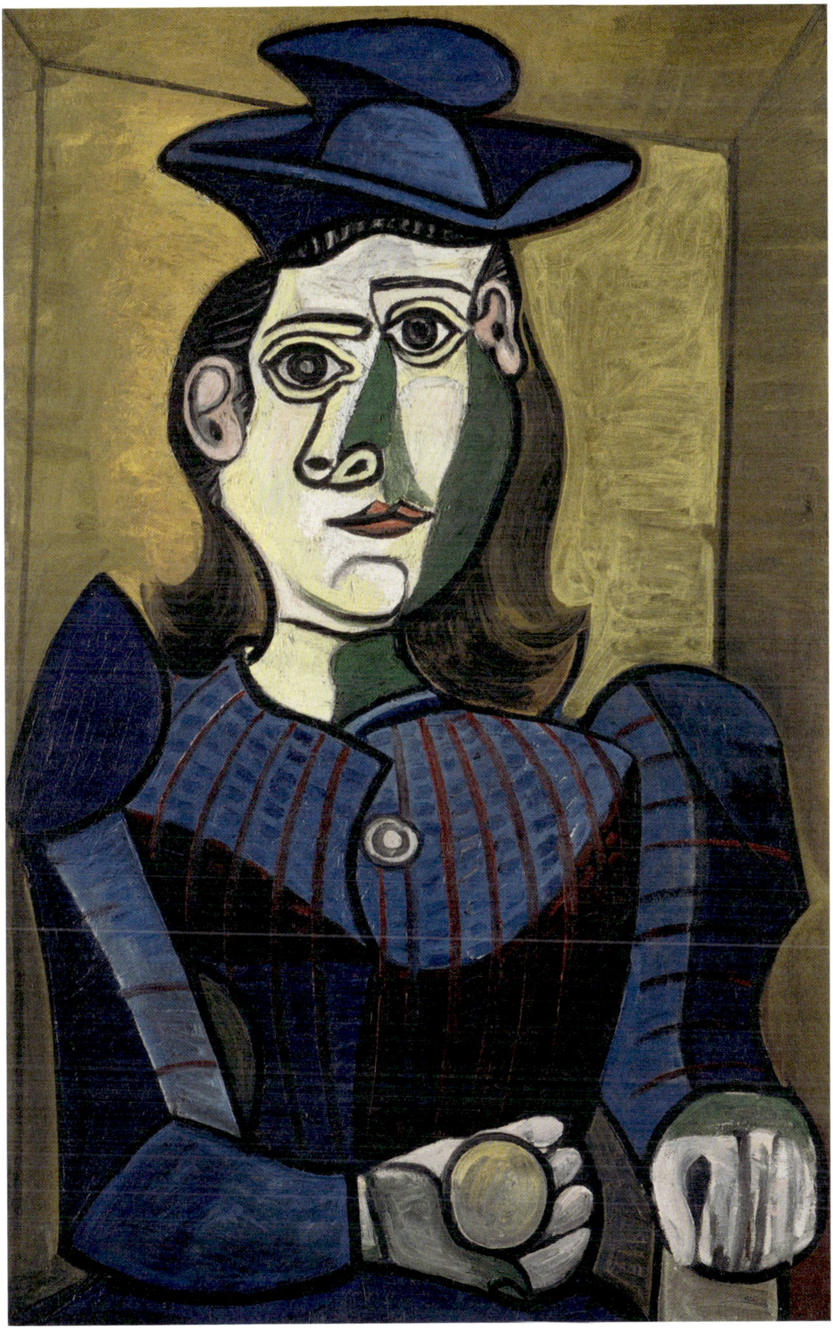

1945

Pitcher and Skeleton

Paris, February 18, 1945
Oil on canvas, 28.7 × 36.3 in (73 × 92.2 cm)
Dation Pablo Picasso, 1979. MP194

It is believed Picasso once told Pierre Daix that a saucepan could scream. This still life, executed in grisaille, an ancient technique based on contrasting values of the same gray, which he often employed for tragic works—the most famous example of which being *Guernica* (1937, Museo Nacional Centro de Arte Reina Sofía, Madrid), seems to howl in its icy coldness. This piece, made after Paris was liberated but before the end of the Second World War, was thus painted around the same time as one of Picasso's three major historical and political works: *The Charnel House* (1944–45, MoMA, New York), another grisaille painting, which refers to the discovery of the concentration camps. Can a "skeleton" really be seen? Looking like anything but an anatomy book, only the title of the painting allows the shape next to the "pitcher" to be considered as a pile of bones. These were most likely of an animal and are sitting on a table, bringing to mind the human skulls of the *Memento Mori* tradition, displayed in still lives to symbolize inescapable death. With this strange and unknown object, Picasso therefore suggests the unrepresentable. **E.B.**

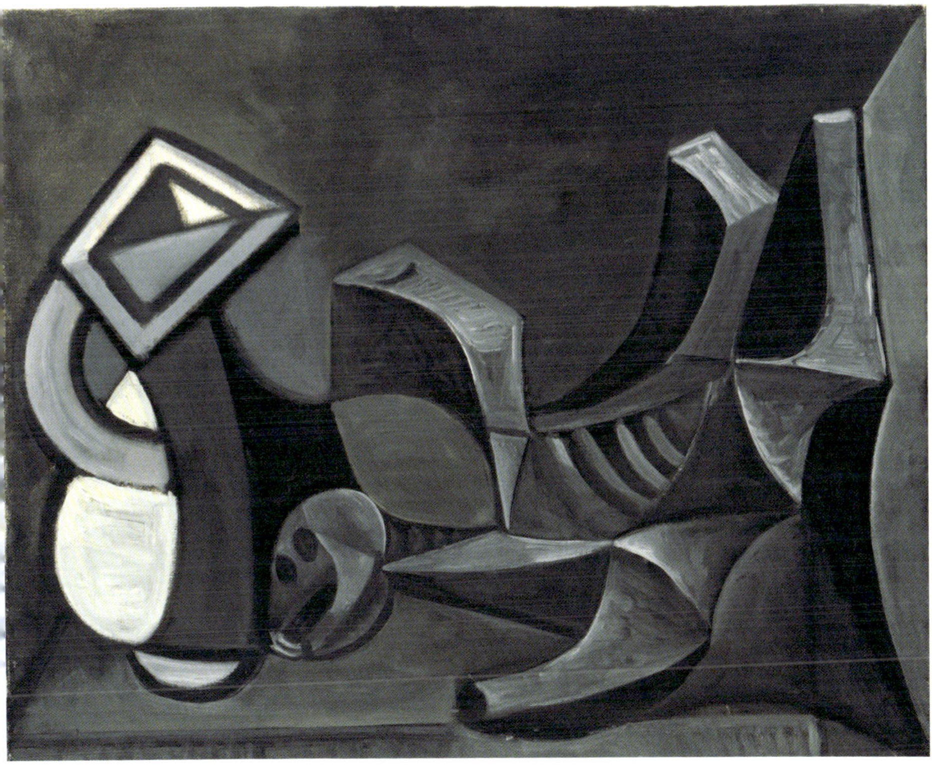

Picasso, a political artist?

No, painting is not meant to decorate apartments. It is a tool for both an offensive and a defensive war against the enemy.

Pablo Picasso in Simone Téry, "Picasso n'est pas officier dans l'armée françaises," *Les Lettres françaises*, no. 48, March 24 1945, n.p.

1901: Black Spain?

During his first visits to Paris, Picasso was part of the "Spanish colony." He lived at 130b Boulevard de Clichy, in a building where many Spanish artists, probably anarchists, lived. The anarchist movement is of major importance in Spain's political history. However, the artistic groups Picasso was acquainted with in Barcelona, at the El Quatre Gats café, were not so much anarchists, as they were marked by a Nietzschean fin-de-siecle spirit and an urge for Catalan independence. In Montmartre, these ideas circulated within the Spanish colony, but Picasso was above all confronted by the insolent spirit of the Chat Noir, of Alfred Jarry, Alphonse Allais and the Incoherents, and then Guillaume Apollinaire.

1937–1939: Spanish Republicans

Picasso truly entered the political arena during the Spanish Civil War. From 1927 to 1933, the Surrealist movement was committed to the French Communist Party. Dora Maar, an anti-fascist activist, played a major role in the artist's first political engagements, starting in 1935, until Paul Éluard took over. In September 1936, Picasso agreed to being appointed honorary director of the Prado Museum by the Republicans, clearly stating who had his support. In January 1937, a Spanish Republican government delegation visited him in Paris, to commission a painting for the Spanish Pavilion at the International Exhibition of Arts and Technology, opening that summer.
The small Basque town of Guernica was bombed on April 26, 1937: Black-and-white photos of the destruction and the massacre of the population were published in newspapers, leading to the creation of *Guernica*. The painting was exhibited on the ground floor of the pavilion from July 1937. Seldom had Picasso used such a large canvas (137.5 × 305.7 in.). It was exhibited with the engraved plates entitled *The Dream and Lie of Franco*, a Republican satire as a series of comic strips of the civil war as conducted by Franco. Franco is caricatured as a sort of tuber-mollusk and brings to mind the literary tyrant King

Ubu by Alfred Jarry. Immediately, *Guernica* is a crucial political tool, even though nothing in its composition explicitly alludes to either side. The viewers at the International Exhibition and the critics compare the engravings with Goya's painting *The Disasters of War* (1810-1815), a dark account of the Spanish War of Independence against Napoleon's troops.

1944–1953: the French Communist Party

In October 1944, Picasso joined the French Communist Party, the "party of 75,000 murdered" Resistance fighters. Pierre Daix, Hélène Parmelin and her husband the painter Edouard Pignon constitute Picasso's Communist circle. He lent his image to the Communist-led pacifist movement (World Congress of Intellectuals in Defense of Peace, Wroclaw, 1948, World Congress of Advocates of Peace, Paris, 1949). He let Louis Aragon, committed to the party since 1927, choose a dove in his studio, which became the movement's emblem, and he painted *Massacre in Korea* (MP203, see p. 136), on January 18, 1951, to condemn American military involvement in Korea. During these years, Pablo Picasso frequently appeared in Communist publications, *L'Humanité* and *Les Lettres françaises*: he helped the image of the movement. In 1953, to commemorate the death of Stalin, Picasso publishes an unrealistic portrait of the Soviet leader in *Les Lettres françaises*. The painting caused a scandal, and Picasso gradually moved away from the French Communist Party.
Was Picasso a political artist? With a few famous exceptions, his art was not political. In his life, as a public man, he supported movements, including financially. However, he remained perfectly independent artistically. The lingering image of Picasso being political may rely on the sense of total autonomy and absolute liberty he had. His artistic commitment was radical and such an attitude is, in itself, a great political lesson, as the ideal of staying true to oneself. **E.B.**

1946

Portrait of Françoise

Paris, April 22 and 23, 1946 and May 22, 1946
Graphite pencil on thick vellum drawing paper, 26 × 19.9 in. (66 × 50.5 cm) and 26 × 20 in. (66 × 50.8 cm)
Dation Pablo Picasso, 1979. MP1350, MP1349, MP1351

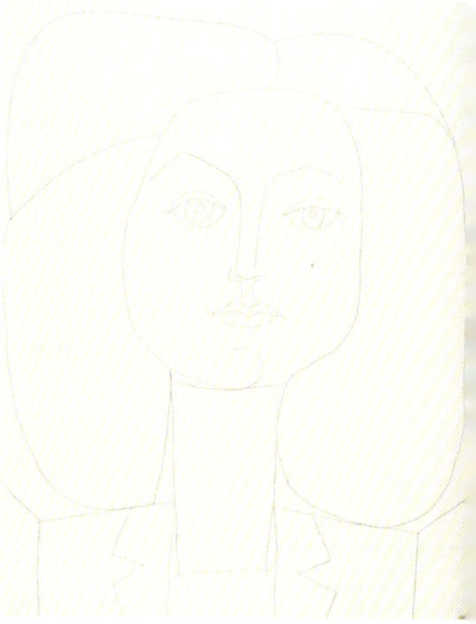

In the spring of 1946, Françoise Gilot and Pablo Picasso had been together for a year, at the Grands-Augustins. The young woman had become a huge part of Picasso's life and art, especially in his drawings, relayed and amplified by lithography. When the artist met the master printer Fernand Mourlot in the fall of 1945, it gave him the opportunity to rediscover this technique he hasn't used for twenty-five years. He thus started making hundreds of lithographs. The face of Françoise appeared quite soon: a delightful oval, radiant eyes, and rich hair, as suggested by a few Matisse-like lines that hold back the blank of the paper. The young woman is in fact an admirer of Matisse and had visited him a few weeks earlier with her lover. Unlike Picasso's other models, Françoise is not sitting in a chair. She surrenders to the artist's pressing desire to give life to his creations, through the multiplication of portraits on vellum paper: Picasso sometimes drew up to ten in one day (June 14, 1946). Meant for lithography, they all reveal, thanks to their diversity, the young woman's beauty and personality. **N.L.**

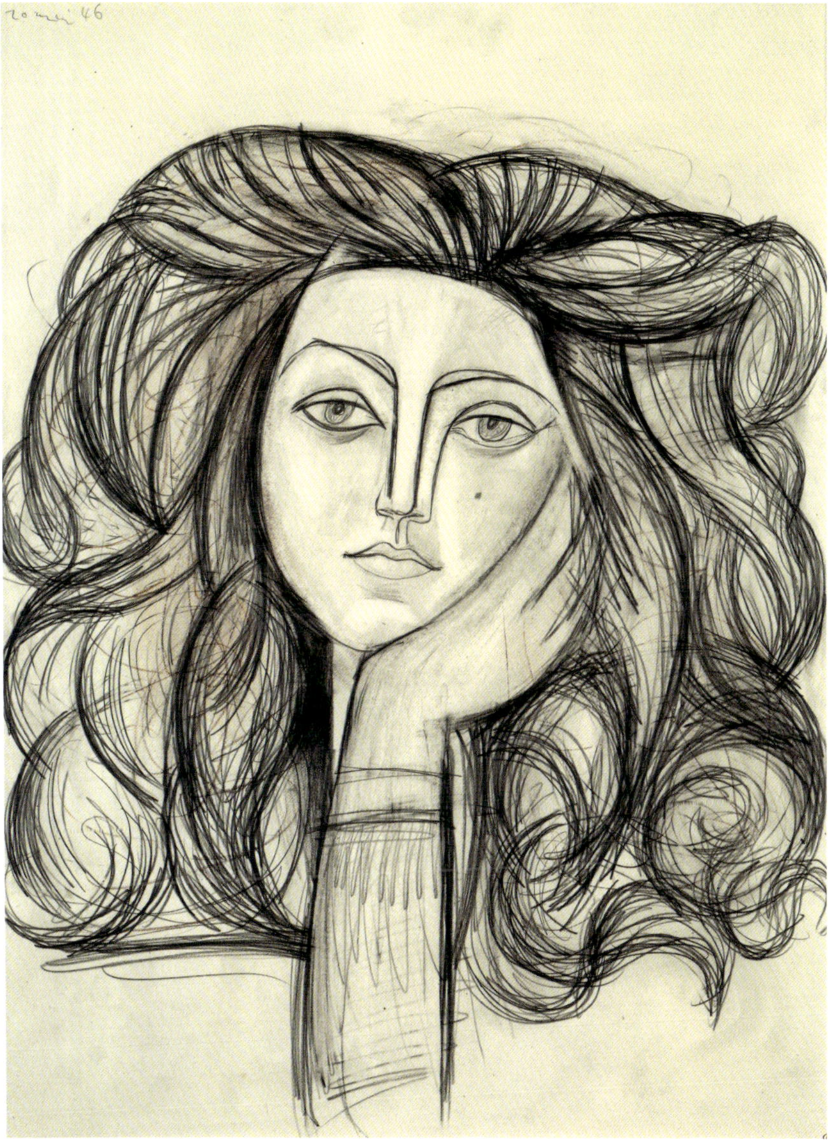

1947

Vase: Woman with Amphora

October, 1947–48
White clay, thrown element, modeled and assembled. Decorated with slip and white enamel, incisions and glazed after firing. 16.7 × 12.8 × 6.1 in. (42.5 × 32.5 × 15.5 cm)
Dation Pablo Picasso, 1979. MP3679

In 1936, Picasso discovered pottery studios in the town of Vallauris, in the South of France, while taking a walk with Paul and Nusch Éluard. Ten years later, he returned there to work, making some 2,000 pieces in only a few months at the Madoura studio. *Vase: Woman with Amphora* is part of a series of ceramics, inspired by the anthropomorphic curves of a vase, which extend the metaphor, with touches of paint highlighting lines and contours, turning the ceramics into actual sculptures of women. Picasso, far from betraying the practical dimension of the original object, uses it to make an object in-between artifact and artwork, in which each element is both function and symbol. Its black lines and sheen recall antique ceramics, while the shape of the vase hints towards the Hellenistic Tanagra figurines from Boeotia, which strongly influenced the artist. **E.P.**

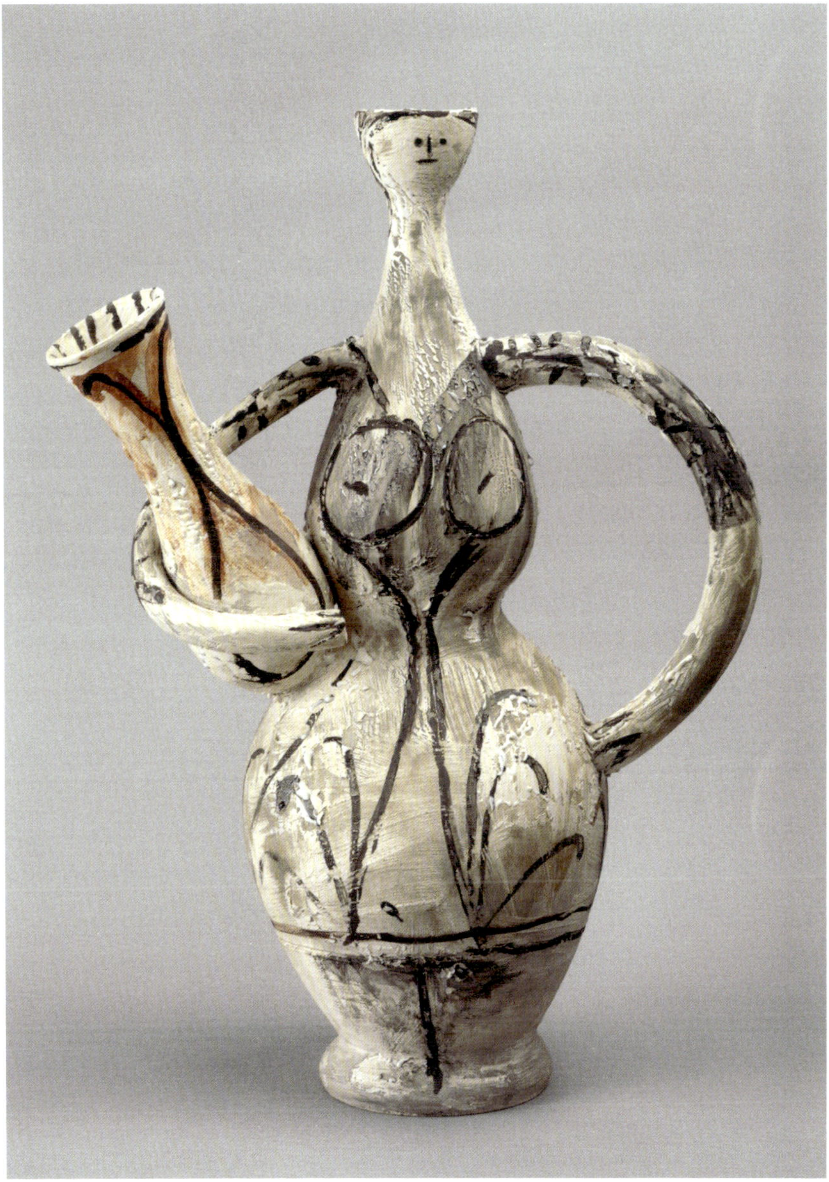

1948

The Kitchen

Paris, November 1948
Oil on canvas, 68.9 × 99.2 in. (175 × 252 cm)
Dation Pablo Picasso, 1979. MP200

This large gray painting is composed of tangled lines, which create contrast and transparency among the shapes. It brings to mind Pablo Picasso's experimentations with the painted line and with space in the late 1920s (*The Painter and His Model*, 1926, MP96, the series of *Figure* [project for a monument to Apollinaire], 1928, MP263 and MP264).
The shades of gray in themselves stress the shape and contours of the objects in the light, rather than their material. Picasso however represents a prosaic, everyday living space: the kitchen. More specifically, his kitchen at the Grands-Augustins studio, with its ceramic plates hanging on the wall. He explained to his partner, Françoise Gilot: "If you focus on what is full, meaning the object as a positive shape, the environment is reduced to almost nothing. If you focus on the space surrounding the object, then the object is reduced to almost nothing. Which of the two is most interesting, what is inside or outside the shape?"
Here, these plastic interrogations lead Pablo Picasso to near abstraction, except for the owl, the turtledoves and the plants, that are said to have been painted by Françoise Gilot.
A second version of this painting was made some time later, after a copy by Françoise Gilot and Javier Vilató, Picasso's nephew. **E.B.**

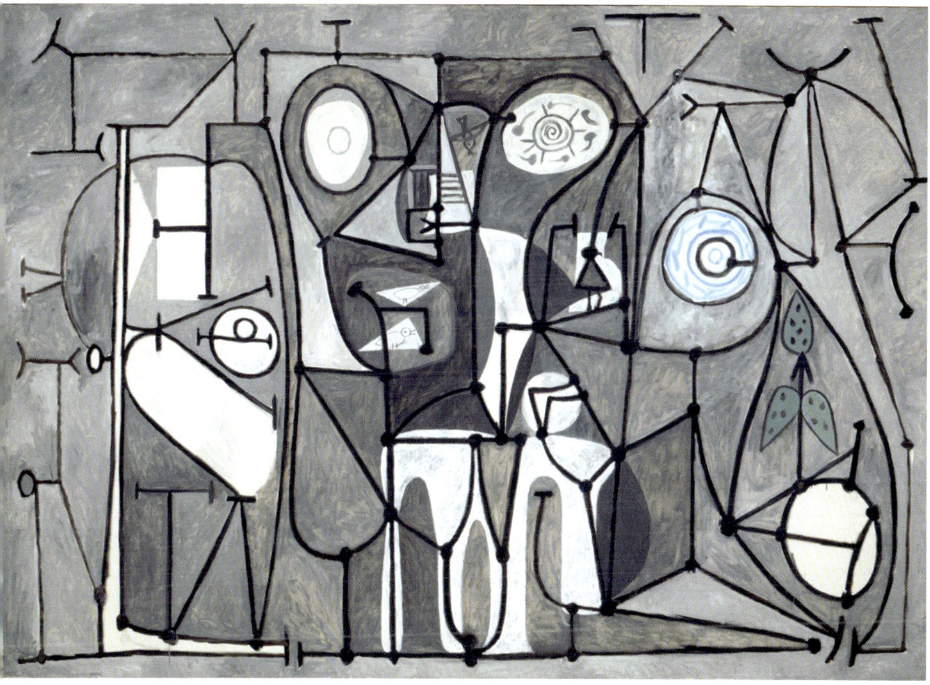

1949

Owl

Vallauris, December 30, 1949
Turned white clay, decorated with slip and white enamel, incisions, and painted under the glaze. 7.5 × 7.1 × 8.7 in. (19 × 18 × 22 cm)
Dation Pablo Picasso, 1979. MP3692

In the ceramics studio of Madoura in Vallauris, where three years earlier the potter Jules Agard had initiated Picasso in the technique of the wheel, the artist made animal-like objects, among which the owl emerges as a favorite topic. Its irregular surface shows incisions, reinforced by touches of paint that mark the relief of the feathers and the eyes of the bird. This reminds the viewer that the artist is never looking for a smooth, classical result. Picasso, who perfectly mastered traditional pottery techniques, used them for heightened effect, as is the case here with the unusual choice of decoration, glaze on enamel. Furthermore, these animal subjects were most likely inspired by the history of pottery, especially that of pre-Colombian and Hispanic-Moresque. Thus, the dove will in turn find its place naturally, after the war, in Picasso's ceramic productions. **E.P.**

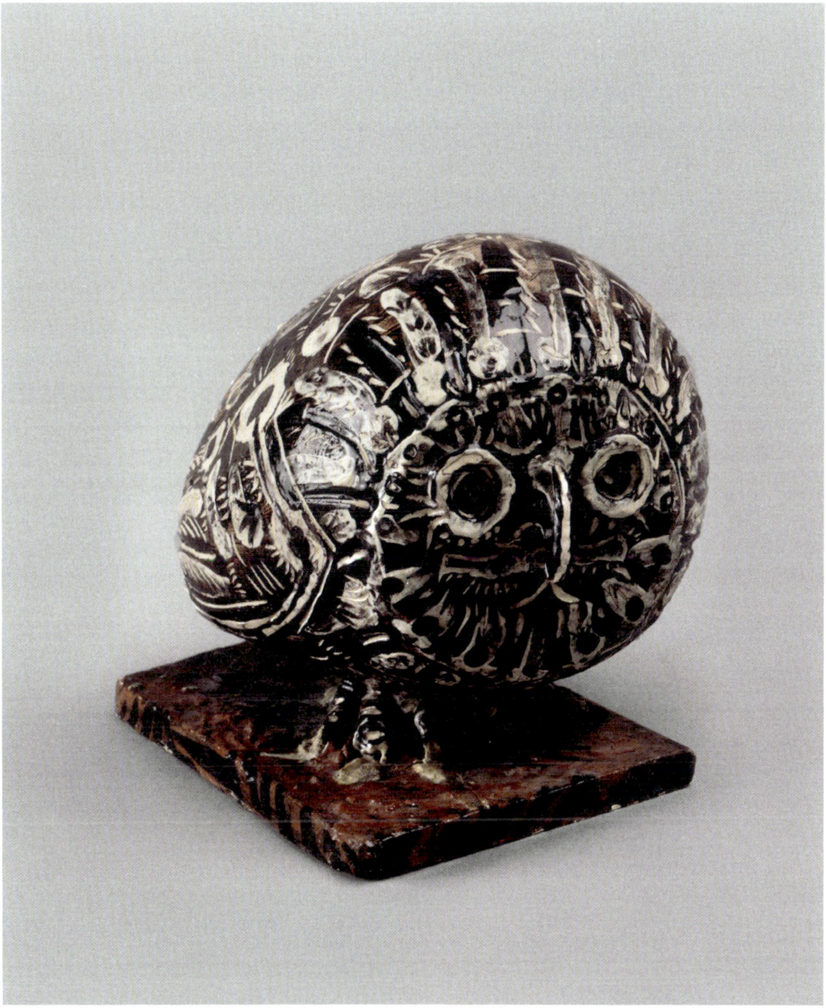

1950

The Goat

Vallauris, 1950
Original plaster: wicker basket, ceramic pots palm leaf, metal, wood, cardboard and plaster
47.4 × 28.3 × 56.7 in. (120.5 × 72 × 144 cm)
Dation Pablo Picasso, 1979. MP339

The goat is an emblematic animal, very familiar in the artist's work. This piece in itself shows the great power of assemblage, which can give life to a sculpture. Thanks to the sculptor's "divinatory look," always keeping an eye out for a found object that can impersonate its plastic metaphor, a surprisingly realistic goat takes shape. Beneath a plaster coating, it bears within its womb all the elements that compose it: its angular skeleton is encircled with metal bars; a palm tree rod serves as backbone; a wicker basket forms its heavy belly; vine stocks curl its horns; while old milk cans figure its teats. Contrary to the 1942 *Bull's Head* (p. 117), for which Pablo Picasso had seen a bull when discovering a bicycle seat and handlebars, here the idea of the goat preceded the research for objects, found in a junkyard on Rue Fournas. They are chosen specifically for their capacity to embody a scrawny goat, the way Picasso has designed it in Antibes in 1946. The myth thus becomes reality: much like Amalthea nursing Zeus in Ancient Greece, the goat is also Esmeralda, a flesh and bone animal given to Picasso one Christmas. This present appears in David Douglas Duncan's photographs: it is wittily leashed to the tail of the bronze sculpture goat, in the garden of La Californie. **V.P.**

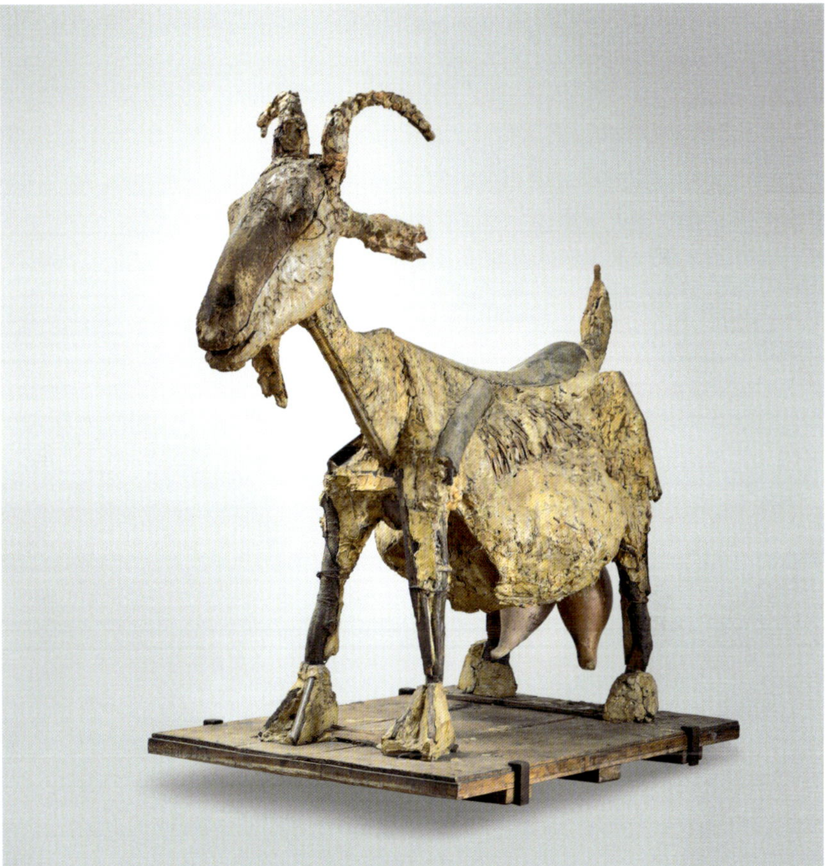

1951

Massacre in Korea

Vallauris, January 18, 1951
Oil on plywood, 43.3 × 82.7 in. (110 × 210 cm)
Dation Pablo Picasso, 1979. MP203

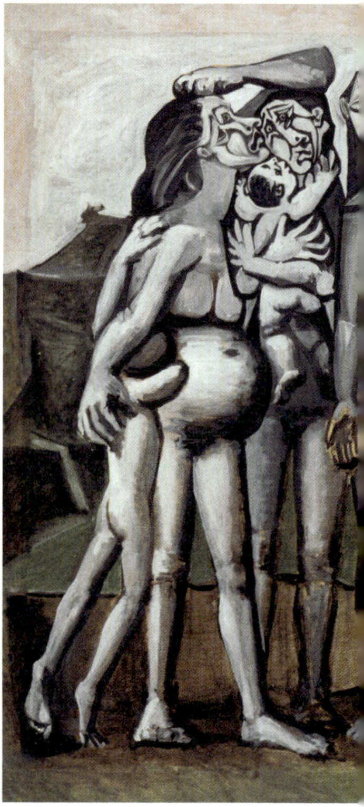

The Korean War was one of the first localized conflicts during the Cold War. In the painting, two groups of the same gray are opposed. The cluster of women and children hold hands, their faces so close to one another that they merge, in an already cadaveric gray. The nudity and the pregnancy stretch marks are eternal, much like the children's plumpness and the way they hang on to their mothers. Facing them, the soldiers hold guns resembling arquebuses, wear helmets much like those of medieval knights, and one on the far right is even waving a sword. This painting follows in the footsteps of a famous and modern line, as its composition quotes Goya's *Tres de Mayo* (1814, Prado Museum, Madrid) and Manet's *The Execution of Emperor Maximilian* (1868–69, Städtische Kunsthalle, Mannheim). Much like *Guernica* (1937, Museo Nacional Centro de Arte Reina Sofía, Madrid) or *The Charnel House* (1945, MoMA, New York), these two examples belong to the history of contemporary painting. Goya, Manet and Picasso set themselves apart from the grand historical genre that evokes ancient battles and tales, and choose to depict the war in their own day and age. As the USSR and the United States were testing their military and industrial equipment's efficiency on Korean territory, true danger is perceptible in the bodies of the medieval and robotic cyborgs: it is the technocratic alliance between industry and armament, the technicist shift, the paradox of a flourishing industry in the "Glorious thirty," making death weapons. Here, the contemporary completely disappears, leaving way for the ancient and mythological. **E.B.**

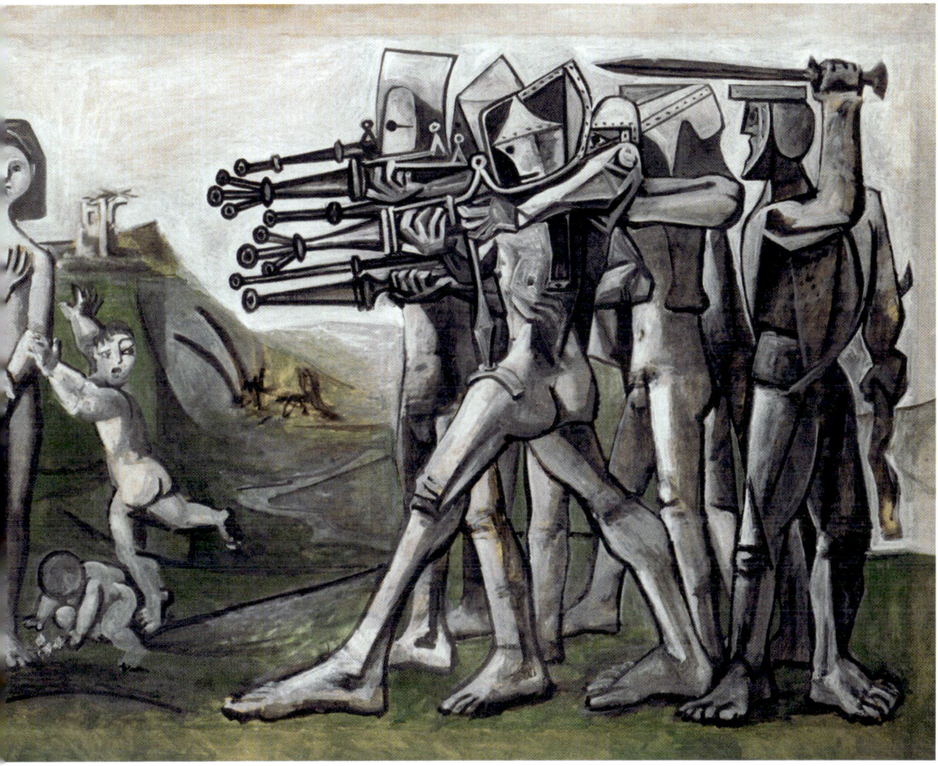

1952

Study for War and Peace

May 1, 1952
Graphite and oil pencil on paper
10 × 13.94 in. (25.4 × 35.4 cm)
Dation Pablo Picasso, 1979. MP1409

In 1952, Picasso began decorating the walls of an abandoned chapel in Vallauris on the theme of war and peace. He carried out long preparatory work, choosing his motifs among traditional and pagan symbols. Three drawing notebooks with 279 sketches in them constitute the major part of this work, but also loose medium-sized sheets, such as this one. Three scenes appear in the space separated in a cinematographic manner, with several sequences. One shows a circle of little girls in a tense, close, frenetic dance, that brings to mind the representations of medieval peasant circles symbolizing peace and harmony. Then, a warrior armed with a sword and a dove-adorned shield. Last, a horned man-owl holding a basket full of heads. These three groups of figures are allegories of war and peace, both intertwine here, thus building a pictorial epic before our eyes. They unveil what shall become the graphic strength, the dynamism and the practically mythological eloquence of the final result. **C.F.**

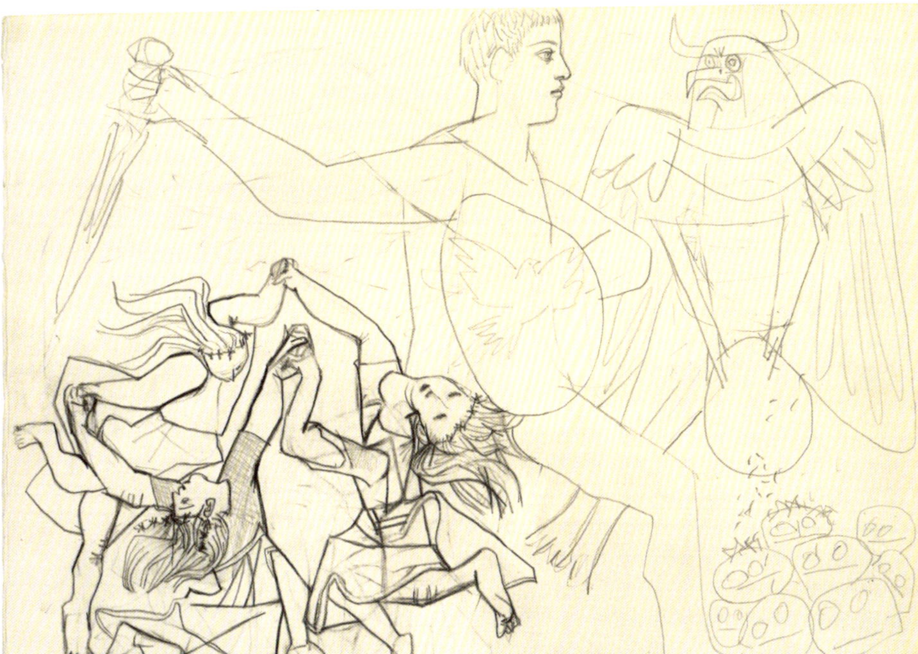
Ier Mai 52.

1953

The Shadow

Vallauris, December 29, 1953
Oil and charcoal on canvas, 51 × 38 in. (129.5 × 96.5 cm)
Dation Pablo Picasso, 1979. MP208

The Shadow was born during a lonely winter. Françoise Gilot, Picasso's partner since the end of the war, had left him and the Villa Galloise a few weeks earlier. The scene takes place at Vallauris, as proven by the toy and the vase. The painter and model configuration is familiar, but the composition is new. A massive silhouette dominates the perspective in which stands a female figure, reminder of the *Pink Nude* by Matisse (1935, Museum of Art, Baltimore). She becomes the focal point of a multi-framed vision, by the door and by the white lines that delineate more spaces. The painter is thus the master of the piece. He is off-stage as he is not represented, and at the same time included by his shadow. He constitutes the hinge between reality and a fictional confrontation—whether carnal encounter or aesthetic fantasy—that seems meant to stay latent, just like the shadow on the doorstep. **N.L.**

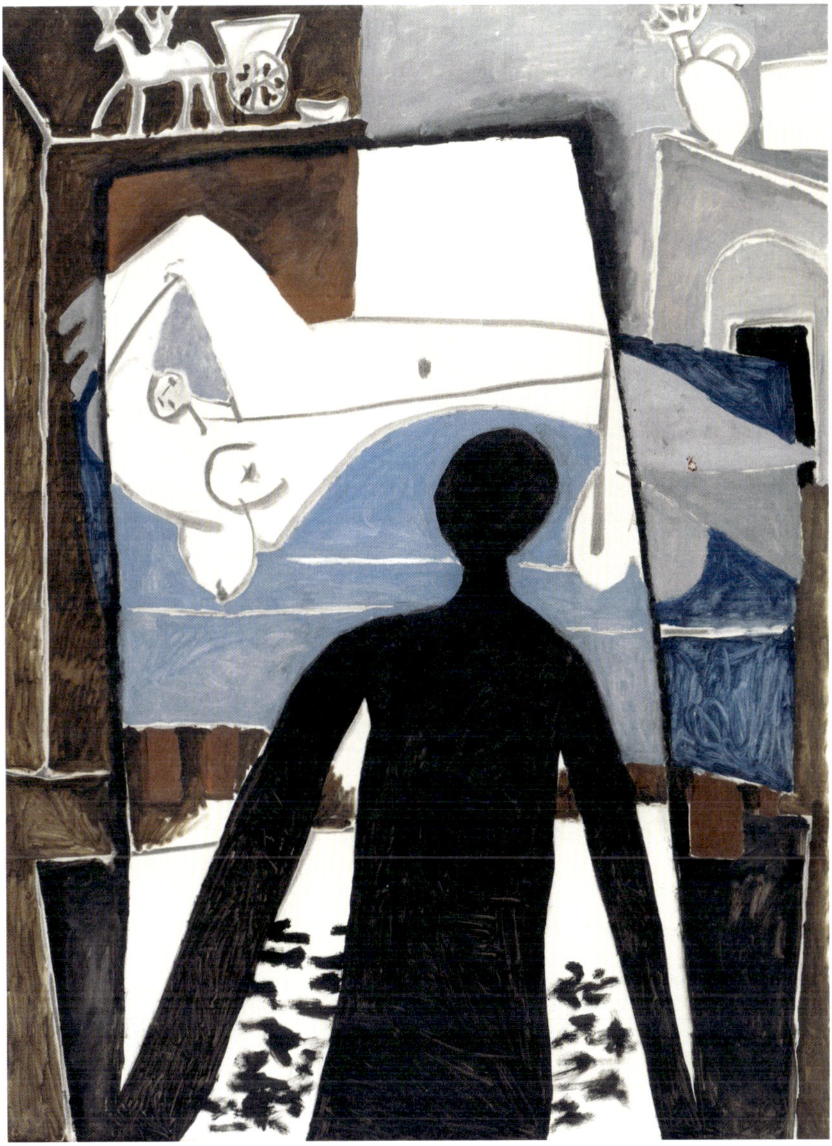

1954

Jacqueline with Hands Crossed

Vallauris, June 3, 1954
Oil on canvas, 45.7 × 34.8 in. (116 × 88.5 cm)
Dation Jacqueline Picasso, 1990. MP1990-26

This portrait is among the first of Jacqueline Roque, Pablo Picasso's last partner. Her position, her high neck, the knees held in her hands and the choice of sharp edges and angles, will come and go in the representations of her: alternately, there are portraits in which the young woman sits in a rocking chair, often wearing a black scarf, hinting towards an ancestral Spain and reigniting Picasso's graphic style, that he invented during his stay in Gósol, in the summer of 1906. Thus Jacqueline Roque immediately has two faces. In fact, this sort of sculptural, three-quarter "Sphinx," had already been tried a few weeks earlier in the series of portraits of the young Sylvette David. Moreover, this portrait of Jacqueline, sitting on a tile floor and wearing a shimmering yellow striped tunic, also follows the tradition of the Odalisques, dear to Matisse and Delacroix, which Picasso passionately drew a few days later in his notebook. In December 1954, he inaugurated a great graphic and pictorial series after *Women of Algiers in Their Apartment* (1834, Musée du Louvre, Paris). Finally, can we perhaps see in this rough silhouette an echo to the works of the then-fashionable painter Bernard Buffet? This assertive character is thus built with an intertwining of complex references and becomes a marvelous object of projection for the artist. **E.B.**

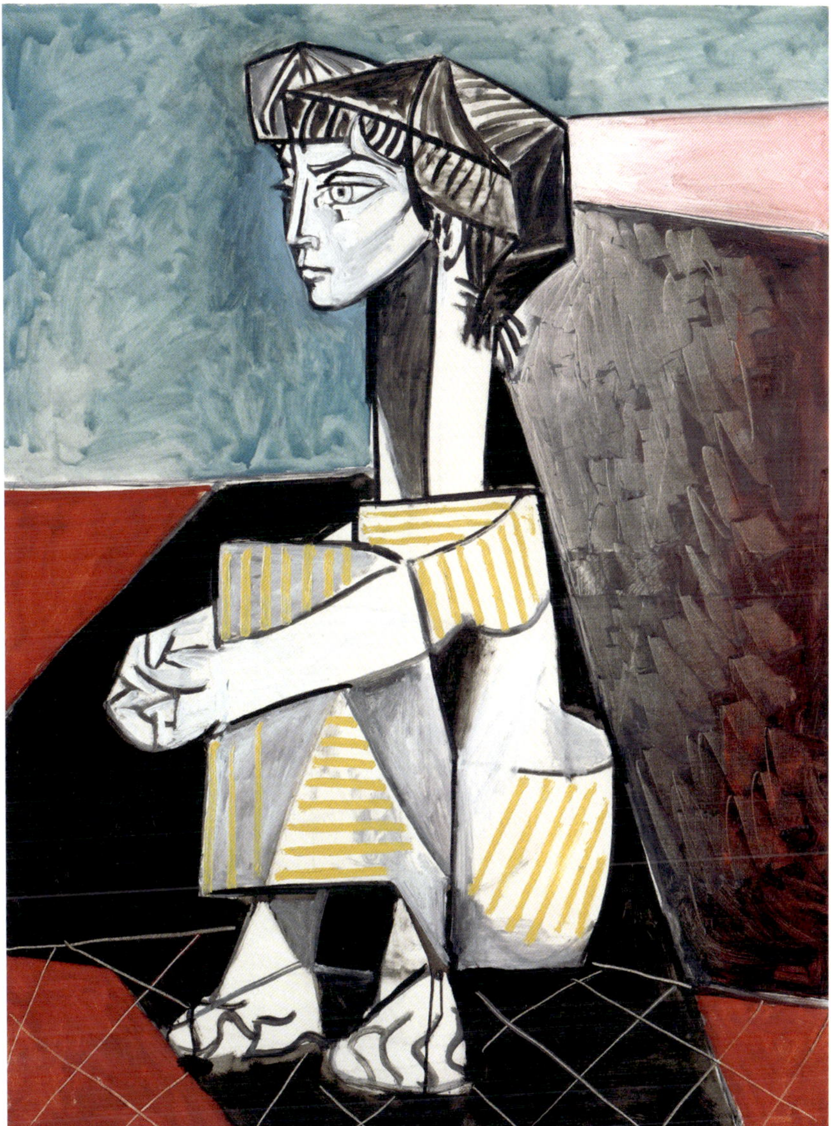

Picasso and women

Most of the time I spent in the studio watching him draw and paint. 'I almost never work from a model, but since you're here, maybe I'll give it a try. ... Pablo stood off, three or four yards from me, looking tense and remote. His eyes didn't leave me for a second. He didn't touch his drawing pad; he wasn't even holding a pencil. Finally he said, 'I see what I need to do. You can dress now. You won't have to pose again.'

Françoise Gilot and Carlton Lake, *Life with Picasso*, New York, McGraw-Hill, 1964, p. 115.

The prostitute and the model

Pablo Picasso received the conventional sex education of a young European man in the late nineteenth-century: that of a brothel. Prostitutes were the first women he saw naked, nude models being banned from art schools. The experience of brothels and their whole process left a lasting mark on the men of that generation. In particular, the "presentation" of the women, under electric lights, amidst an ostentatious decor and reflections from the many mirrors.
Edgar Degas made a series of very crude monotypes representing such scenes, and eleven of his works were in Picasso's personal collection, and now held in the Musée National Picasso-Paris.
When Picasso arrived in Paris in 1900, he was confronted with a completely different mercantile relationship between men and women: models were rented out to artists, and their activity was not always far from prostitution. In Picasso's imagination, the erotic relationship between painter and model tended to mix the fantasies of the introduction at the brothel with that of the model posing before the painter's eyes. This image recurs in his 1960s paintings and engravings (*The Painter and His Model*, November 15, 1964, MP1990-31; the series of prints "Variations on the *Unknown Masterpiece*: Painter, Model, Couple and Two Painters", MP3050 to MP3052). Picasso staged creation as the gaze of a man on a woman. In this he was consistentwith the male tradition of Western art, in which sexual roles define the man as the creator, the subject, and the woman as the model, the object.

Art and life

However, Picasso pushes the confusion between art and eroticism, or rather, love, further. In the nineteenth century, the model had no name. She was merely a tool to the artist. For a handful of artists though, beloved and admired by Picasso, their models became involved in their personal lives: Raphael and La Fornarina, Rembrandt and his partner, Hendrickje Stoffels.
Impressionists, followed by Gauguin and Van Gogh, represented their loved ones. Picasso took this logic to the next level and intentionally merged his life, and his "life as a painter."[1]
A "domestic" artist, he confounds his home with his studio, and represents those who surrounded him, especially his lovers, in an almost obsessional way. As Pierre Daix showed, existential break ups are also stylistic, life being constantly submitted to artistic interpretation. He almost never had a model pose, but worked from photographs. From 1945, Françoise Gilot, and later Jacqueline Roque, appeared by his side in the media, and he drew the link himself between his art, his love life and family, which he exhibited for paparazzi. Photo books were published. Roland Penrose, Pierre Daix, and John Richardson carved out this biographical approach to Picasso's life and art, at the suggestion of Picasso himself, as he built his own myth.

Picasso and gender

In his radical and surreal—or perhaps conceptual—fusing of art and life, artist and model, Picasso remained marked by an ancient separation of the traditional division of the social roles of men and women, representing them in all their instinctual archaism. His way of representing masculinity, and relationships between men and women (many rape scenes are associated with the Minotaur's violence, for instance *Minotaur Raping a Woman*, June 28, 1933, MP1133), reveal a male psyche that at the very least implies a masculine conception of creation, which may partly explain why the painter Françoise Gilot left him in 1953.
Picasso's obsession with women and models leads us to also confuse the model, the woman, and her representation. We forget that Fernande Olivier was renowned in Montmartre, that Olga Khokhlova was a wonderful dancer in the Ballets Russes company, that Dora Maar was a photographer, a poet, a Surrealist and an activist, and that Françoise Gilot was a painter. They all influenced Picasso. **E.B.**

1. Pierre Daix, *La Vie de peintre de Pablo Picasso*, Paris, Seuil, 1977.

1955

Study for Women of Algiers *after Delacroix*

In the 1950s, Picasso reinterpreted a series of existing paintings: *Women of Algiers* (1834, Musée du Louvre, Paris) by Delacroix. The museum has only a few traces of these variations, except for a remarkable set of seventy-two *Studies for* Women of Algiers *after Delacroix*. They reveal the extraordinary string of film-like sequences of motifs that constitute the composition. Comprising fifteen paintings, nine engravings and two lithographs, this cycle inspired by Delacroix is the first of its size in the artist's career. It was probably triggered by the death of Matisse, his friend and creator of the Odalisques. The series was achieved in only a few weeks, from December 1954 to February 1955. In these variations, Picasso underlines the resemblance between Jacqueline Roque and the woman with the water pipe. It offers a new contemporary interpretation of oriental painting. Throughout the studies, the fluidity and fertility inherent to the artist's creative process appear. A process revealed on screen over the summer of 1955, in the documentary by Henri-Georges Clouzot, *The Mystery of Picasso*. **E.Ph.**

Study for* Women of Algiers *after Delacroix

Paris, December 26, 1954
Pen and Indian ink on paper,
8.3 × 10.6 in. (21 × 27 cm)
Dation Pablo Picasso,
1979. MP1443

Study for* Women of Algiers *after Delacroix

Paris, December 31, 1954
Pen and Indian ink on paper,
8.3 × 10.6 in. (21 × 27 cm)
Dation Pablo Picasso,
1979. MP1468

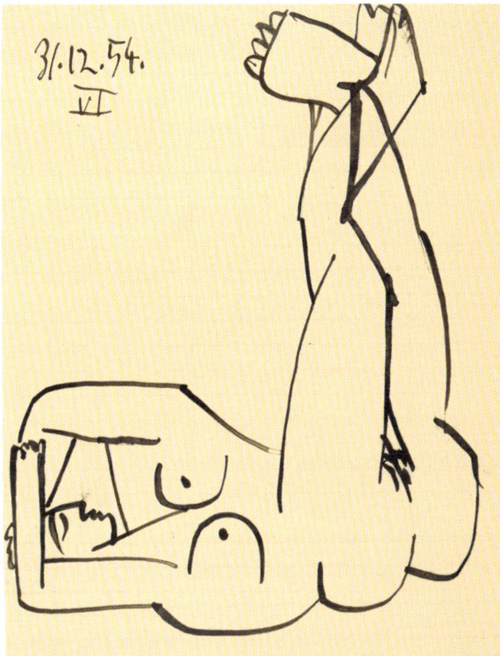
31.12.54.
VI

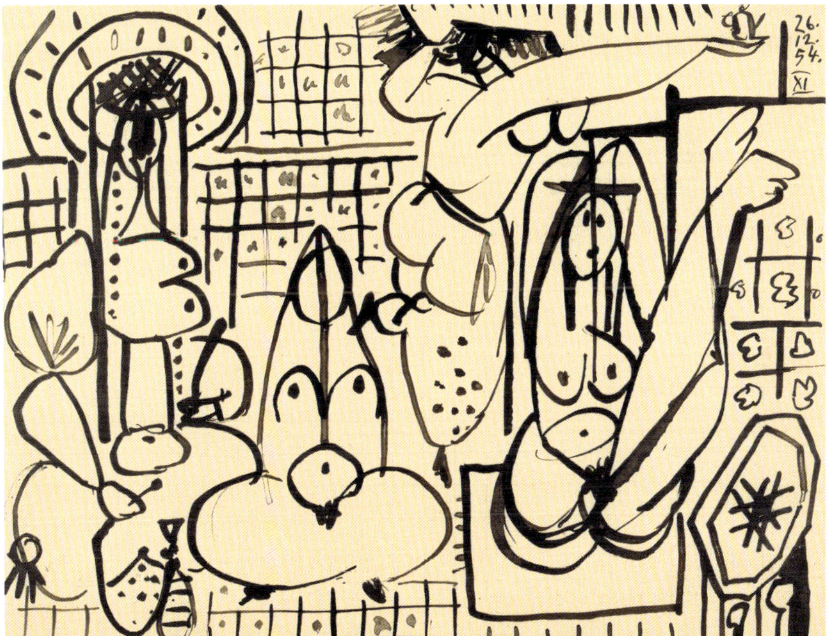
26.
12.
54.
XI

1956

The Bathers

Cannes, summer 1956
Bronze, C. Valsuani foundry
between 1957 and 1959
Dation Pablo Picasso,
1979. MP352 à MP357

In 1955, during the shooting of *The Mystery of Picasso*, by Clouzot, Picasso created a series of improvised works before the camera, among which were *The Centaur* (1955, Los Angeles County Museum of Art), a large wooden sculpture. It announces the upcoming series of *Bathers*, made the next summer in Cannes. This group of six indissociable characters was represented in a series of drawings in September 1956, revealing the key to the setting of the scenes: the Diver and the Man with his hands clasped stand on the pier, the Woman with her outstretched arms and the Young Man are on a diving board, the Fountain Man and the Child are in the water. The use of recycled materials and the assembling of flat surfaces were not new to Picasso, whose 1912 cut-out iron and cardboard assemblage we know. Here, the plastic process becomes a constructive principle taken to a monumental level. The expressive character of this outdoor Mediterranean theater is so powerful that it recalls the Cycladic marble idols of ancient Greece, of which Picasso owned a figurine. **V.P.**

The Diver
103.9 × 32.9 × 32.9 in.
(264 × 83,5 × 83,5 cm)

Man with Clasped Hands
84 × 28.7 × 14.2 in.
(213,5 × 73 × 36 cm)

The Fountain Man
89.8 × 34.6 × 30.5 in.
(228 × 88 × 77,5 cm)

The Child
53.5 × 26.4 × 18.1 in.
(136 × 67 × 46 cm)

Woman with Outstretched Arms
78 × 68.5 × 18.1 in.
(198 × 174 × 46 cm)

The Young Man
69.3 × 25.6 × 18.1 in.
(176 × 65 × 46 cm)

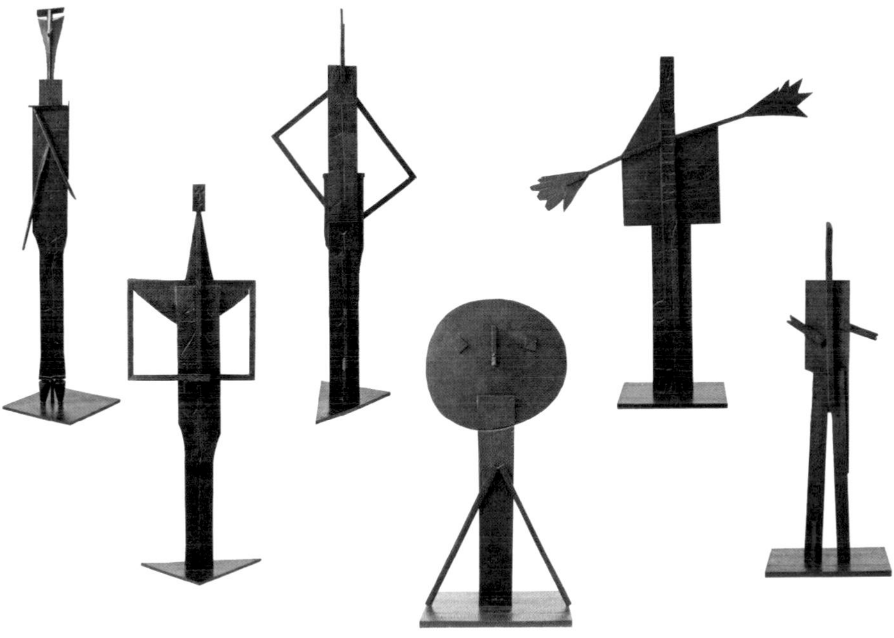

1957

Woman's Head

Cannes, 1957
Cut and painted wood, 31 × 13.4 × 14.2 in.
(78.5 × 34 × 36 cm)
Dation Pablo Picasso, 1979. MP350

Woman's Head is the heir to Cubist faceted heads and open volumes. On a monumental level, it reactivates the creative dialogue between the two- and three-dimensional. When Pablo Picasso met the Norwegian sculptor Carl Nesjar in January 1957, this sculpture became the experimental model of the first engraved concrete pole (9 ft), erected in 1958 in Viksjø Park, in Gor Larvik (Norway). With the solemn and angular portraits of Jacqueline Roque as a starting point, a new perspective on the vocabulary of painting is again created through the selecting and distributing of painted elements and the disposition of the face's facets in space, as well as around the axis. The visual and material frugality of *Woman's Head* contributes to its perfect monumental adaptation in its designed environment: its open structure gives it a visibility in the landscape from any angle, while the contrasting colors take into account variations in natural light. This was proven by the 40 ft model installed in 1991 in Flaine, an alpine ski resort. **N.L.**

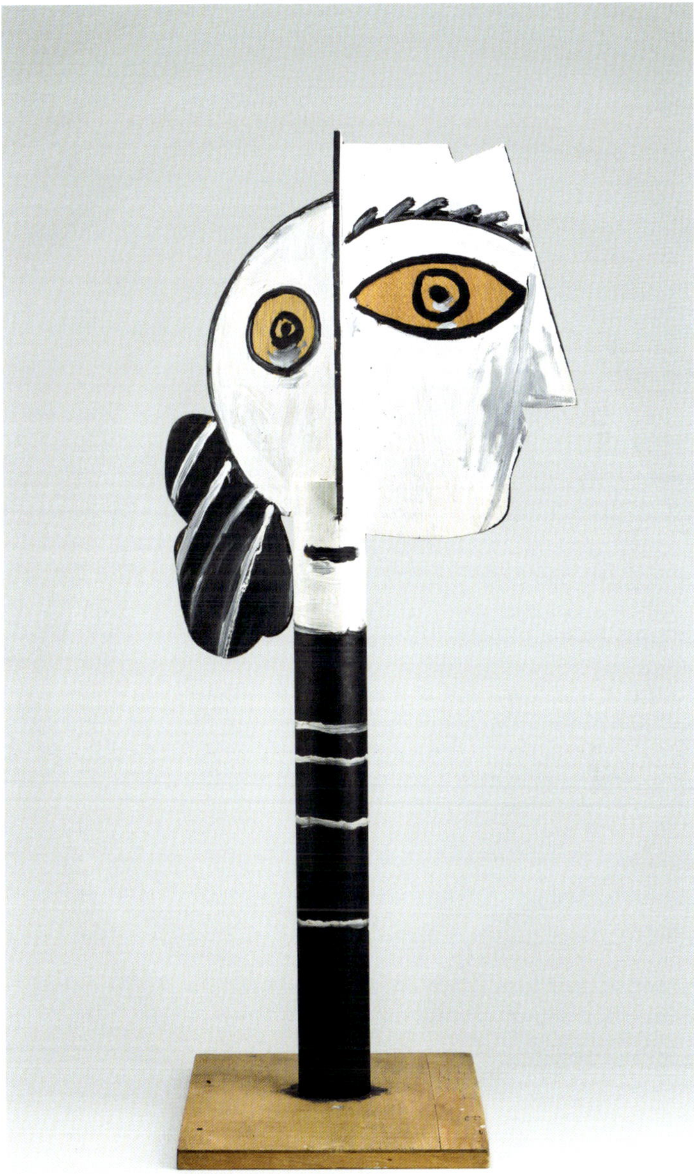

1958

Still Life with Bull's Head

Cannes, May 25–June 9, 1958
Oil on canvas, 64 × 51.2 in. (162.5 × 130 cm)
Dation Pablo Picasso, 1979. MP213

This work was painted just as Picasso finished a cycle of fifty—eight paintings inspired by Velázquez's *Las Meninas*—a series he donated in 1968 to the new Picasso Museum in Barcelona. It is also one of the rare moments when he agreed to take a public commission: *The Fall of Icarus* is inaugurated in September 1958 at the headquarters of the UNESCO in Paris.
This *Still Life* acts as a pause and the resuming of a conversation with Matisse, Picasso's old friend and foe who passed away four years earlier. The still life before an open window and the shimmering Mediterranean-like scenery are recurring motifs in Matisse's art, from his first Fauvist work (*The Open Window*, 1905, National Gallery of Art, Washington) until after the war (*Red Interior: Still Life on a Blue Table*, 1947, Kunstsammlung Nordrhein Westfallen, Düsseldorf).
Traditionally, the open window is a metaphor for painting: in Matisse's works, it could be window or painting. Here, Picasso borrows from his friend a frequent red-and-blue contrast, but outside there are only a few clouds. Furthermore Picasso displays the head of a bull on the windowsill. The omnipresent red leads suggests the presence of blood, on this head that draws the attention of every gaze. This painting has something ferocious about it, as the voluptuous tranquility of Matisse's world is disturbed by one of Picasso's corrida emblems. **E.B.**

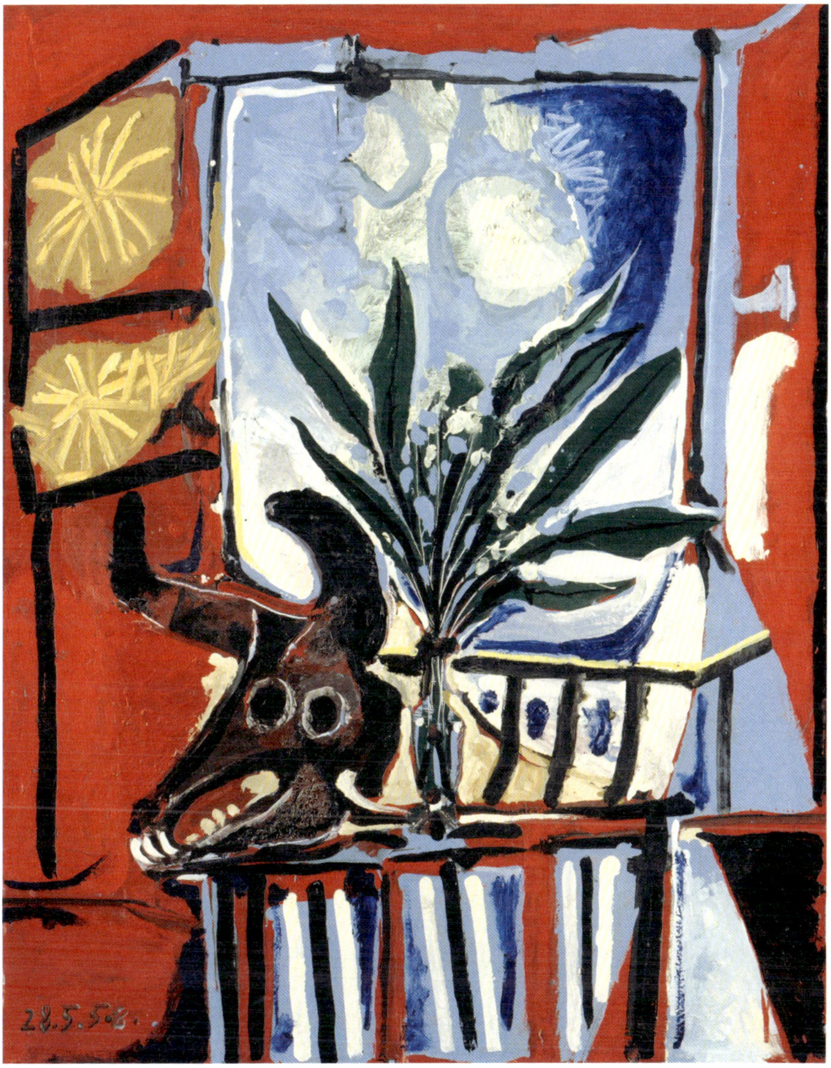
28.5.58.

1959

Paseo de cuadrillas (illustration for *La Tauromaquia*, plate 3)

May 1957
Sugar aquatint on copper
Proof on paper watermarked by a bull, printed by Lacourière-Frélaut
13.7 × 19.8 in. (34.9 × 50.3 cm)
Dation Pablo Picasso, 1979. MP3568-3

In the spring of 1957, after having gone to the Easter corrida in Arles, Picasso undertook the illustration of *La Tauromaquia o arte de torear*, by Jose Delgado, also known as Pepe Illo, published by Gustavo Gili in 1959. True to the text, Picasso most accurately tackles each step of the corrida, through twenty-six aquatints, showing every intention of covering the entire ceremonial: the field in which the bulls rest, the arenas where the aficionados gather, the *paseo*—procession of matadors, picadors and bandilleros—the execution of the bull, and then the *arrastre* and the triumph parade.

In a sugar aquatint, Picasso grasps the movement and the fleetingness of what takes place in the arena. This technique, close to wash drawing, helps Picasso create different grains which appear as nuances, thus creating depth and shades. He therefore illustrates the confrontation between light and shadow, the terrible tension in the bullfighting ritual. **J.-Y.S.**

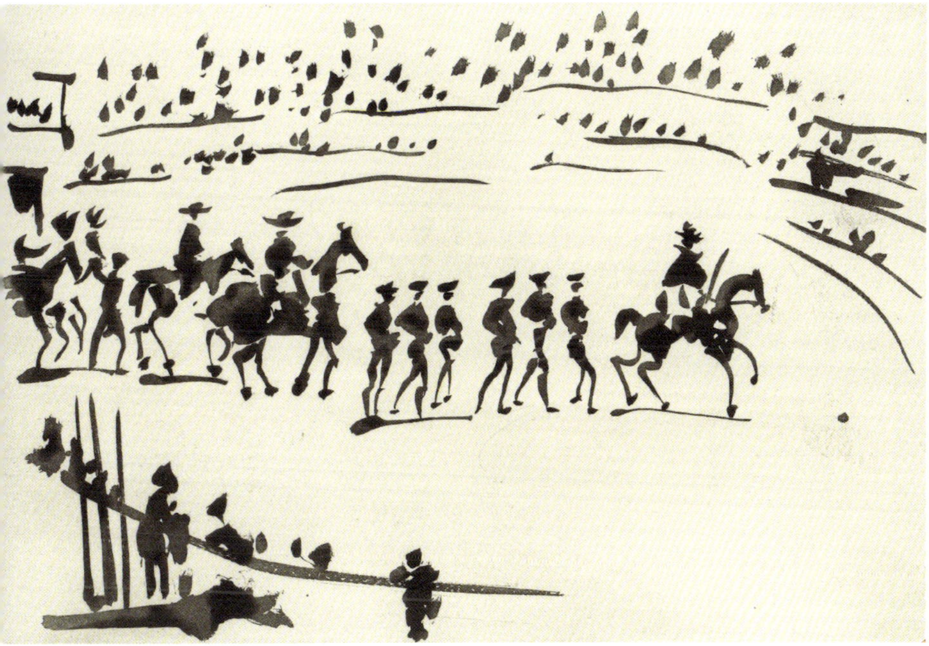

1960

The Dresser at Vauvenargues

Cannes-Vauvenargues, March 23, 1959–January 23, 1960
Oil on canvas, 76.8 × 110.2 in. (195 × 280 cm)
Dation Pablo Picasso, 1979. MP214

The heavy baroque dresser sitting in the dining room at Vauvenargues Castle becomes a major motif in Picasso's new studio. Its ringed columns, carvings, moldings, balusters and bas-relief sculptures supply an endless gallery of shapes. The piece of furniture is flanked with two quotes that evoke explicitly Picasso's favorite theme: that of the model. The moving child is yet another evolution of the seated-woman theme, begun with the artist's first pieces. The woman's bust, perched on a pedestal, makes for a distant echo to the antique figures in the "Vollard Suite" engravings, made thirty years earlier. Bright bottle-green, yellow, orange and red are typical of the Vauvenargues period, and share a palette enhanced by a radiant Ripolin, an enamel paint that builders introduced to Picasso in 1912. The large *Dresser at Vauvenargues* was thought of in Cannes, after Picasso's first stay in Vauvenargues, early 1959. It took about ten months to complete, and was finished in this castle near Aix-en-Provence. On the back of the canvas, Picasso kept track of every step of the creation: dates, places and even time. **N.L.**

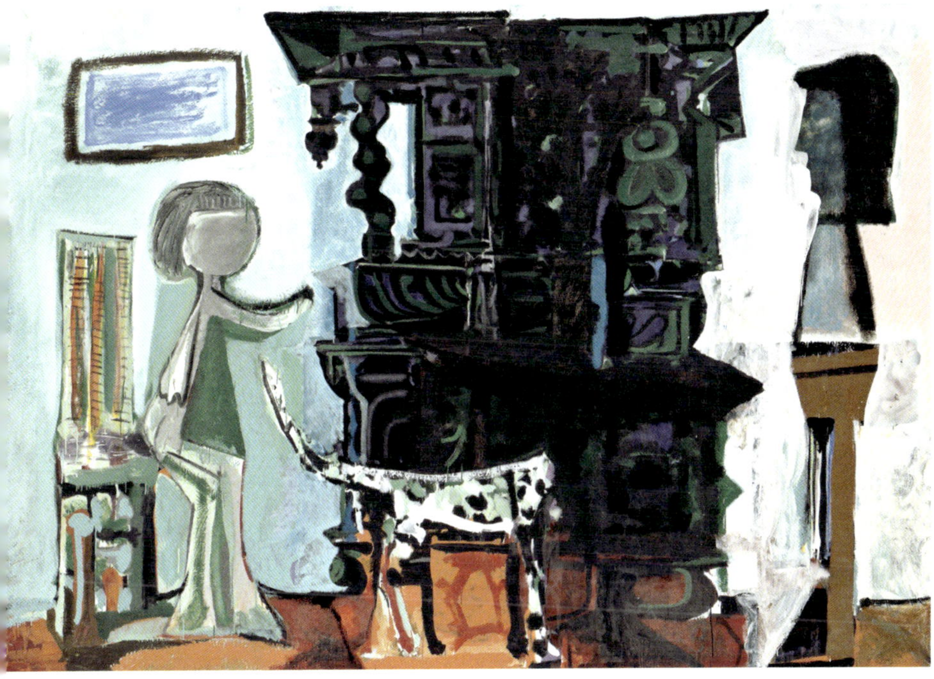

1961

The Chair

Cannes, 1961
Cut, folded and painted sheet of metal,
43.9 × 45.1 × 35 in. (111.5 × 114.5 × 89 cm)
Dation Pablo Picasso, 1979. MP359

This chair is made with a sheet of paper and a piece of charcoal. When Pablo Picasso designed it on the wrapping of a plywood board, the seat was still maturing. Its shape and nature are not determined: animal, plant, or object? Moving on to the third dimension literally set the chair on its legs. The artist cuts out and folds the paper until the drawing gives birth to its latent volume. Transferring the profile to a painted metal sheet, cutting the iron and soldering the crucial points contribute to the strengthening of this radical transmutation. Picasso had already used metal sheets, to create depth in his compositions. In the early 1960s, this material is sometimes used with enamel paint and oil pencils. It turns out to be favored by the artist, giving many diverse creations, including heads of women, soccer players and full-length figures. Picasso often cuts out these sculptures directly with scissors. They share a certain lightness, a playful and roguish spirit, much like this chair and its unbalanced shape. **N.L.**

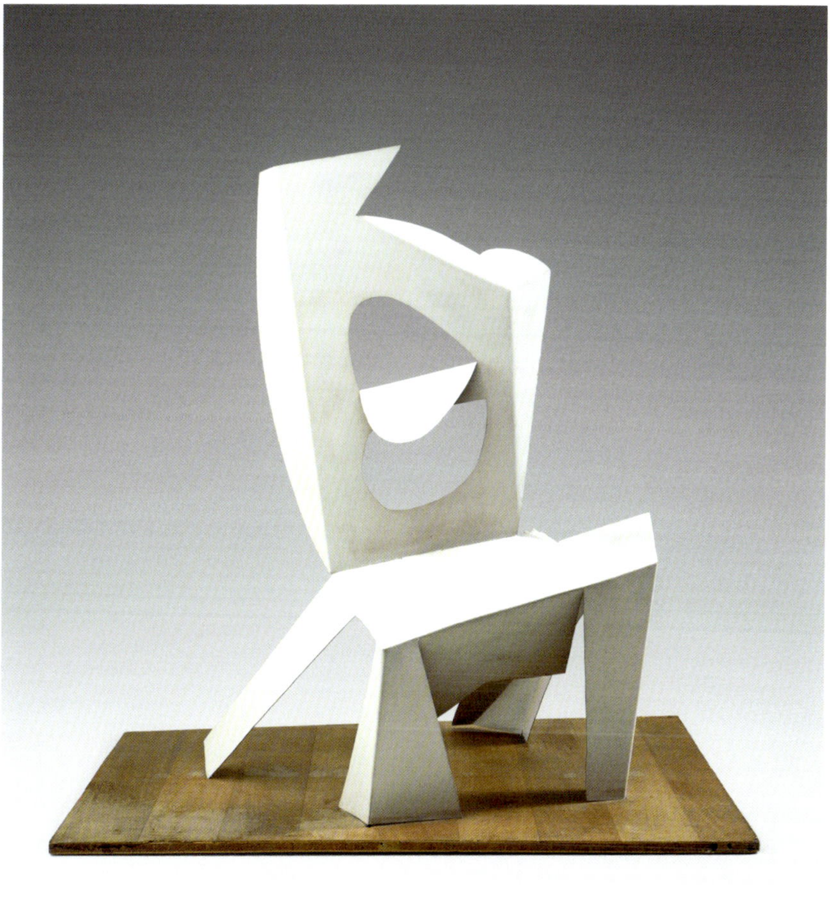

1962

Diurnes (cover)

Jacques Prévert (author)
Pablo Picasso (illustrator)
André Villers (photographer)
Paris, Berggruen, 1962
Musée National Picasso-Paris Library

Published in 1962 by the collector Heinz Berggruen, the book *Diurnes* (*Diurnal*) was born of the collaboration between Pablo Picasso, the poet Jacques Prevert (1900–1977) and the photographer Andre Villers (born in 1930).
In 1953, Picasso met Andre Villers: he gave him his first Rolleiflex camera and encouraged him to pursue his experimental works, playing with cutting, superimposition and transparency effects.
From 1954 to 1961, Villers made hundreds of photographs, cuttings—a technique in between drawing and sculpture, most appreciated by Picasso—assemblages, and photographic transfers. Among these photograms, the artists chose about thirty that they composed together: masks, heads, fairies and portraits are then given a name by Prevert, who invents a story for each of these thirty ephemeral characters, giving its title to the whole set. The book thus allies the texts by Prevert and the thirty reproductions of the photographic cut-outs. Picasso draws the title *Diurnes*, as well as a face for the slip-case. **J.-Y. S.**

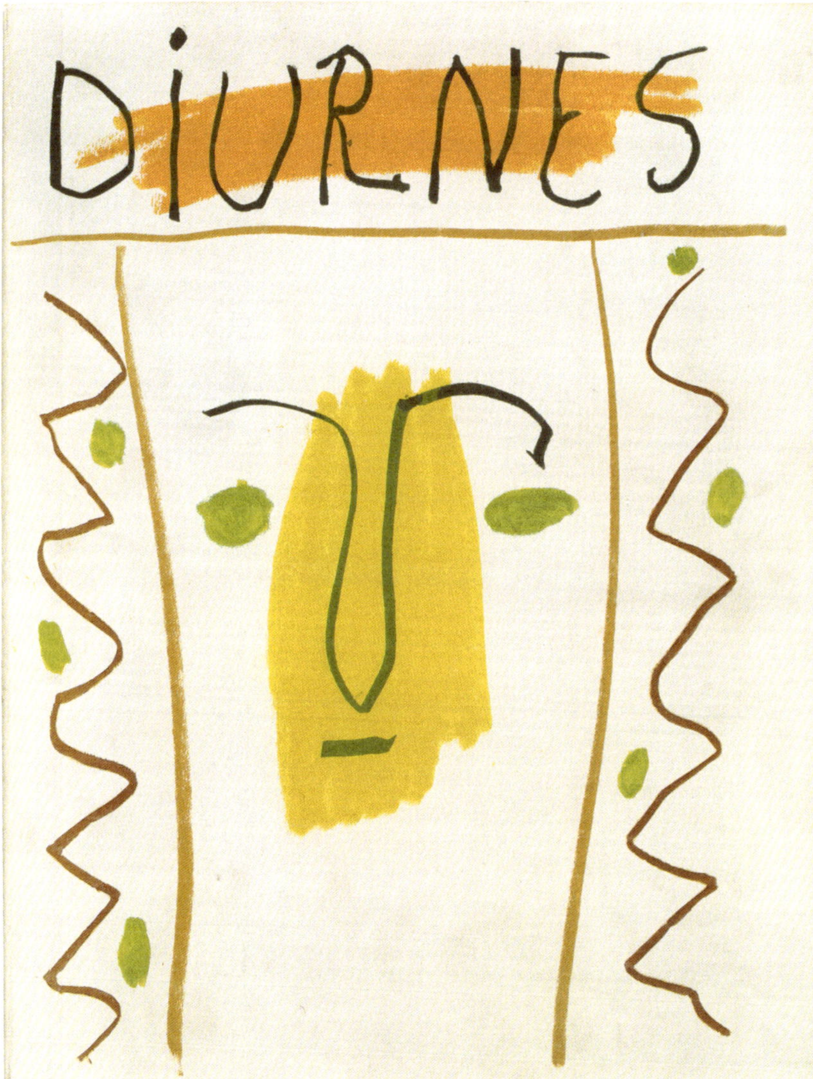
DIURNES

Picasso and childhood

One day in 1946, Picasso was visiting an exhibition of children's drawings curated by the British Council. He looked at them with his ambiguous smile and said: "As a child, never could I have taken part in such an exhibition: when I was twelve I could already draw like Raphael. It took me my whole life to learn how to draw like a child."

Antonina Vallentin, *Picasso*, Paris, Albin Michel, 1957, p. 14.

Pablo Picasso's childhood drawings

The Musée National Picasso-Paris holds a few drawings by teenage Picasso. There are three types. As a young virtuoso who "draws like Raphael," Picasso made academic nudes that reveal his artistic precociousness (*Academic Study of a Cast Imitating an Antique*, 1893–94, MP405). Other drawings depict bulls (*Citado al quiebro*, 1893–95, MP404) and bullfights (*Corrida*, September 2, 1894, MP401) in a realistic and dynamic style. Third, he created small magazines, *La Coruña* and *Azul y Blanco*, resembling comic books, in which caricatural characters tell short stories. Of these three types of works, only the latter appear childish: their humor is naïve, the boxes of the comic strips are clumsily displayed and the drawing seems spontaneous. It is only an appearance however, as Picasso has already mastered academic drawing. It took him decades to reconcile this childish, free manner with academic, technical subjects.

The twentieth century's "child's play"

In the early twentieth century, the "primitivism" of artists as well as of critics and theoreticians, was on the rise, demonstrating their rejection of academicism. Primitivism illustrated a wide interest in anything that Western civilization considers "other" and thus rejects: the insane, prisoners, children, women, prehistoric men and "savages."

Childlike productions thus met with growing interest. In 1900, Kandinsky showed children's drawings at the Universal Exhibition. In his 1924 *Surrealist Manifesto*, André Breton writes that: "Childhood may be the closest thing to 'real life'." Michel Leiris, a good friend of Picasso's, lauded the childish spirit of the Catalan Joan Miró's paintings. In the 1920s, innocence, spontaneity and purity, supposedly linked to childhood, were acclaimed in the art world, fueled by contemporary studies of children's psychology. Christian Zervos, who edited the magazine *Cahiers d'art*, developed the idea that the same "creative impulse [exists] in children's drawings, prehistoric paintings, tribal sculptures, mythical stories and modern artists' works."[1] Georges Bataille took that theory further, adding that they all bear the same "cruelty" and violence.

Back to childhood

The childlike dimension in Picasso's work is the subject of progressive development. It is primarily based on the liberal display of body parts, organs and orifices (*Woman with Ruff*, Summer 1926, MP97; *Sleeping Woman*, 1927, MP98; *Woman in an Armchair*, 1927, MP99). The line is gradually simplified. For his Dinard bathers (summer 1928, MP107-110, p. 86-87), Picasso seeks geometrical shapes that call to mind construction games and playing jacks, as well as a form of raw expressionlessness. The distorted faces in the second half of the 1930s also suggest monsters drawn by children (*Sleeping Woman with Shutters*, April 25, 1936, MP152; *Head*, May 1, 1936, MP154). In a certain way, the childlike drawing—remnants of a fantasy rather than faithful depiction of reality—tallies with Picasso's idea of an artistic work. In the 1950s, he built life-size toys such as *The Goat* (MP339) and *Little Girl Jumping Rope* (MP336). Picasso's sculptures are enlivened by their playful, combinatorial, imaginative and humorous aspects.

Picasso and Françoise Gilot raised Claude and Paloma in a modern way, encouraging their creativity. Some paintings depict them drawing (*Claude Drawing, Françoise and Paloma*, MP209). Picasso occasionally clearly imitates a child's style (*Mother and Children at Play*, MP1990-24). However, it is his last phase that is the most flamboyantly childlike. The brightly colored paint spurts and smears the canvas, spreads fluidly and becomes tactile. Is it the re-found pleasure of making a mess? The imitation of little children's enjoyment of bright colors? The outlined bodies tend to transform into childish figures, made up of nonrealistic symbolic shapes, tangible signs (*Couple*, MP1990-41). So when Pablo Picasso painted himself in 1972 as a *Young Painter*, at the twilight of his life, he managed, after an enormous amount of work to "draw like a child." **E.B.**

1. Elza Adamowicz, *Ceci n'est pas un tableau. Les écrits surréalistes sur l'art*, Lausanne, L'Âge d'homme, p. 87.

1963

Notebook 56

February 10–December 16, 1963
Graphite, colored pencils and wax crayon on paper
21 × 27 cm
Folio 11(r), 21(r), 22(r), 27(r), 30(r), backcover
Dation, 1979. MP1886

Picasso's final period started in 1954, when he met Jacqueline, his last partner, whom he married in 1961. It is dominated by the themes of the workshop and confrontation with masters, Delacroix, Velázquez and Manet. The 1963 notebook is one of the collection's gems and is almost entirely dedicated to the encounter between painter and model, a subject the artist also covers in painting, in a series of workshops that give birth to a major exhibition at Galerie Louise Leiris in 1964. This gallery, named after the art dealer Kahnweiler's sister-in-law and collaborator, highlights the friendship between Picasso and Kahnweiler, dealer of early Cubism, and showed the painter's work from 1948. In this notebook, the theme of the art studio is a pretext for a series of amusing scenes (canonical images of the noble painter), but also dramatic ones (old man with glasses and a monkey), in which Picasso signs his artistic legacy, all the while exploring a reflection on the creative process. With an unmatched technical skill, mixing pastel and wax pencil that exalt the colors, the drawing reveals a steady hand, contradicting the last sentence on the cover: "Painting is stronger than me, it dictates my every move." Isn't it rather Picasso who, as stated by Michel Leiris, "can now make painting whatever he wants"? **E.Ph.**

Painter and Monkey
December 16, 1963
Folio 11(r)

The Studio: The Painter and His Model
February 17, 1963
Folio 20(r)

The Studio: The Painter and His Model
February 17, 1963
Folio 22(r)

The Studio: The Painter and His Model
February 20, 1963
Folio 27(r)

The Painter
February 21, 1963
Folio 30(r)

Backcover with inscription
March 27, 196
Wax crayon on beige cardboard
Folio 3(c)

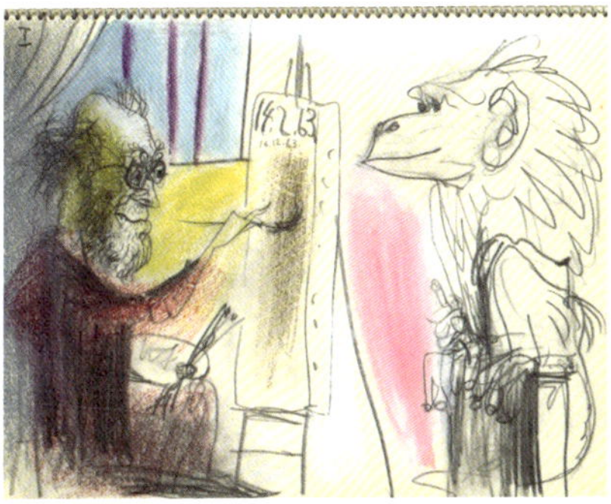

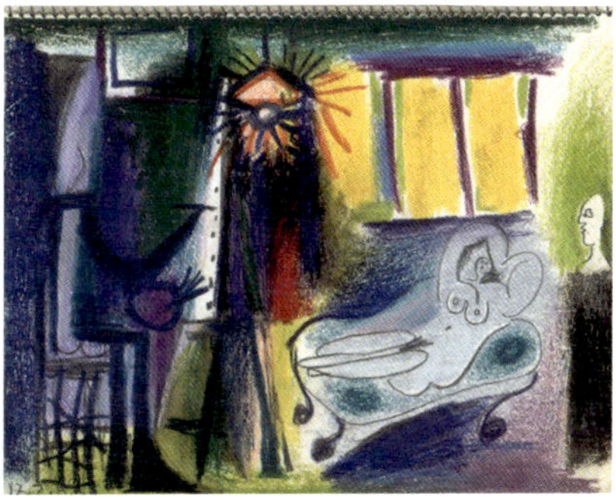

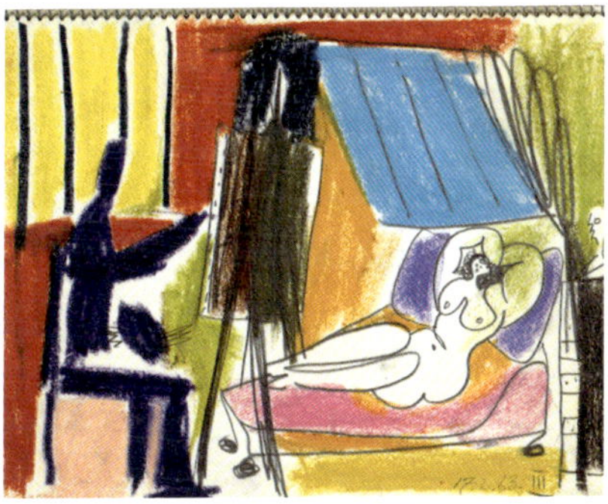

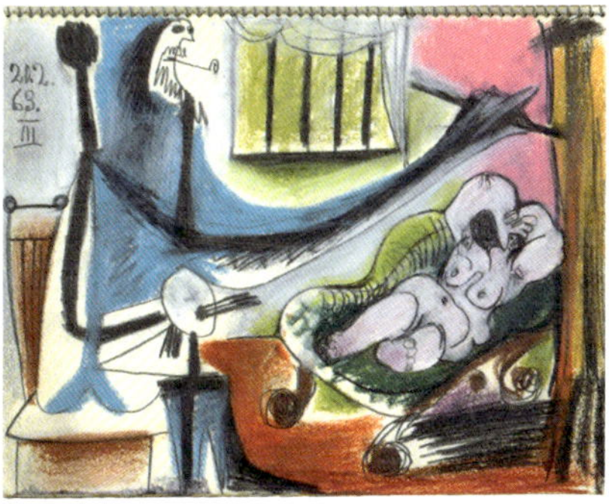

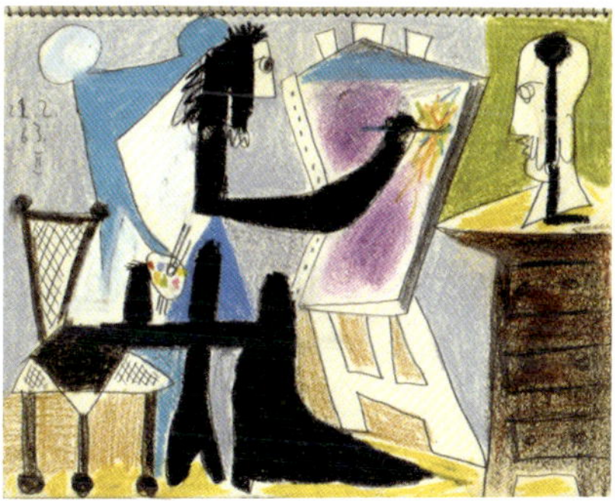

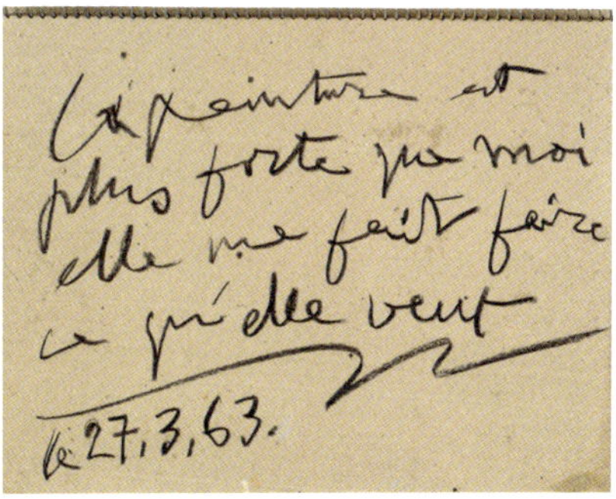
La peinture est
plus forte que moi
elle me fait faire
ce qu'elle veut
le 27.3.63.

1964

Man Smoking a Cigarette, with a Gray and Blue Striped Shirt

Mougins, August 27, 1964
Sugar aquatint on copper. Artist's proof on watermarked paper, printed in color, dedicated "Pour Aldo Crommelynck," signed
Édition Galerie Louise Leiris 1965, 22.36 × 16.3 in.(56.8 × 41.4 cm)
Purchase 2013. MP20131-1-1-5

Even though this engraving is not explicitly introduced as a self-portrait, everything indicates that it is indeed himself that Picasso depicts here, as a juvenile man smoking, wearing the famous striped shirt that is one of his distinctive features in the eyes of the public. As early as the 1950s, he often appeared wearing this shirt in widely published photographs. This jersey—perhaps a derivative of Harlequin's costume, who was for a while Picasso's alter ego?—appears in fact as early as 1938 in *The Artist before his Canvas* (MP72), a dark and frugal self-portrait of Picasso at work, asserting the necessary commitment of the painter facing a coming History. Acquired in 2013, this print, signed by the artist, came directly from Aldo Crommelynck, a famous printer who moved his studio to Mougins in 1963 to be closer to Picasso, who then lived in Notre-Dame-de Vie. The collaboration between the two men was very intense and notably resulted in the first-rate suites of engravings: *The Magnificent Cuckold*, *Celestina*, *Suite 347* and *Suite 156*. **E.Ph.**

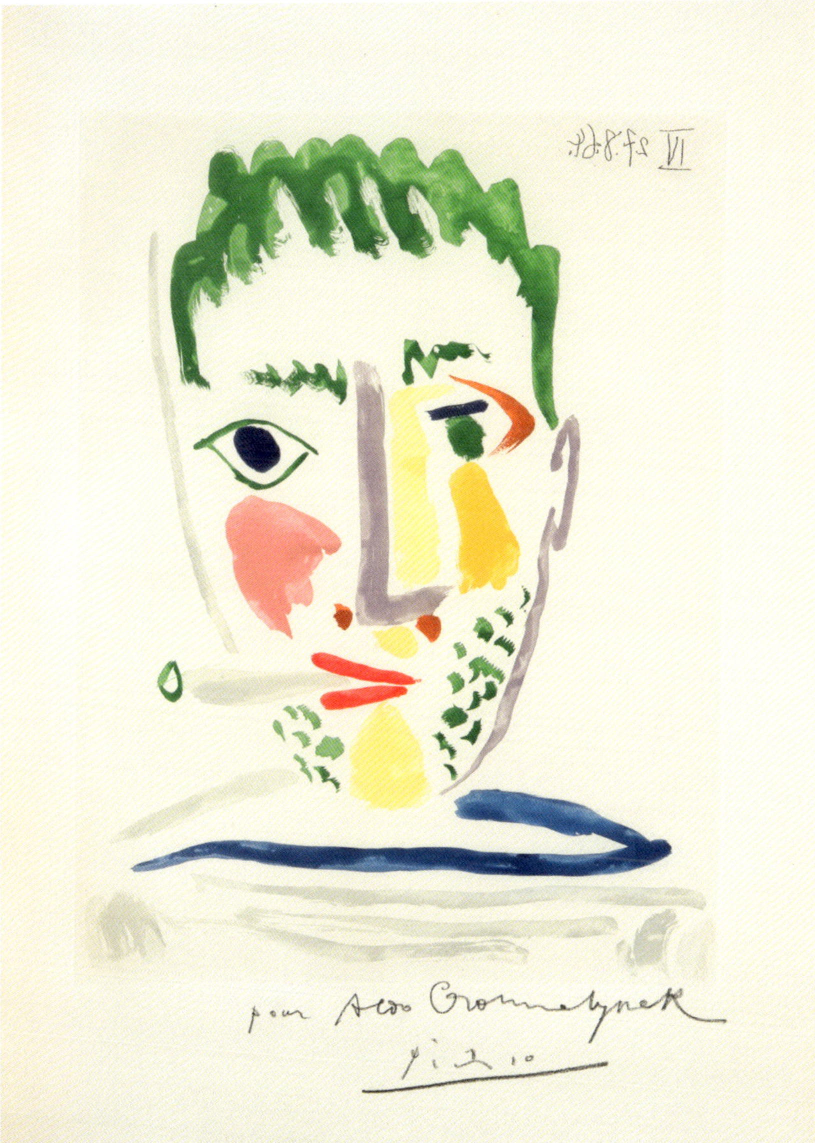
pour Aldo Crommelynck
Picasso

1965

The Model

Mougins, March 1, 1965
Aquatint and etching on copper
Proof on watermarked paper, printed by Crommelynck, dedicated "Pour Aldo Crommelynck," signed
Édition Galerie Louise Leiris 1965, 22.6 × 17 in. (57.5 × 43.3 cm)
Purchase 2013. MP2013-1-5

This engraving shows once again the importance of the theme of the model, which returns a lot in the late 1960s, and of the collaboration with the printers Aldo and Piero Crommelynck. The model sits in a classical fashion, although she is revealing her genitals to a large, bearded, male face. Presented both front and sideways, he seems to be looking in several directions at the same time. The woman appears to be indifferent, but the white shape coming from her face extends to meet the man—the artist—in the telling of a pictorial story. The outlining of the model's body and the man's face give them an ancient, classical dimension, bringing to mind the characters on ancient ceramics despite the relative disorganization of the woman's body, and despite the man being reduced to a lustful face, eyes and lips. Picasso has already traced these lines over the previous years, in his Vallauris works. A proof of how "ceramics work like engraving. The cooking is the printing. That is the moment in which you know what you have actually done. When you hold the print in your hands, already you are no longer the engraver. You have changed. And you have to redo it. But with ceramics, you cannot change anything." (Remarks by Picasso, published by Pierre Daix in *Dictionnaire Picasso*, Paris, Bouquins, 1995, p. 171). **E.B.**

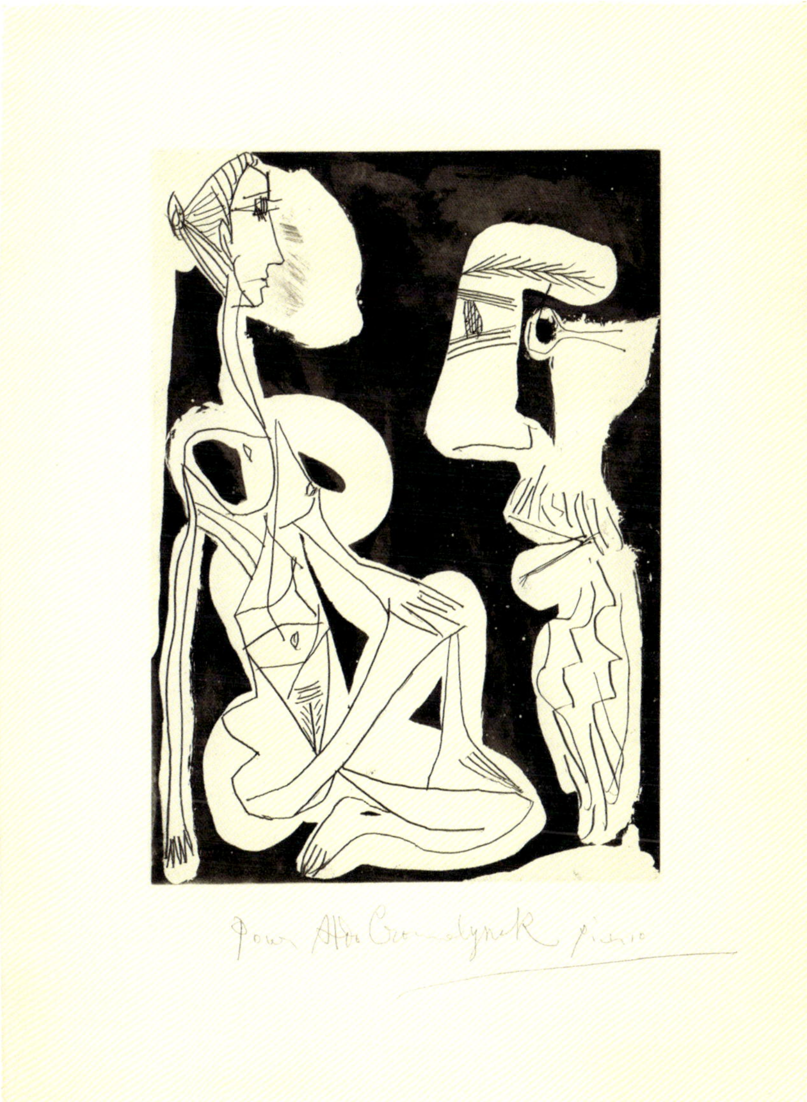
Pour Aldo Crommelynck Picasso

1966

The Magnificent Cuckold

In 1966, Picasso drew twelve illustrations for the play *The Magnificent Cuckold*, by Fernand Crommelynck, published in 1968 by the playwright's sons. This farce, written in 1920, tells the story of a husband tormented by jealousy, who tries his wife's fidelity in every possible way. The old cuckold, bearing horns and a phallic scepter, sits cross-legged in the center. He is attending the trial of his naked wife, chained by an executioner. The trial takes place before the Inquisition, represented by austere Spanish dignitaries and a jester, straight out of History. As in all his illustrations, the text is a springboard for Picasso's creativity, never caught up in literal interpretation. The cuckold is here seen as prey to elaborate erotic fantasies, despite his old age. It may just represent the artist himself, who, although aging, is still a tireless, vigorous creator. This is an etching, the technique of which is close enough to drawing. The line is engraved in varnish, and then the board is dipped in acid, which bites the copper where the varnish has been removed. The rapidity of the execution and the energy of Picasso's graphic drawing are evident in this print. **A.M.**

The Cuckold Witnessing the Trial of a Naked Woman Chained by an Executioner, before the Inquisition

Mougins, December 11, 1966
Etching on copper. Proof on paper, printed by Crommelynck
11.4 x 14.9 in. (289 × 37.9 cm)
Dation Jacqueline Picasso, 1990. MP1990-144

At the Theater, a Scene in the Manner of "The Arabian Nights"

Mougins, November 16, 1966
Aquatint, lithography pencil and etching on copper. Proof on paper, printed by Crommelynck
11 x 14.9 in. (28 × 37.9 cm)
Dation Jacqueline Picasso, 1990. MP1990-143

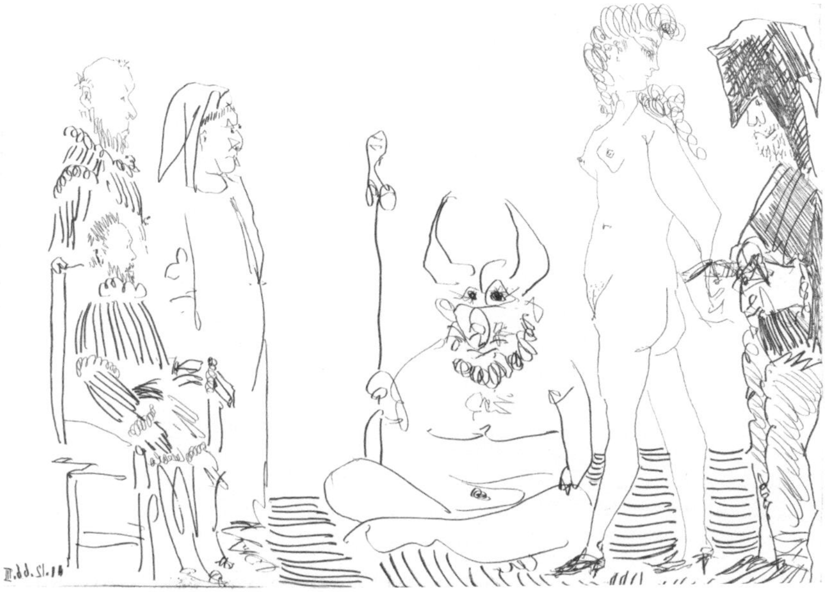

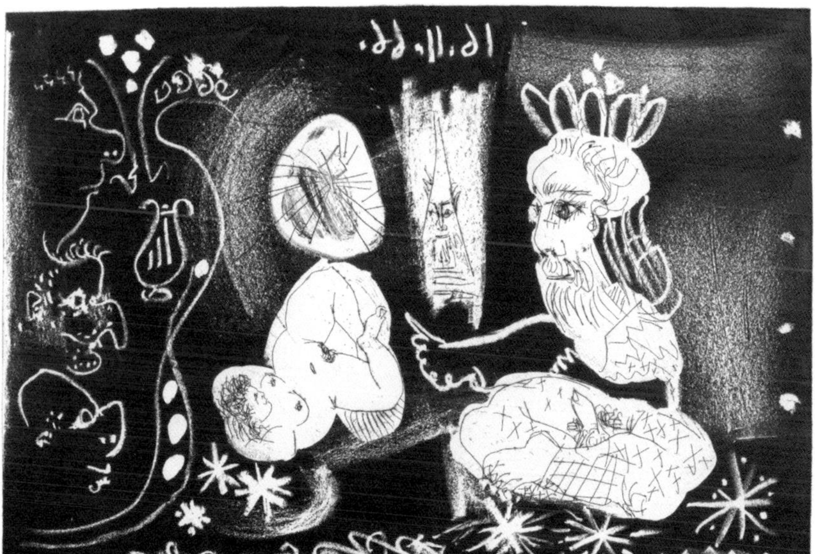
16.III.66.

1967

Reclining Nude

Mougins, June 14, 1967
Oil on canvas, 76.8 × 51.2 in. (195 × 130 cm)
Dation Pablo Picasso, 1979. MP219

This *Reclining Nude* was painted in the summer, in Mougins, Picasso's last home where he lived with Jacqueline Roque. Her genitalia is offered in the center of the frame. A black slit and curled hair echo the black, close together, mischievous eyes. Her arms, feet and breasts, underlined with lilac pink, spring sideways towards the top of the painting and become disproportionately, comically, large. This body, an invitation to scour its exuberant relief, has been kneaded, felt and imagined more than actually seen. The theme of the reclining female nude has a long history in painting. Here, Picasso refers both to Titian and to Goya: Titian, for his "Venus with Musician" series, which he reinterpreted on October 27, 1970 in *Reclining Nude* and *Man Playing the Guitar* (MP224), and Goya for his two *Maja* (1790–1800 and 1800–03). Sexual desire, desire to see and desire to paint all come together, and inspire one another, in the intimacy of the libido. This nude is a form of revolution as it is facing the artist in an openly erotic, ostentatious, seductive position. Sexual liberation is in the air. May '68 is around the corner and 1969 is an "erotic year," as sung by Serge Gainsbourg. That Picasso would then set his fantasies free is thus in the spirit of his time, and the sign of persisting life. **E.B.**

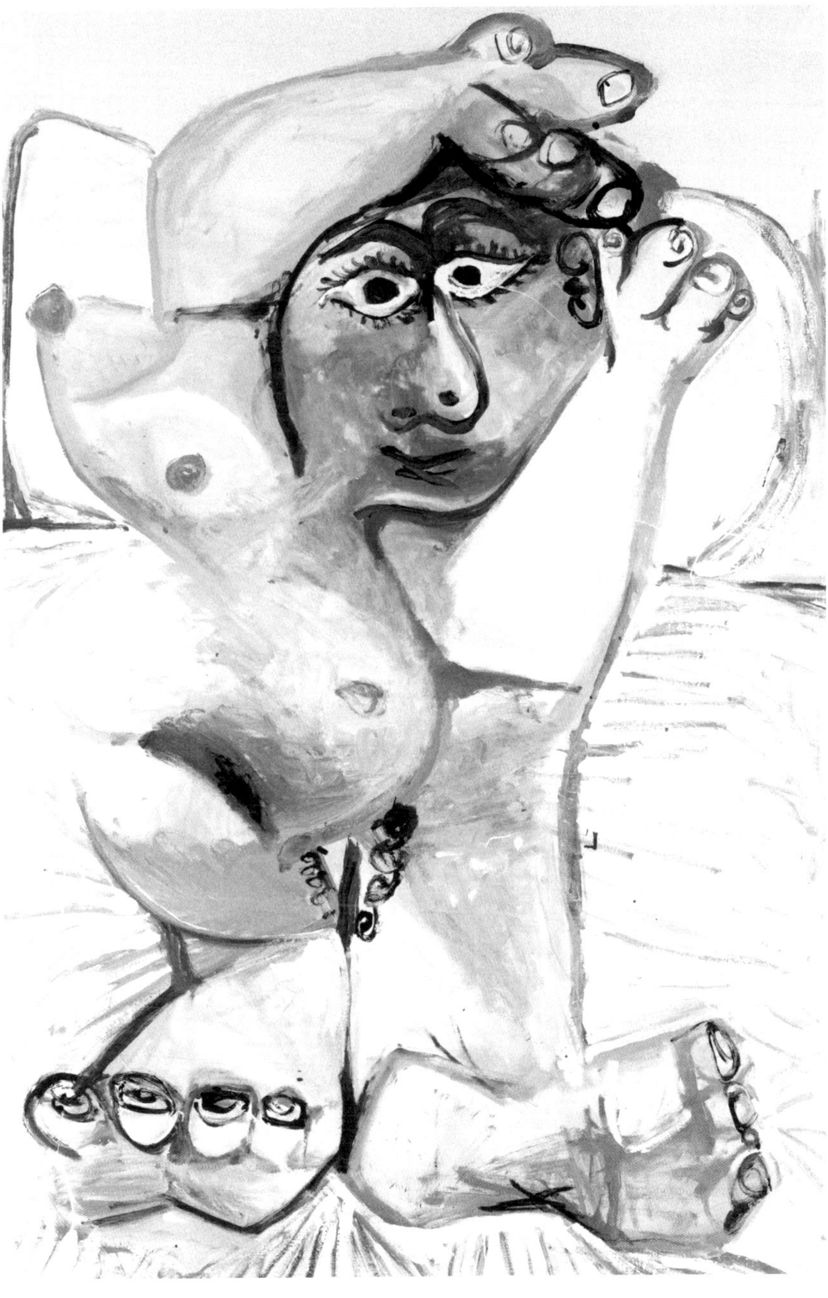

1968

Celestina

April 11–August 18, 1968
Etching, aquatint, scraper and drypoint on sixty-six copper plates. Proof on watermarked paper, printed by Crommelynck, dated "9.9.70," numbered "1/9," signed
29.2 x 40.9 cm (74.2 × 104 cm)
Dation Pablo Picasso, 1979. MP3053

This exceptional collection of sixty-six engravings was chosen by Picasso to illustrate *Celestina* by Fernando de Rojas.
It is not the first time Picasso showed interest in the character of Celestina, the old witch-like matchmaker, whom he represented in an unsettling and cold manner in 1904 (MP1989-5, p. 32). Here, on the contrary, the tone is lighter, almost caricatural. Half-way between the critical vision of the novel and the comedy of situations defying the rules of good behavior, Picasso depicts expressive characters in scenes alluding to the romantic encounters of gentlemen, soldiers and prostitutes.
The disposition of the engravings all together on one single print displays at a glance the great diversity of techniques Picasso used: etching, aquatint, scraper and engraving.
Thus this panorama offers a remarkable overview of all the contradictory effects that can be achieved with the art of print. **E.Ph.**

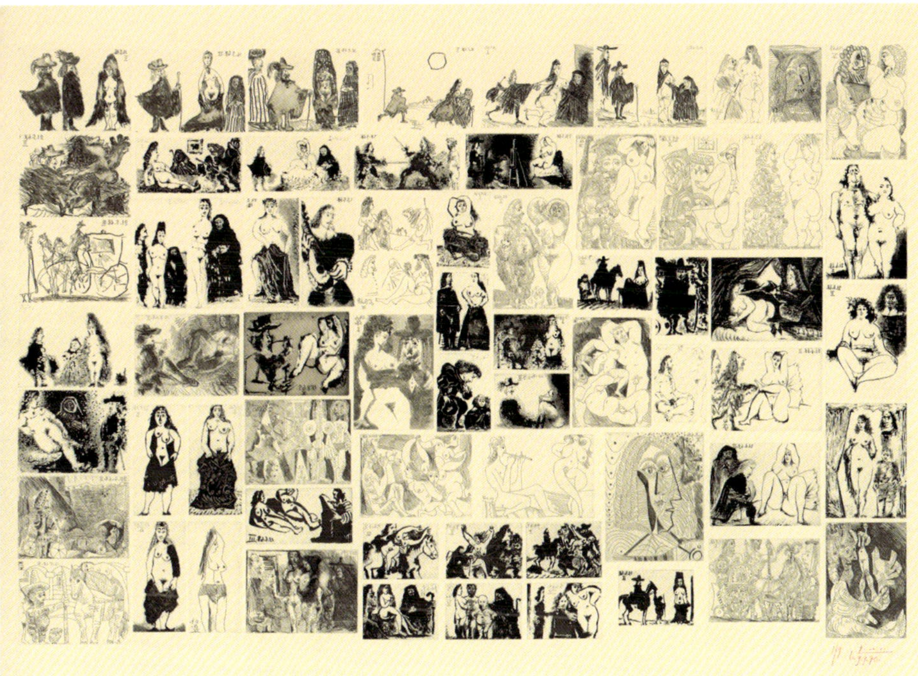

1969

The Kiss

Mougins, October 26, 1969
Oil on canvas, 38.2 × 51.2 in. (97 × 130 cm)
Dation Pablo Picasso, 1979. MP220

This last *Kiss* amongst the collection resonates with the violent way Pablo Picasso has handled this theme since 1925 (p. 177). The previous year, eroticism had blossomed in Picasso's art: after the great nudes, he made a series called "347," in the Crommelyncks' studio: 347 obscene encounters between naked women and musketeers. He then tackled the love of Raphael and La Fornarina in twenty-five images, exhibited at the end of 1968 at Galerie Louise Leiris, but hidden behind a curtain. The death of his friend Sabartés seemed to accelerate his productivity even more. Among the 165 paintings exhibited by Picasso at the Palais des Papes in Avignon in 1970, this *Kiss* (there are two of them) holds the place of honor. It shows, up close, the faces of two people, in a cream-white material crossed with black lines that entangle the two heads in a way that conveys a strong sexual connotation. However, the black, dense eyes that we often find in Picasso's works are empty. They do not look at each other. And if the woman seems to be lying down, the man on the other hand stands in a vertical position. The fusion of the intertwined lines evokes sexual union and pleasure, all the while causing great tension, as Picasso seizes the ultimate moment of the kiss, its climax before the bodies separate. **E.B.**

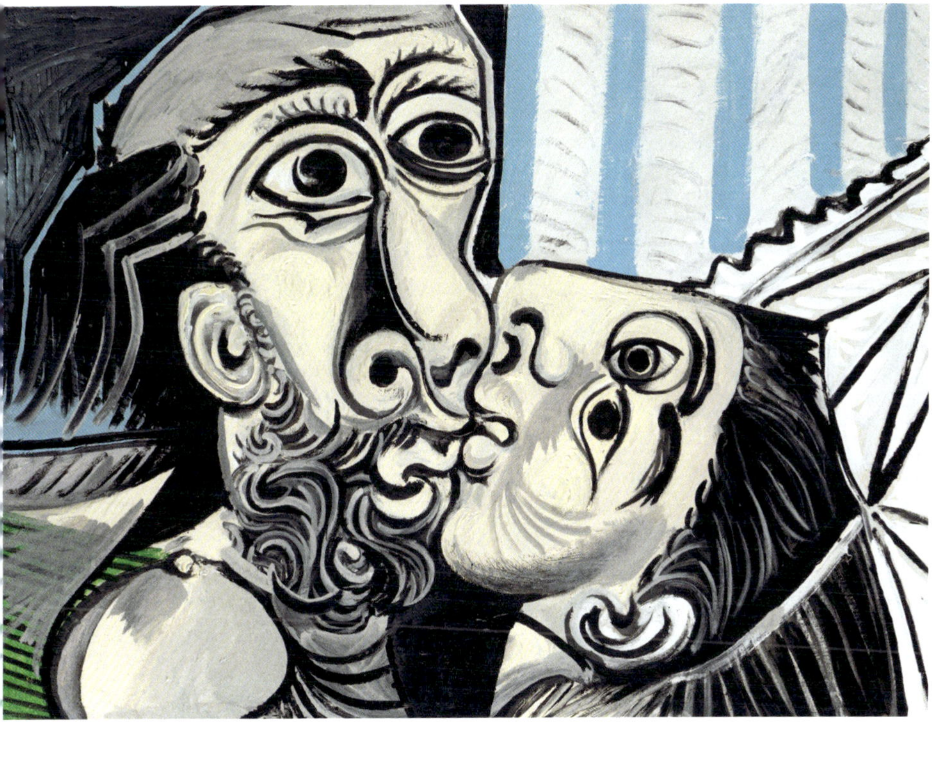

1970

The Matador

Mougins, October 4, 1970
Oil on canvas, 57.3 × 44.9 in. (145.5 × 114 cm)
Dation Pablo Picasso, 1979. MP223

Matador, musketeer, or Spanish Grandee? This eccentric character from another era, with his hat, sword, ruff and lace, smokes detachedly—resembling Picasso's usual pose in photographs. Picasso was a corrida aficionado and it is not surprising to see him return to this theme towards the end of his life, as it embodies masculinity and a fight to the death. It also takes on a sexual connotation with Picasso, as revealed here by the evidently phallic symbols that are the sword and the cigar. This mocking character, made of apple-green and a typically seventies orange, seems endowed with a sense of irony. But it is also an ancient figure straight out of a painting by Goya or Diego Velázquez. It could also be a literary reference, as Picasso enjoyed writers from the Spanish Golden Age. Thus, this character could be from a play by Pedro Calderón de la Barca—or by Molière. The well-read Picasso was introduced to sixteenth- and seventeenth-century French literature by Max Jacob and Guillaume Apollinaire. He became passionate about it, and gives his matador the traits of a musketeer. The "last Picasso" therefore in many ways resembles fantastical time-traveling. **E.B.**

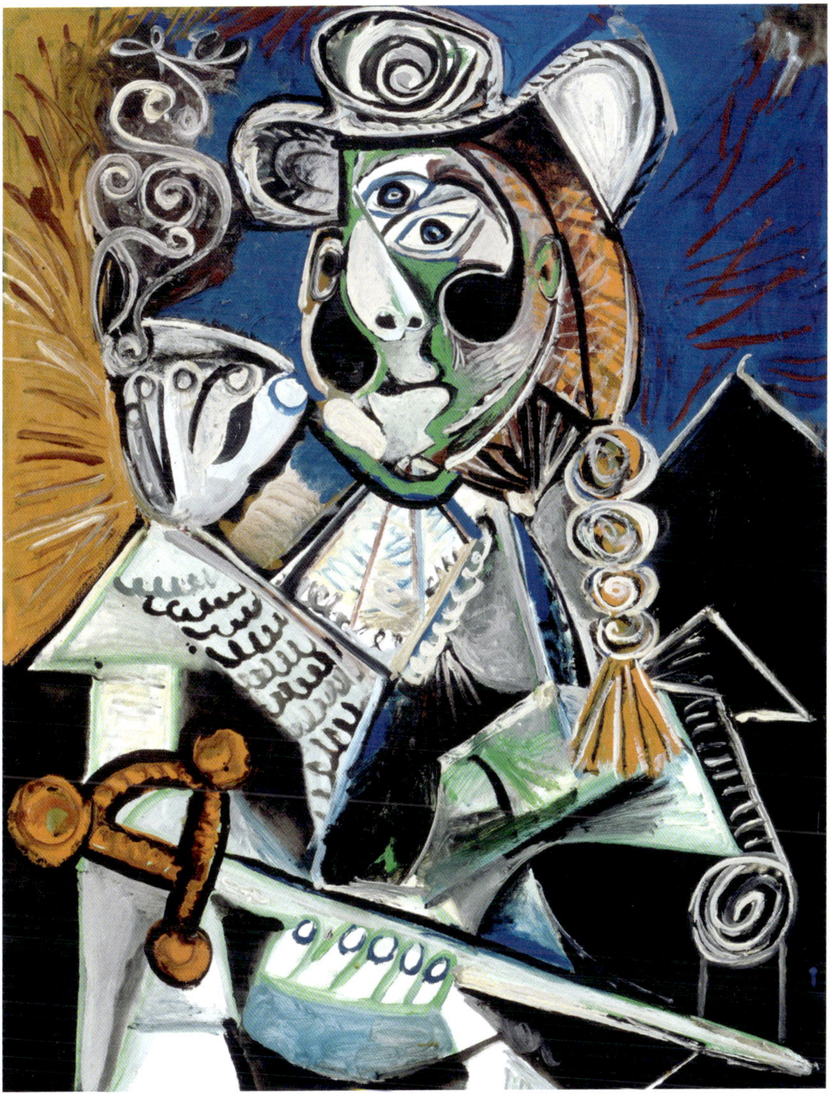

1971

The Couple

Mougins, 1970–71
Oil on plywood, 64.4 × 51.8 in. (163.5 × 1315 cm)
Dation Jacqueline Picasso, 1990. MP1990-41

Eye, nose, vulva, breast, leg, penis, hand, toe: this *Couple* seems to spell out a human body and all its crudely naked parts. Picasso, particularly in two series from the 1930s, "Anatomies" and "Mating," had already decomposed the human figure so much so that the—especially sexual—interaction of the bodies becomes impossible. In the early 1960s, in his notebooks, he drew similar odalisques, whose luscious body parts seem dissociated one from another. This experiment appears as a search for each part's essence, through its form but also through its symbolic importance to the person—here, that of the genitals. Picasso has learned such a lesson from two influences: African art in the 1900s and its overly identified and symbolic body parts in sculpture, and mostly, starting in the 1950s, children's drawings, the naïveté of which Picasso sought his entire life, inspired by children's psychology studies that develop after the war. This couple thus formulates a grammar of the body, confirming the symbolic and conceptual dimensions in Picasso's art. **E.B.**

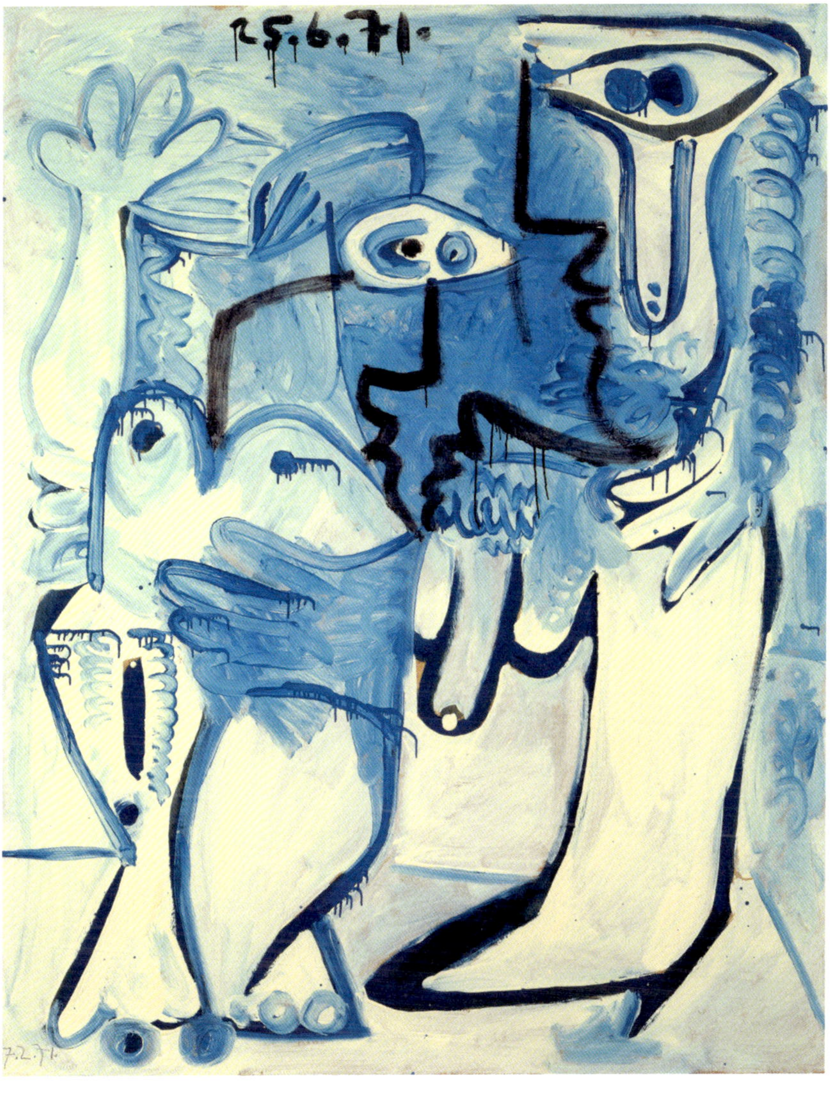

1972

The Young Painter

Mougins, April 14, 1972
Oil on canvas, 35.8 × 28.5 in. (91 × 72.5 cm)
Dation Pablo Picasso, 1979. MP228

A year before Picasso's death, a juvenile figure appears in his paintings, amidst flamboyant Musketeers and torrid embraces: a young painter with the characteristic features of the hat and the paintbrush. His cape brings to mind seventeenth-century Spanish realist novels and their picaros, while his hat hints toward Vincent van Gogh or Auguste Renoir. At that time, Picasso represented himself more or less realistically, with different postures and at various ages, including with these two oversized pupils and this calm smile, in a completely new embodiment of the passion that drove him for over eighty years. Amidst his contemporary production, this portrait, with its economy of means, is a sharp contrast. The canvas's white base coat makes up most of the painting. The young painter emerges graciously from limbo, with a few touches of the brush, uniform colors and thin layers of paint, through which the weave of the canvas shows through. A figure of youth, this testamentary work seems to smile to the future. **N.L.**

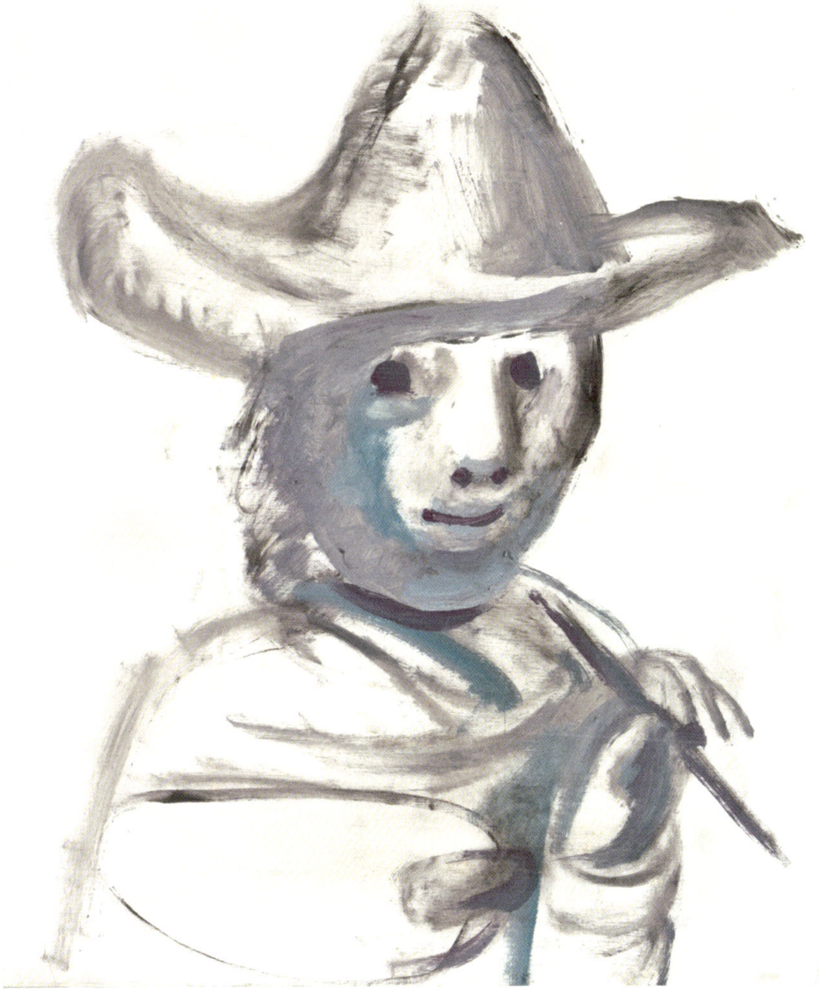

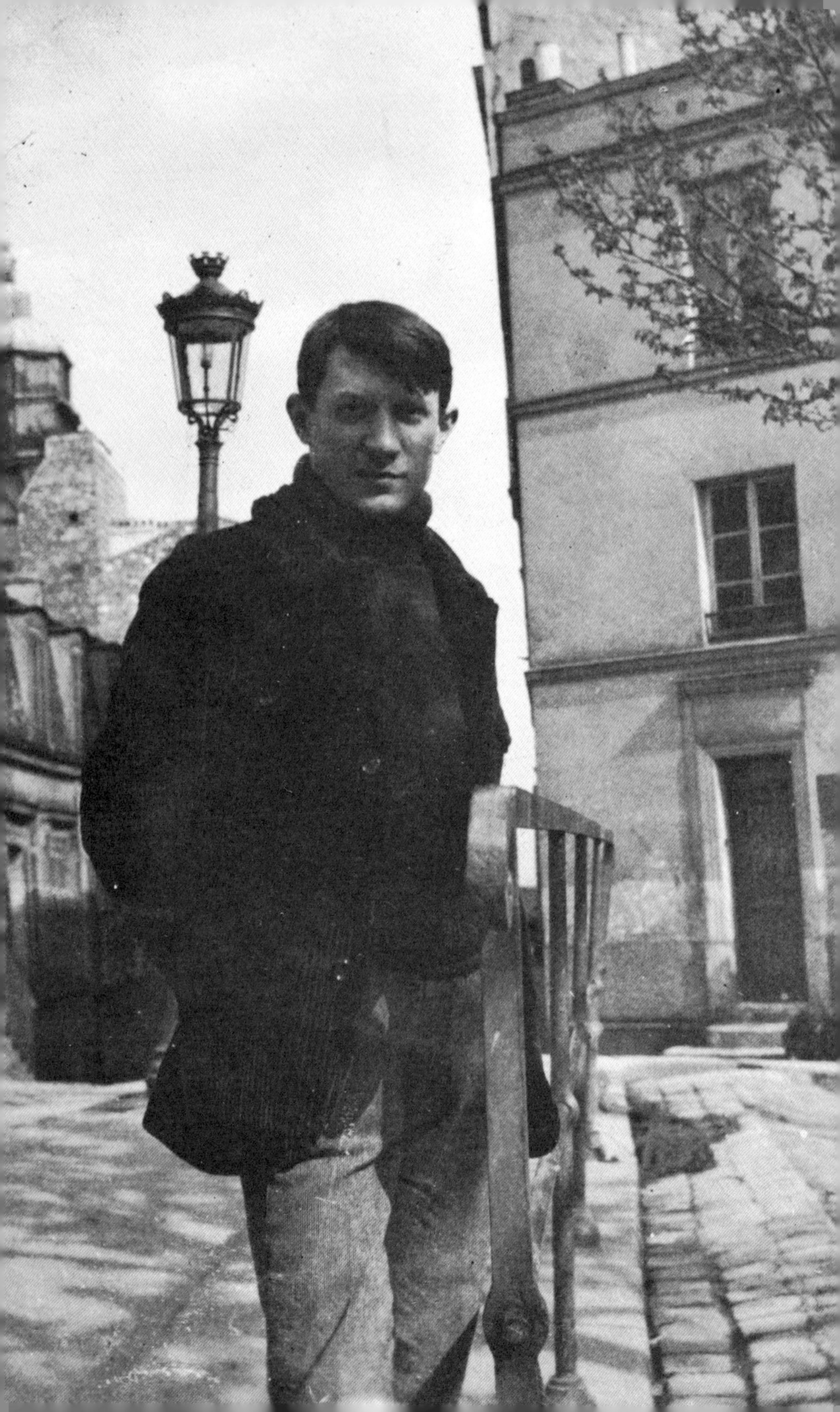

Chronology

1881
Birth of Pablo Picasso on October 25 in Málaga. He is the son of teacher and painter José Ruiz Blasco and of Maria Picasso y Lopez.

1884
Birth of his sister Dolorès, nicknamed Lola.

1887
Birth of his second sister, Concepción, nicknamed Conchita.

1888
First paintings, under the influence of his father.

1892
Begins at La Corogne School of Fine Arts, where his father teaches.

1893
Creation of the illustrated magazine *Azul y Bianco*, for family and friends.

1895
Death of Concepción. Moves to Barcelona : is admitted to La Lonja School of Fine Arts, majoring in classical art and still life, where his father teaches.

1896
First studio, shared with Manuel Pallarès.

1897
Admitted to the San Fernando Royal Academy of Fine Arts in Madrid. First large canvas: *Science and Charity* (Museu Picasso, Barcelona).

1898
First stay in Horta de Ebro, with Manuel Pallarès.

1899
Returns to Barcelona: avant-garde circle *Els Quatre Gats*. Meets Carlos Casagemas.

1900
First stay in Paris with Carlos Casagemas, for the Universal Exposition. Stays in Montmartre and meets Berthe Weill.

1901
Paints *The Death of Casagemas* (MP3) as a tribute to his friend who committed suicide. Meets Max Jacob. Beginning of the Blue period: Self-Portrait (MP4).

1902
First exhibition of his blue paintings at Berthe Weill's and first clay sculpture: *Seated Woman* (MP230).

1903
Returns to Barcelona: *Life* (Museum of Arts, Cleveland).

1904
Moves to the Bateau-Lavoir in Montmartre. Meets André Salmon, Guillaume Apollinaire and Fernande Olivier, his model who becomes his partner for seven years. Transition from the Blue period: *Celestina* (MP1989-5), to the Rose Period: *The Actor* (Metropolitan, New York).

1905
Visits the Van Gogh and Seurat retrospective exhibitions at the Salon des Indépendants and the Ingres retrospective at the Salon d'Automne. Meets Leo and Gertrude Stein. First bronze piece: *The Jester* (MP231).

1906
Visits an exhibition at the Louvre on Iberian sculpture. Influence of primitivism, use of ethnographic and orientalist photography. Meets Henri Matisse. *Portrait of Gertrude Stein* (Metropolitan, New York).

Unknown
Portrait of Pablo Picasso at Place Ravignan in Montmartre in 1904
Undated print
Gift Succession Picasso, 1992. APPH15301

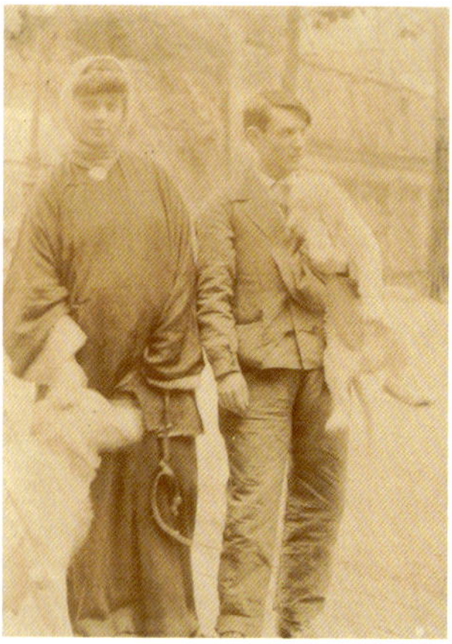

1907
Buys two Iberian head sculptures, without knowing they were stolen from the Louvre. Discovers African painting at the Musée du Trocadéro. Meets Georges Braque. *Les Demoiselles d'Avignon* (MoMA, New York).

1908
Banquet organized for Henri Rousseau, with Guillaume Apollinaire, Marie Laurencin, André Salmon, Georges Braque and Gertrude Stein.

1909
Moves in with Fernande to a new studio in Paris, 11 Boulevard de Clichy.

1910
Signs a deal with Daniel-Henry Kahnweiler, his art dealer: *Portrait of Kahnweiler* (Art Institute, Chicago). Last exhibition at the Vollard gallery: refuses to be shown in Paris until 1916.

1911
Exhibitions in galleries in Berlin and New York. Affair with Eva Gouel. Meets the Futurists and begins lettering.

1912
Exhibitions in Moscow, Munich, Berlin and Cologne. Moves to Montparnasse and starts constructions: *Still-Life With Chair Caning* (MP36).

1913
Exhibits in New York at the Armory Show. First retrospective in Munich. Death of his father.

1914
Stays in Avignon with Eva. Beginning of the First World War. The *Absinthe Glass* series.

1915
Godfather of Max Jacob, who converts to Catholicism. Death of Eva Gouel.

1916
Affair with Gaby Lespinasse. Meets Diaghilev, director of the company Ballets Russes. First exhibition of *Les Demoiselles d'Avignon*, organized by André Salmon.

1917
Makes the scenery and costumes for the ballet, *Parade* in Rome. Visits Naples and Pompeii. Affaire with Olga Khokhlova, dancer in the Ballets Russes company.

1918
Exhibition with Matisse at the Paul-Guillaume gallery. Marries Olga: *Portrait of Olga in a Chair* (MP55). Armistice.

1919
Meets Joan Miro. New pieces for ballets, *The Three-Cornered Hat and Pulcinella.*

1920
Stays in Saint-Raphaël with Olga.

1921
Birth of Paul. First monograph dedicated to Picasso in Munich. *Three Women at a Fountain* (MoMA, New York).

1922
Stays in Dinard with Olga and Paul. *Two Women Running on the Beach (The Race)* (MP78). Works with Cocteau on the scenery of his

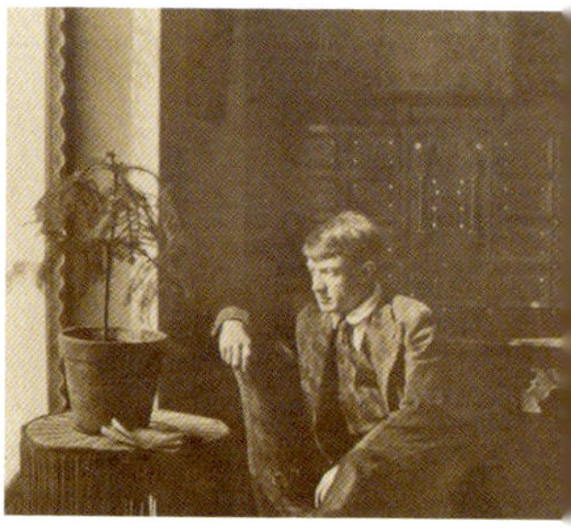

Unknown
Picasso and Fernande Olivier with their dogs, Féo and Frika, in Montmartre, Paris, c. 1904–06
Undated print
Purchase, 1998. MP1998-96

Unknown (?)
Picasso in his studio in the Rue Schœlcher, Paris, c. 1914–15
Undated print
Gift Succession Picasso, 1992. MP1998-

play, *Antigone*. Writes letters to Man Ray.

1923
Stays at Cap d'Antibes with Olga and Paul. *Pan Pipes* (MP79). Liaison with Sara Murphy.

1924
Support from the Surrealists for the scenery of the *Mercury* ballet.

1925
Stays in Monte Carlo with Olga and Paul to see the Ballets Russes. Paints *The Dance* (Tate Gallery, London). Moves to Juan-les-Pins. Active with the Surrealist group.

1926
Picasso's works are regularly published in the magazine *Cahiers d'art*. Series of assemblages, *Guitar* and *Workshop of the Milliner* (Musée National d'Art Moderne – Centre Pompidou, Paris).

1927
Meets Marie-Thérèse Walter. Illustrates Balzac's *Unknown Masterpiece* with engravings.

1928
Artistic work with Julio Gonzalez. Stays in Dinard with Olga and Paul—and secretly, Marie-Thérèse. Birth of the theme of the Minotaur and first iron sculptures.

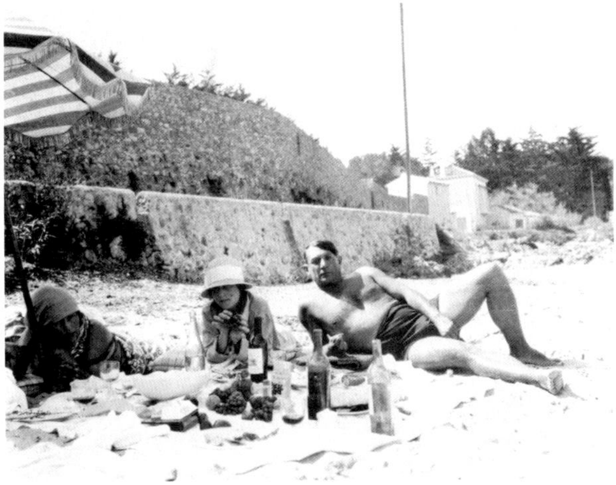

1929
Decay in his relationship with Olga. Stays in Dinard with Marie-Thérèse.

1930
Buys the Château de Boisgeloup. Illustrates Ovid's *Metamorphoses* for the publisher Albert Skira. *The Acrobat* (MP120).

1931
Sets up a sculpture studio in the Château de Boisgeloup. Engraving series: *Vollard Suite*.

1932
First retrospective of his works in Paris, at the Georges Petit gallery. Publication of the first volume of the catalogue raisonné 1895–1906, by Christian Zervos.

1933
Summer in Cannes at the Majestic, then at the Ritz in Barcelona, with Olga and Paul. Publication of the memoirs of Fernande Olivier, *Picasso and his friends*.

1934
Discovers the Roman paintings of the National Museum of Catalan Art in Barcelona. Appearance of political themes in his works. *Woman with Leaves* (MP314).

1935
Stops painting. Writing phase, poetry in particular. Separates from Olga, without getting divorced. Birth of Maya. Meets Dora Maar.

1936
Friendship with Paul Éluard. Nominated as the head of the Museo del Prado in Madrid. Affair with Dora Maar. Beginning of the Spanish Civil War.

1937
New art studio, 7 Rue des Grands-Augustins. Quick and intensive

Unknown
Picasso with Olga and Sara Murphy on Garoupe Beach, Cap d'Antibes, August 1923
Undated print
Gift Succession Picasso, 1992. APPH6564

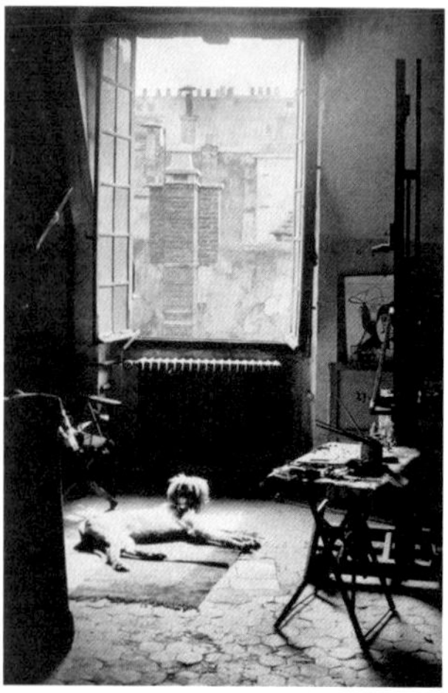

work for *Guernica* (Museo Nacional Centro de Arte Reina Sofía, Madrid), photographed by Dora Maar, for the Spanish Pavilion at the International Exhibition dedicated to Arts and Technology in Modern Life in Paris.

1938
The Surrealists split due to political reasons.

1939
Death of his mother. *Guernica* (Museo Nacional Centro de Arte Reina Sofía, Madrid) exhibited in the United States for the show *Picasso: 40 years of His Art* at the Museum of Modern Art in New York. Beginning of the Second World War.

1940
Moves to his studio on Rue des Grands-Augustins during the Occupation.

1941
Writes *Desire Caught by the Tail*, an illustrated play in six acts.

1942
Attacked by Vlaminck in an article published in *Comœdia*; young painters, intellectuals and members of the Resistance support Picasso. *Bull's Head* (MP330).

1943
Decay of his relationship with Dora Maar. Meets the young painter Françoise Gilot. *Man with Sheep* (MP331).

1944
Joins the Communist Party. Major retrospective at the Salon d'Automne: violent reactions against his work and his political commitment. Becomes president of the management committee of the Front National des Arts, which investigated the cases of artists who were compromised by their collaboration.

1945
Stays in Antibes with Dora Maar before returning to Paris and to Françoise. End of the Second World War. *The Mass Grave* (MoMA, New York).

1946
Art and Resistance exhibition at the Palais de Tokyo, Paris, and the major exhibition at the Museum of Modern Art in New York.

1947
Gives ten major paintings to the Musée d'Art Moderne. Birth of Claude. Intense ceramics activity in Vallauris.

1948
Paul Haesaerts films *Visite à Picasso*. Venice Biennale: (first exhibition in Italy). Participates in the Congress of Intellectuals for Peace, in Wroclaw, with Paul Éluard. Visits Krakow and Auschwitz with Pierre Daix.

1949
The Dove is chosen by Aragon as the poster for the Congress for Peace in Paris. Birth of Paloma. Buys the Fournas studios to enlarge his house in Vallauris.

1950
Takes part in the second Peace Conference in

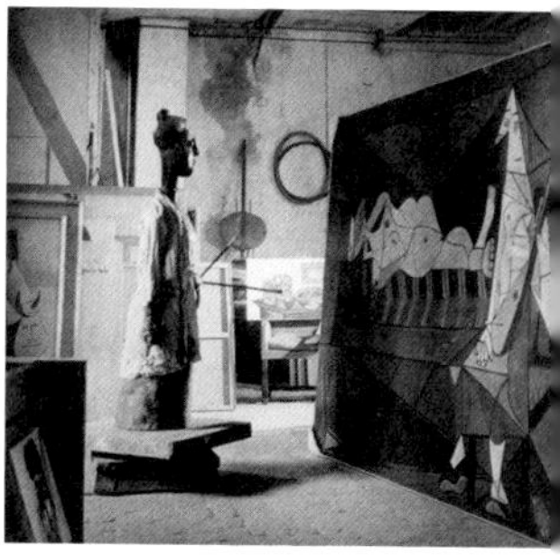

Brassaï (HalászGyula, known as)
Woman in a Long Dress facing *The Serenade* oil on cavas in the Grands-Augustins studio, Paris, 1946
Vintage print
Purchase, 1986. MP1986-36

Brassaï (Halász Gyula, known as)
Kazbek, the dog, in the Grands-Augustins studio, Paris, May 3, 1944
Print c. 1968
Purchase, 1986. MP1986-29

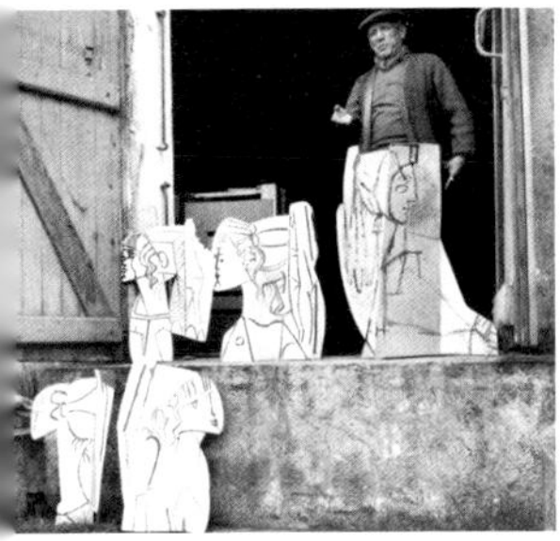

Great Britain. Receives the Lenin Prize for Peace. Series of large sculptures with recycled objects: *The Goat* (MP340). Beginning of the Korean War.

1951
Stays in Paris and Vallauris with Françoise. Large retrospective exhibition in Japan. *Massacre in Korea* (MP203).

1952
Paints an abandoned chapel in Vallauris: *Temple for Peace*. Meets Jacqueline Roque.

1953
Cubism 1907-1914 at the Musée National d'Art Moderne. Distances himself from the Communist Party after his portrait of Stalin is published on the cover of *Lettres françaises*.

1954
Meets Sylvette David and makes numerous portraits of her. Moves in with Jacqueline Roque in Paris.

Unknown
Picasso and Carl Nesjar, with the maquettes for the monumental sculpture *Sylvette* in the Fournas studio, Vallauris, 1962
Undated print. Gift Succession Picasso, 1992. APPH5455

1955
Buys La Californie house in the hills of Cannes. *Women of Algiers* series, inspired by Delacroix.

1956
Collective letter to the French Communist Party on the situation in Hungary. First retrospective in Barcelona.

1957
Las Meninas series, inspired by Velázquez. Major retrospective in the United States.

1958
Inauguration of the UNESCO mural, *The Fall of Icarus*. Buys the Château de Vauvenargues near Aix-en-Provence and to Cézanne sites.

1959
Inauguration of *Monument to Apollinaire (Head of Dora Maar)* in Saint-Germain-des-Prés and of *Temple for Peace* in Vallauris. Beginning of

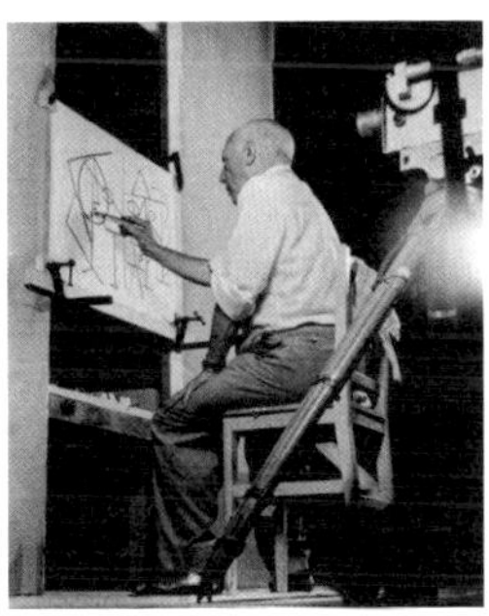

Unknown
Picasso drawing *Woman and Jester* during the filming of *The Mystery of Picasso* by H.-G. Clouzot, Studio de la Victorine, Nice, 1955
Undated print. Gift Succession Picasso, 1992. APPH8883

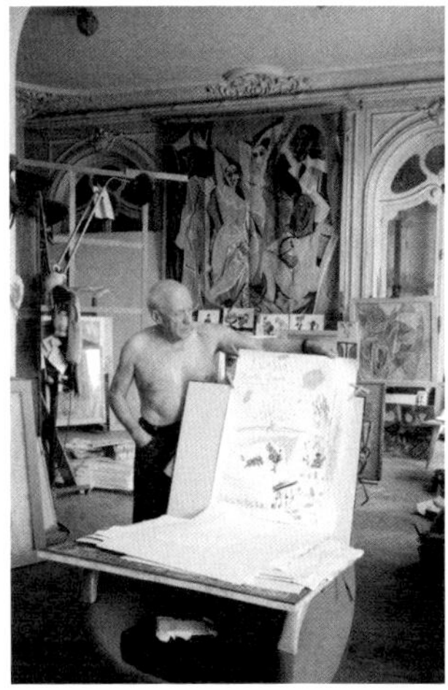

his series *Luncheon on the Grass, After Manet*.

1960
Exhibition at the Sala Gaspar Gallery, in Barcelona. *The Vauvenargues Buffet* (MP214).

1961
Marries Jacqueline Roque in Vallauris. Beginning of the metal sheets, painted and cut out: *Woman With Her Arms Spread* (MP360).

1962
Receives second Lenin Prize for Peace.

1963
Opening of the Museu Picasso (Barcelona), thanks to donations by Sabartés of Picasso works. Beginning of an engraving collaboration with the Crommelynck brothers.

1964
Publication of *Conversations with*

Edward Quinn
Picasso in the studio of La Californie, Cannes 1960, on the poster for *Engraved Works*, Galerie des Ponchettes
Undated print. Gift Succession Picasso, 1992. APPH1619

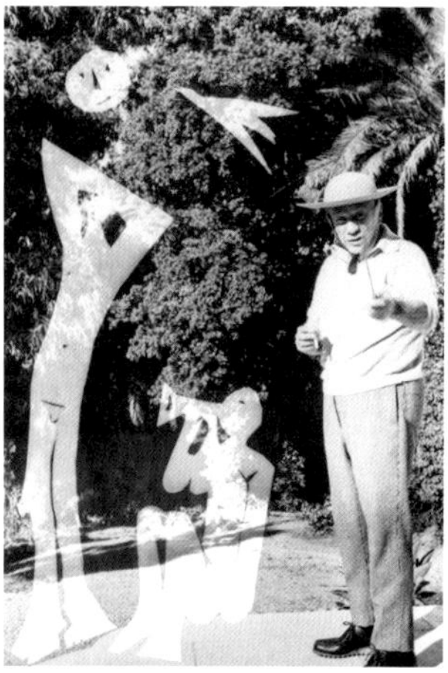

Picasso by Brassaï. Series *The Painter and his Model.*

1965
Publication of *Life with Picasso* by Françoise Gilot, despite Picasso's objections. Engraved enlargements on concrete by Carl Nesjar of *Luncheon on the Grass, After Manet*.

1966
Inauguration of the *Hommage to Picasso* exhibition at the Grand and Petit Palais by André Malraux, minister of cultural affairs.

1967
Refuses the Legion of Honor. Inauguration of *Woman's Head* in Chicago.

1968
Death of Jaime Sabartés: as a tribute, the exceptional donation of the entire *Meninas* series and of a portrait of Sabartés by Picasso to the Museu Picasso in Barcelona.

1969
Writes and illustrates a "literary fantasy": *El Entierro del Conde de Orgaz. The Kiss* (MP220).

1970
Donates his early works to the Museu Picasso (Barcelona). Exhibition of his recent works at the Palais des Papes in Avignon. *Family* (MP222).

1971
Donates his first metal construction, *Guitar*, to MoMA. Donates 57 drawings to the Musée Réattu in Arles. Major exhibition at the Louvre for his 90th birthday.

1972
Works in Mougins. Large exhibition of the collection at MoMA. *The Young Painter* (MP228).

1973
Dies at home in Notre-Dame-de-Vie in Mougins on April 8. Buried in the garden of Vauvenargues. Major posthumous exhibition : *Pablo Picasso 1970–1972* at the Palais des Papes in Avignon. Donation of Picasso's personal collection to France.

André Villiers
Picasso in the garden at La Californie Cut and superimposed, Cannes, 1961, undated print. Undated print. Gift Succession Picasso, 1992. APPH2283

Roberto Otero
Portrait of Picasso in a yellow dressing gown in front of the painting *The Matador and Women with a Bird*, 1970. Print c. 1987 Purchase, 1989. MP1989-7(4)

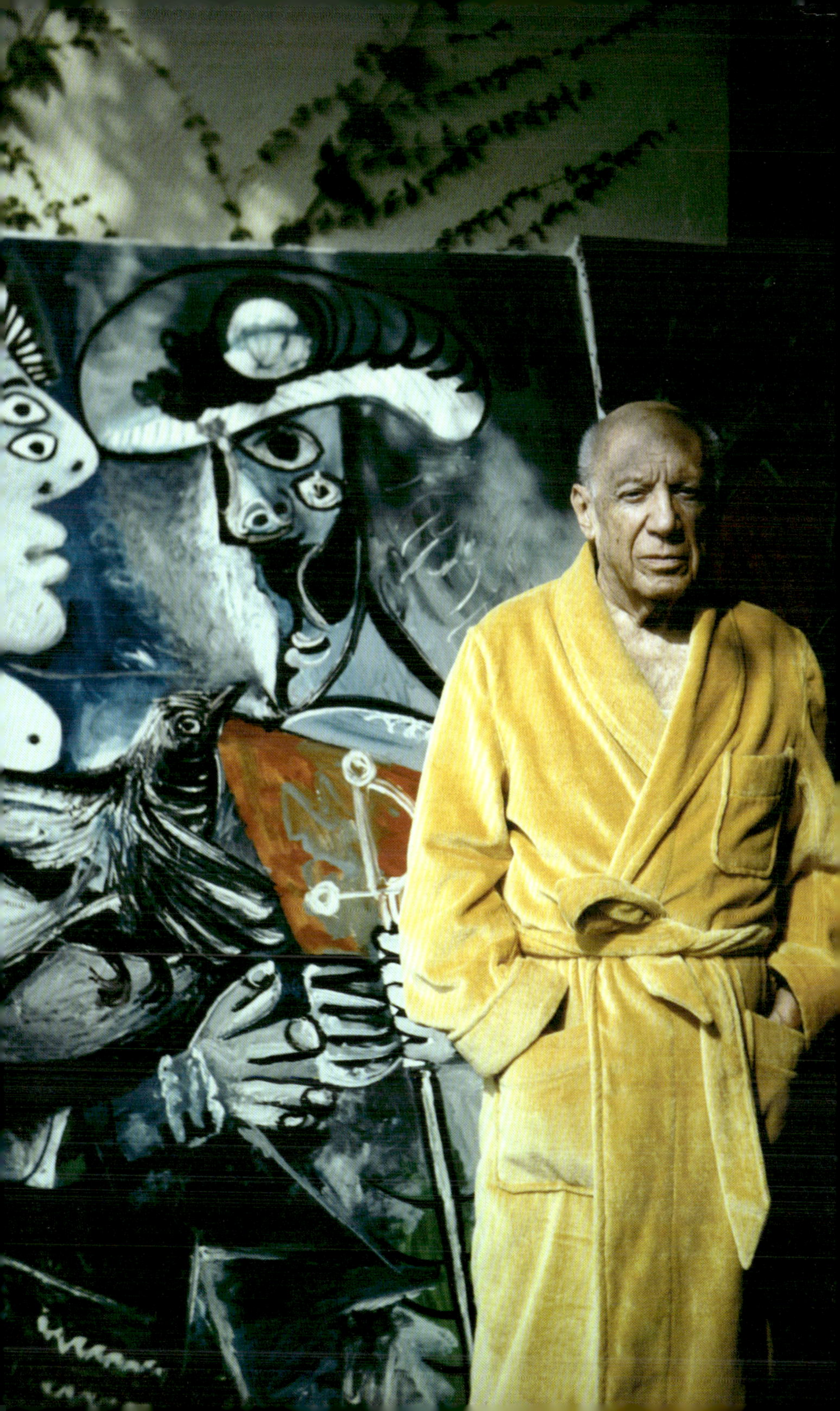

THE STAFF OF THE MUSÉE NATIONAL PICASSO-PARIS
Charles Akilimali Ali-Kanda, Violette Andres, Sophie Annoepel-Cabrignac, Ananay Arango, Orgest Azizaj, Anne Bantignie, Abass Barro, Marie Bauer, Chérifa Belkhiri, Tommaso Benelli, Lacdar Benhenda, Anaïs Bertrand, Hicham Bitari, Guillaume Blanc, Denis Bobicov, Sébastien Bonnard, Anne Boucley, Naïma Boudaoui, Yann Bouget, Élodie Bouilloux, Joëlle Bourrée, Émilie Bouvard, Marie Cazard, Riad Chaoub, Thierry Chauvin, Soraya Chibah, Camille Citerici, Chantal Clerc, Laure Collignon, Alice Cormenier, Anne Cornet, Camille Corteggiani, Laura Couvreur, Jordan Dambra, Jean-René David, Sophie Daynes-Diallo, Sandrine Delacroix, Julie Delclaux, Thomas Denise, Dominique Desseaux, Virginie Duchêne, Young Duvernois, Audrey Ego, Pierrot Eugène, Maxime Fellion, Sergio Fernandes, Michel Fernandez, Lionel Fonvieille, Najoua Ftaiti, Abdelghani Gardani, Claire Garnier, Vidal Garrido, Francette Girault, Grégory Gladone, Audrey Gonzalez, Stéphane Grégoire, Léo Guezi, Constantin Guyonnet, Jamel Hammiche, Margot Harrari, Quentin Havet, Prasith Hin, Miradji Issa, Nathalie Jimenez, Isis Jourda, Benjamin Karczewski, Michel-Nestor Kossi, Robert Kuevidjen, Claude Lachaise, Sarah Lagrevol, David Lair, Marie-Angèle Lassource, Jean-Marie Le Bars, Laurent Le Bon, Leslie Lechevallier, Marie Leclerc, Rita Leforestier, Nathalie Leleu, Émilie Lenne-Joly, Ibrahim M'Bapandza, Robin Magnani, Olivier Mas, Jean-Paul Mercier-Baudrier, Stéphanie Molins, Valérie Moro, Lydie-Inès Motuhi, Erol Ok, Béatrice Paasch, Eve Paperman-Pchibich, Srinivas Pascal, Laurent Passelergue, Pierre-Simon Pellissier, Virginie Perdrisot, Sandra Perlemoine, Gilles Petit, Élodie Petrose, Émilia Philippot, Jannick Pierre, Gilbert Pinault, Anne-Sophie Pinçon, Virginie Polak, Fred Privat, Yaël Pustilnicov, Sonny Raharison, Zohreh Ramezani, Cathy Reinold, Géraldine Sandras, Thomas Scaramuzza, Marie-Hélène Schmitt, Nabila Senane, Jeanne-Yvette Sudour, Ludovic Suppato, Matthieu Vahanian, Anne-Sophie Vernon, Steve Victor, Antoine Villette, Clémentine Wyka, Mehdi Yemmi, Damien Zhang.

MUSÉE NATIONAL PICASSO-PARIS
Scientific Direction
Émilie Bouvard

Editorial coordination and iconography
Virginie Duchêne

ÉDITIONS ARTLYS
Editorial Direction
Séverine Cuzin-Schulte

Editing
Emmanuelle Maffesoli

Translation
Mathilde Fassin

Copy editor
Bronwyn Mahoney

Design and graphic production
Prototype: Aurore Jannin and Laurent Pinon

DTP
Catherine Enault

Photo-engraving
Printmodel, Paris

Manufacturing
Hugues Charreyron

Printed in March 2016 by the printing house Die Keure, Bruges, Belgium.
Legal Deposit: April 2016

EN Musée national Picasso-Paris: 979-10-93056-11-1

EN Artlys: 978-2-85495-619-1